HITLER'S WAR MACHINE

PANZERS
1936-1945

BOB CARRUTHERS

BOOKS LTD

This book is published in Great Britain in 2013 by
Coda Books Ltd, Office Suite 2, Shrieves Walk, Sheep Street,
Stratford upon Avon, Warwickshire CV37 6GJ.
www.codabooks.com

Copyright © 2013 Coda Books Ltd

ISBN 978-1-78158-316-6

A CIP catalogue record for this book is available from the British Library.
All rights reserved. No part of this publication may be reproduced or
transmitted in any form or by any means (electronic or mechanical,
including photocopy, recording, or any information storage and retrieval
system, without the prior permission in writing from the publisher.

CONTENTS

INTRODUCTION 5

THE PANZER I 20
- Development history 21
- Combat history 26
- Variants 35

THE PANZER II 36
- History 36
- Design 37
- Variants 39
- Legion Condor 51
- Contemporary Documents 73

THE PANZER III 95
- Germany's Medium Tank 95
- Development History 116
- Combat Use 146

THE PANZER IV 159
- The Workhorse of the Panzerwaffe 159
- Development History 185
- Combat history 210
- Variants 218

THE PANTHER 223

Guderian's Problem Child 223
The Panther Manual: The Pantherfibel 229
The Re-building Programme 235
The Development Process 250
The Panther In Production 257
The Panther In Combat 262
Building The Panther 281

THE TIGER I 308

Production Of The Tiger 310
Deployment 322
The Mechanics Of The Tiger I 325
Production History 330
Design Features 336
Getting To The Battlefield 341
Design review 362
Combat History 367
Tiger Aces 379
Inside The Tiger 389
"Yank" magazine 393
Tiger I Tanks in Sicily 396
Armour And Armament 403
The Two Extremes 406
Tiger I Tanks in Normandy 412
The Soviet Response 418
Tigers In Italy 423
Tank Losses 426
Notable Variants 428

INTRODUCTION

This book is the compendium edition featuring complete reprints of five of the titles from the series entitled 'Hitler's War Machine.' The aim of the series is to provide the reader with a varied range of materials drawn from original writings covering the strategic, operational and tactical aspects of the weapons and battles of Hitler's war. The concept behind the series is to provide the well-read and knowledgeable reader with an interesting compilation of related primary sources combined with the best of what is in the public domain to build a picture of a particular aspect of that titanic struggle.

I am pleased to report that the series has been well received and it is a pleasure to be able to bring original primary sources to the attention of an interested readership. I particularly enjoy discovering new primary sources, and I am pleased to be able to present them unadorned and unvarnished to a sophisticated audience. The primary sources such as Die Wehrmacht and Signal, speak for themselves and the readership I strive to serve is the increasingly well informed community of reader/historians which needs no editorial lead and can draw its own conclusions. I am well aware that our community is constantly striving to discover new nuggets of information, and I trust that with this volume I have managed to stimulate fresh enthusiasm and that at least some of these facts and articles will be new to you and will provoke readers to research further down these lines of investigation, and perhaps cause established views to be challenged once more. I am aware at all times in compiling these materials that our relentless pursuit of more and better historical information is at the core our common passion. I trust

A Panzer I in action during the Spanish Civil War

that this selection will contribute to that search and will help all of us to better comprehend and understand the bewildering events of the last century.

In order to produce an interesting compilation giving a flavour of events at the tactical and operational level I have returned once more to the wartime US Intelligence series of pamphlets, which contain an intriguing series of contemporary articles on weapons and tactics. I find this series of pamphlets particularly fascinating as they are written in, what was then, the present tense and, as such, provide us with a sense of what was happening at the face of battle as events unfolded.

The first vehicle to be produced in any numbers for the Panzerwaffe was, of course, the tiny Panzer I, which at the time was known as the MG Panzerwagen. Delivery of 318 of these had been made by August 1935, along with 15 of the Zugfuhrerwagen, which was later to become the Panzer III. One aspect of tank design which the Germans got absolutely right from the very outset was to identify the importance of radio communications. Although initially only the command tanks were fitted with radios that could both transmit and receive, the other vehicles were at last equipped with receiving radio sets, and this was a major advance upon the thinking of many of the countries which would come to oppose Germany. Throughout 1934 exercises continued with the experimental tank units and a number of other valuable lessons quickly became apparent, particularly the need for close co-operation between the air forces and the tanks on the ground. At this point the first serious tank tactics which were to bring so much success during the Second World War began to appear. It was soon obvious that the tanks needed to be employed on a relatively narrow front. A divisional front was estimated at about three kilometres, a great change from the wide fronts of the Great War. It was still obvious to the German High Command that the decisions which were being made, were based on theory, rather than practice. Germany - and indeed every other nation of the time - had no practical experience to draw upon, therefore a number of educated guesses were made.

In January 1936 General Beck reported to the High Command, his findings being based on a study of a French organisation. He was also very critical of the slow rise in production capacity which was hampering the development of the tank force. Interestingly, the debate about which tasks tanks were suitable for, and whether specialist machines had to be developed for each task, was already beginning to take shape. Beck's report clearly stated that the three main tasks of the Panzers were supporting infantry, operating in units with other mobile weapons and, finally, combating other tanks. Beck himself was unable to come to a decision about whether a single tank should be developed with the capability to take on each of these purposes or whether a specialist vehicle should he designed for each purpose.

Ultimately the decision was that the light tanks would be used in a scouting role and that an infantry support tank would be developed which was later to come to fruition in the form of the Panzer IV; this decision cast the Panzer III in the role of main battle tank. Amazingly the decision was taken that the 3.7cm gun which initially equipped the Panzer III would be sufficient for the battle conditions. The various types of German tank design were to cater for most eventualities on the battlefield. Initially the Panzer I was considered to be fit for training purposes only, however manufacturing proceeded very slowly and eventually both the Panzer I and II were earmarked for the reconnaissance role. The Panzer III was essentially designed for break-through and anti-tank operations and the Panzer IV was designed to provide close support for the infantry battling their way forward against dug-In positions. Almost from the outset the limitations of the design for the Panzer I were obvious. The armament in the form of two machine guns, was inadequate for most purposes on the battlefield. In addition the very thin armour gave protection only against rifle bullets: almost any battlefield weapon could penetrate the armour. More significant was the fact that the crew was comprised of only two men.

In October 1935 General Liese, head of the Heere's Waffenamt issued a report which gave the limitations of the tanks. He noted that the MG Panzerwagen (Panzer I), although fitted out only with two 7.9mm machine guns, could be adapted to attack armoured cars and other light tanks if it was issued with special S.M.P. steel core ammunition. In the case of the MG Panzer II, it was noted that the muzzle velocity of the 2cm gun could penetrate up to 10mm of armoured plate at a range of up to 700 metres. It was therefore decided that the Panzer II could engage armoured cars with success, and was also fully functional for combat against tanks with approximately the same armour as itself. Liese noted that the tanks most likely to be encountered in

A Panzer II in flames following a hit near Tobruk 1941.

large numbers in a war against the French were the light Renault Ml7 and Ml8 tanks, of which there were about three thousand operational in the French forces at the time. It was also thought that the Panzer II would be the equal of the Renault NC37 and NC31 tanks. Against the heavier French tanks, including the Char B, it was noted that the Panzer II was practically worthless. Despite these reservations large-scale delivery of the Panzer II was already in train and was expected to commence from 1st April 1937.

The Panzer I actually entered active service in 1937 with the Legion Condor and proved to be an efficient machine within its highly proscribed limits. There are those who state that the Panzer II was also deployed in Spain although I can find no evidence to support this claim. Perhaps there is someone out there who can resolve the debate, for the time being I continue to err on the side of caution.

Delivery of fifteen Zugfuhrerwagen, which was later to become the Panzer III was completed by August 1935. One

Brand new Panzer III Ausf.F roll off the production line and out of the factory.

aspect of tank design which the Germans got absolutely right from the very outset was to identify the importance of radio communications. Although initially only the command tanks were fitted with radios that could both transmit and receive, the other vehicles were at last equipped with receiving radio sets, and this was a major advance upon the thinking of many of the countries which would come to oppose Germany. Throughout 1934 exercises continued with the experimental tank units and a number of other valuable lessons quickly became apparent, particularly the need for close co-operation between the air forces and the tanks on the ground. At this point the first serious tank tactics which were to bring so much success during the Second World War began to appear. It was soon obvious that the tanks needed to be employed on a relatively narrow front. A divisional front was estimated at about three kilometres, a great change from the wide fronts of the Great War. It was still obvious to the German High Command that the decisions which were being made, were based on theory, rather than practice.

Germany - and indeed every other nation of the time - had no practical experience to draw upon, therefore a number of educated guesses were made.

In January 1936 General Beck reported to the High Command, his findings being based on a study of a French organisation. He was also very critical of the slow rise in production capacity which was hampering the development of the tank force. Interestingly, the debate about which tasks tanks were suitable for, and whether specialist machines had to be developed for each task, was already beginning to take shape. Beck's report clearly stated that the three main tasks of the Panzers were supporting infantry, operating in units with other mobile weapons and, finally, combating other tanks. Beck himself was unable to come to a decision about whether a single tank should be developed with the capability to take on each of these purposes or whether a specialist vehicle should he designed for each purpose.

Ultimately the decision was that the light tanks would be used in a scouting role and that an infantry support tank would be developed which was ultimately to come to fruition in the form of the Panzer IV. This decision cast the Panzer III in the role of main battle tank. Amazingly the decision was taken that the 3.7cm gun which initially equipped the Panzer III would be sufficient for the battle conditions. The various types of German tank design were to cater for most eventualities on the battlefield. The Panzer I and II were earmarked for the reconnaissance role. The Panzer III was essentially designed for break-through and anti-tank operations and the Panzer IV was designed to provide close support for the infantry battling their way forward against dug-In positions. Almost from the outset the limitations of the design for the Panzer I were obvious. The armament in the form of two machine guns, was inadequate for most purposes on the battlefield. In addition the very thin armor gave protection only against rifle bullets: almost any battlefield weapon could penetrate the armor. More significant was the fact that the crew was comprised of only two men.

In October 1935 General Liese, head of the Heeres Waffenamt issued a report which gave the limitations of the tanks. He noted that the MG Panzerwagen (Panzer I), although fitted out only with two 7.9mm machine guns, could be adapted to attack armored cars and other light tanks if it was issued with special S.M.P. steel core ammunition. In the case of the MG Panzer II, it was noted that the muzzle velocity of the 2cm gun could penetrate up to 10mm of armored plate at a range of up to 700 metres. It was therefore decided that the Panzer II could engage armored cars with success, and was also fully functional for combat against tanks with approximately the same armor as itself. Liese noted that the tanks most likely to be encountered in large numbers in a war against the French were the light Renault Ml7 and Ml8 tanks, of which there were about three thousand operational in the French forces at the time. It was also thought that the Panzer II would be the equal of the Renault NC37 and NC31 tanks. Against the heavier French tanks, including the Char B, it was noted that the Panzer II was practically worthless. Despite these reservations large-scale delivery of the Panzer II was already in train and was expected to commence from 1st April 1937. As regards the new Panzer III, which was designed to be the main battle tank, it was obvious that, even in 1935, Liese was already beginning to have reservations about the effectiveness of the 37mm gun. Originally the 37mm L/45 had been planned for this vehicle, but it was urged that the experimental tanks be upgraded to include the L/65 version, which gave a much higher muzzle velocity and some real prospect of penetrating the 40mm thick armored plate of the new French medium tanks. With this in mind it was obvious at this stage that a 50mm gun would be a better proposition for the Panzer III; however the addition of the

The Panzer III Ausf B was unusual as it incorporated eight small road wheels arranged in pairs. The design was unsuccessful and only 15 were built.

larger gun would demand a significant increase in the diameter of the turret which would in turn mean radical redevelopment of the chassis. Given the pressures of time and the need to equip the formations quickly Liese came to the conclusion that the 37mm L/65 was the favoured route, although it is interesting that the limitations of its design had already been noted.

The PzKpfw III (Panzerkampfwagen III Sd.Kfz.141) was therefore designed to be the Wehrmacht's main combat machine and was developed by Daimler-Benz in the mid 1930s under the pseudonym Zugfuhrerwagen, which means platoon commanders' truck. The first prototype of the PzKpfw III was produced by Daimler-Benz in Berlin 1936.

Following numerous modifications, the Ausf. A (1-Serie) appeared in May 1937 and by the end of 1937, 15 were produced. Only 8 of the Ausf. As were fully armed and the unarmed machines were used for further testing and modification.

Daimler-Benz produced 15 Ausf. Bs (2-Serie) in 1937, 15 Ausf. Cs (3a-Serie) by the beginning of 1938; it continued by introducing the next variant the Ausf. D (3b-Serie), 55 of which

The Panzer IV from the business end. The practice of adding the names of sweet-hearts to the vehicle was widespread in this unit.

were produced in 1939. Of the entire Ausf. Ds production run, only 30 were armed.

All early models of the Panzer III, including the Ausf A/B/C/D were pre-prototypes of the whole series and were unsuitable for large scale production. Every new prototype was a marginal improvement on the last. Each model featured a different type of suspension, a variation on the Maybach DSO, such as the HL 108 TR engine. Only a relatively few vehicles saw combat in the early stages of the war; the Ausf. D saw service during fighting in Denmark and Norway in May 1940 and in Finland in 1941/42. In February 1940, the remaining Panzer IIIs Ausf D were handed over to NSKK for training purposes.

The first Panzer III model to go into anything like full-scale production was the Ausf E of which 96 were produced. With a thicker 30mm frontal armor, a Maybach HL 120TR engine and new suspension and gearbox raising its weight up to 19.5 tonnes, the Ausf. E was the best machine so far.

By 1940, and during the 'E' model production, it was decided to fit all models with a 50mm gun as standard. The L/42 gun was fitted on Ausf. E, F, G and H. In an ill considered deal which would come back to haunt them, the Germans actually sold Two PzKpfw III tanks to the Soviet Union in the Summer of 1940 under the Ribbentrop-Molotov treaty. They were tested by the Soviets alongside the early T-34/76 tanks. The German PzKpfw III proved to be faster than Soviet T-34/76 and BT-7, reaching a maximum speed of 69km/h. However it was obvious that the Soviet T-34 was far superior in armor protection and armament even if lacking in esthetics and overall mechanical reliability, when compared to German PzKpfw III tanks. The PzKpfw III was also found to be far less noisy than Soviet T-34. It was discovered that the T-34 could easily be heard from a distance of 450m, while PzKpfw III could only be heard when it approached to within 150-200m.

From 1941, Hitler insisted that the more powerful L/60 (50mm) gun was fitted on Ausf J-1. In 1942, 104 Ausf J's were converted to Panzerbefehlswagen III (Command Tanks) and in April 1943, 100 Ausf. M's were converted by Wegmann into the Flammpanzer (Flamethrower Tanks); designed to fight in urban areas such as Stalingrad. Although the models produced never actually reached Stalingrad, they did see service on the Eastern Front. Additionally, many Ausf. Ms were converted into the Sturmgeschütz III or the Ausf. N.

The Panzer III provided the main battle tank for the Panzer Divisions in the early years of the war, yet its production was slow and stopped altogether in August 1943, in 1943/44, the Panzer III prototypes were fitted with dozers and were used to clean up the streets of war-torn cities.

The Panzer IV was originally designed as an infantry support tank with a unique tactical role. The Panzer IV was not designed to take part in tank vs tank combat. Although the Panzer IV initially had relatively thin armour, it carried a powerful 75mm gun and could match any other tank at that time. The prototype of

Panzer IV tanks of the SS-Division 'Hitlerjugend' on parade February 1944.

the Panzer IV was given the code name Bataillonfuhrerwagen. The Panzer IV was ordered by Hitler from Krupp, MAN and Rheinmetall Borsig to weigh in at 18 tonnes with a top speed of 35 km/hr. The Krupp design - the VK 200 1 (K) - was eventually selected to enter into full-scale production in 1935. Along with the Panther, it was to become the main combat tank of the Third Reich.

The PzKpfw IV was perceived as the 'workhorse' of all the Panzer divisions and more were produced than any other variant in the 1933-1945 period. The Ausf. A was built as a pre-production vehicle and only 35 were produced. The modifications from this gave rise to the Ausf. B which emerged in 1938 with an increased frontal armour thickness and a six-speed gearbox, which enhanced its cross-country performance. That same year Krupp-Gruson produced the Ausf. C and 134 of this model were in production until 1939.

The Ausf. D/E saw an upgrading of its armour thickness and improved vision blocks for the driver. The Ausf. E was the first of the Panzer IV fitted with turret mounted stowage bins. The Ausf. F(1), produced between 1941-1942 was the last Panzer IV to be based on the short version chassis. 25 of the F Is were converted into Ausf F2s (it had the British nickname of "Mark IV

Special" because, with its high velocity 75mm main armament it was far superior to any other tank at the time). It was followed by the modified version of the Ausf. G in May 1942.

The Ausf. H, introduced in April 1943, was exclusively armed with a newer version of the 75mm KwK 40 L/48 gun and was fitted with steel/wire armour skirts. Over 3,770 of the P/zKpfw IV Ausf H were made and saw action.

As late as 1945 the last model, the Ausf J, was an effective weapon in the hands of an experienced crew. A selected number of the Ausf H and J were also converted into command tanks or observation tanks towards the end of the war period.

The Panzer IV was the only German tank to stay in production throughout the war. It was the real workhorse of the German army and was deployed on every front. Due to its efficient armament, robust armour and outstanding reliability, it was preferred by crews over the Panther, Tiger and King Tiger. The Panzer IV was the most widely exported tank in German service, with around 300 sold to partners such as Finland, Romania, Spain and Bulgaria. After the war, the French and Spanish sold

The Panzer Mark V - The Panther.

A Tiger I deployed in Tunisia. Note the bemused locals to the right.

dozens of Panzer IVs to Syria, where they saw combat in the 1967 Six-Day War.

The Panzer IV was intended to be replaced by the Panzer V The Panther however the numbers produced were never sufficient to replace the mark IV which saw service right to the end of the war.

The Tiger I was a radical departure from other tank designs and was destined to become the most famous heavy tank used in World War II. It was developed in great haste during 1942 by the Henschel & Sohn company as the answer to the unexpectedly formidable Soviet armour encountered during 1941 in the closing stages of Operation Barbarossa. During that titanic campaign an unpleasant surprise for the German armies appeared in the ominous form of the T-34 and the KV-1 to which the German tank designs of the time could provide no answer. The 50mm calibre high velocity gun of the German Mark III lacked projectile mass and penetrating power while the low velocity gun mounted on the German Mark IV was incapable of penetrating the well sloped armour of the T-34 at anything but the shortest range. The high velocity 88mm anti-aircraft gun, which had been forced into action in an anti-tank role in Russia and the western desert, was the only gun which had demonstrated its effectiveness against even the most heavily armoured ground targets such as The KV1.

Rushed into service in August 1942 the Tiger I design at least gave the Panzerwaffe its first tank capable of mounting the fearsome 88mm gun as its main armament. For the hard pressed men of the Panzewaffe however there was a very high price to pay for the Tiger in both literal and metaphorical terms. The highest price of all, or course, was paid by the slave labourers who were forced to build the Tiger.

The Roman numeral I was only officially added in 1944 when the later Tiger II entered production. The initial official German designation was Panzerkampfwagen VI Ausführung H ('Panzer VI version H'), abbreviated to PzKpfw VI Ausf. H. Somewhat confusingly the tank was redesignated as PzKpfw VI Tiger Ausf. E in March 1943. It also enjoyed the ordnance inventory Sonderkraftzug designation SdKfz 181.

The Tiger I first saw action on 22nd September 1942 near Leningrad. It was not an instant success. Under pressure from Hitler, the tank was driven into action in unfavourable terrain, months earlier than planned. Many early models proved to be mechanically unreliable; in this first action most broke down. More worryingly two others were easily knocked out by dug-in Soviet anti-tank guns. Of even more concern was the fact that one disabled tank was almost captured intact by the Soviets. It was finally blown up in November 1942 to prevent it falling into Soviet hands. In any event the Soviets used the battlefield experience well and used the time to study the design and begin to prepare a response which, in due course, would emerge as the fearsome Josef Stalin heavy tank which was to prove equal to the Tiger in every respect.

I trust you enjoy discovering these new sources of information.

Bob Carruthers
Berchtesgaden 2013

THE PANZER I

The Panzer I was a light tank produced in Germany in the 1930s. The name is short for the German Panzerkampfwagen I (armored fighting vehicle mark I), abbreviated PzKpfw I. The tank's official German ordnance inventory designation was SdKfz 101 (special purpose vehicle 101).

Design of the Panzer I began in 1932 and mass production in 1934. Intended only as a training tank to introduce the concept of armored warfare to the German Army, the Panzer I saw combat in Spain during the Spanish Civil War, in Poland, France, the Soviet Union and North Africa during the Second World War, and in China during the Second Sino-Japanese War. Experiences with the Panzer I during the Spanish Civil War helped shape the German armored corps' invasion of Poland in 1939 and France in 1940. By 1941, the Panzer I chassis design was used for production of tank destroyers and assault guns. There were attempts to upgrade the Panzer I throughout its service history,

Testing the capabilities of a Panzer I

including those foreign nations who had been equipped with the Panzer I, to extend the design lifespan. It continued to serve in the armed forces of Spain until 1954.

The Panzer I's performance in combat was limited by its thin armor and light armament of two general purpose machine guns. As a design intended for training, the Panzer I was not as capable as other light tanks of the era, such as the Soviet T-26. Although weak in combat, it nonetheless formed a large portion of Germany's tank strength in numbers and was used in all major campaigns between September 1939 and December 1941. The small, vulnerable light tank would be surpassed in importance by better-known German tanks such as the Panzer IV, Panther, and Tiger. Nevertheless, the Panzer I's contribution to the early victories of Nazi Germany during the Second World War was significant.

Development history

The post-World War I Treaty of Versailles of 1919 prohibited the design, manufacture and deployment of tanks within the Reichswehr. Paragraph Twenty-four of the treaty provided for a 100,000-mark fine and imprisonment of up to six months for anybody who manufactured armoured vehicles, tanks or similar machines, which may be turned to military use.

Despite the manpower and technical limitations imposed upon the German Army by the Treaty of Versailles, several Reichswehr officers established a clandestine General Staff to study the lessons which could be learned from World War I and develop future strategies and tactics accordingly. Although at first the concept of the tank as a mobile weapon of war met with apathy, German industry was silently encouraged to look into tank design, while quiet cooperation was undertaken with the Soviet Union at KAMA. There was also minor military cooperation with Sweden, including the extraction of technical data that proved invaluable to early German tank design. As early as 1926 various German companies, including Rheinmetall and Daimler-Benz, produced a single prototype armed with a large 75-millimeter cannon (the Großtraktor, "large tractor", was so codenamed to veil the true purpose of the vehicle). Only two years later prototypes of the new Leichttraktor ("light tractor"), were produced by German companies, armed with 37-millimeter KwK L/45 guns. The Großtraktor was later put into service for a brief period with the 1 Panzer Division; the Leichttraktor remained in testing until 1935.

In the late 1920s and early 1930s German tank theory was pioneered by two figures: General Oswald Lutz and his chief of staff, Lieutenant Colonel Heinz Guderian. Guderian became the more influential of the two and his ideas were widely publicized. Like his contemporary Sir Percy Hobart, Guderian initially envisioned an armored corps (panzerkorps) composed of several types of tanks. This included a slow infantry tank, armed with a small-caliber cannon and several machine guns. The infantry tank, according to Guderian, was to be heavily armored to defend against enemy anti-tank guns and artillery. He also envisioned a fast breakthrough tank, similar to the British cruiser tank, which was to be armored against enemy anti-tank weapons and have a large 75-millimeter (2.95 in) main gun. Lastly, Germany would need a heavy tank, armed with a massive 150-millimeter (5.9 in) cannon to defeat enemy fortifications, and even stronger armor. Such a tank would require a weight of 70 to 100 tonnes and was completely impractical given the manufacturing capabilities of the day.

Soon after rising to power in Germany, Adolf Hitler approved the creation of Germany's first panzer divisions. Simplifying his earlier proposal, Guderian suggested the design of a main combat vehicle which would be developed into the Panzer III, and a breakthrough tank, the Panzer IV. No existing design

PzKpfw I Ausf. F on display at the Belgrade Military Museum

appealed to Guderian. As a stopgap, the German Army ordered a preliminary vehicle to train German tank crews. This became the Panzer I.

The Panzer I's design history can be traced to 1932's Landwirtschaftlicher Schlepper (La S) (Agricultural Tractor) armored fighting vehicle. The La S was intended not just to train Germany's panzer troops, but to prepare Germany's industry for the mass production of tanks in the near future: a difficult engineering feat for the time. In July 1932, Krupp revealed a prototype of the Landswerk Krupp A, or LKA, with a sloped front glacis plate and large central casemate, a design heavily influenced by the British Carden Loyd tankette. The tank was armed with two obsolescent 7.92-millimeter (.312 in) MG-13 Dreyse machine guns. Machine guns were known to be largely useless against even the lightest tank armor of the time, restricting the Panzer I to a training and anti-infantry role by design.

A mass-produced version of the LKA was designed by a collaborative team from Daimler-Benz, Henschel, Krupp, MAN, and Rheinmetall, exchanging the casemate for a rotating turret. This version was accepted into service after testing in 1934. Although these tanks were referred to as the La S and LKA well beyond the start of production, its official designation, assigned in 1938, was Panzerkampfwagen I Ausführung. A ('model A' or, more accurately, 'batch A'). The first fifteen tanks, produced between February and March 1934, did not include the rotating turret and were used for crew training. Following these, production was switched to the combat version of the tank. The Ausf. A was under-armored, with steel plate of only 13 millimeters (0.51 in) at its thickest. The tank had several design flaws, including suspension problems which made the vehicle pitch at high speed, and engine overheating. The driver was positioned inside the chassis and used conventional steering levers to control the tank, while the commander was positioned in the turret where he also acted as gunner. The two crewmen could communicate by means of a voice tube. Machine gun ammunition was stowed in five bins, containing various numbers of 25-round magazines. Author Lucas Molina Franco states that 833 Panzerkampfwagen I Ausf. A tanks were built in total, Terry Gander assesses the number 818 units while Bryan Perrett estimates the number may have been as low as low as 300.

Many of the problems in the Ausf. A were corrected with the introduction of the Ausf. B. The engine was replaced by the water-cooled, six-cylinder Maybach NL 38 TR, developing 98 horsepower (73 kW), and the gearbox was changed to a more reliable model. The larger engine required the extension of the vehicle's chassis by 40 cm (16 in), and this allowed the improvement of the tank's suspension, adding an additional bogie wheel and raising the tensioner. The tank's weight increased by

0.4 tons. Production of the Ausf. B began in August 1935 and finished in early 1937—Franco writes 840 were constructed, but notes that only 675 of these were combat models, while Perrett suggests a total number of 1,500 (offsetting the low number of Ausf. A he proposes) and Gander a total of 675.

THE NEXT GENERATION

Two more combat versions of the Panzer I were designed and produced between 1939 and 1942. By this stage the design concept had been superseded by medium and heavy tanks and neither variant was produced in sufficient numbers to have a real impact on the progress of the war. These new tanks had nothing in common with either the Ausf. A or B except name. One of these, the Panzer I Ausf. C, was designed jointly between Krauss-Maffei and Daimler-Benz in 1939 to provide an amply armored and armed reconnaissance light tank. The Ausf. C boasted a completely new chassis and turret, a modern torsion-bar suspension and five interleaved roadwheels. It also had a maximum armor thickness of 30 millimeters (1.18 in), over twice that of either the Ausf. A or B, and was armed with a 20-millimeter (0.78 in) EW 141 autocannon. Forty of these tanks were produced, along with six prototypes. Two tanks were deployed to 1 Panzer Division in 1943, and the other thirty-eight were deployed to the LVIII Panzer Reserve Corps during the Normandy landings.

The second vehicle, the Ausf. F, was as different from the Ausf. C as it was from the Ausf. A and B. Intended as an infantry support tank, the Panzer I Ausf. F had a maximum armour thickness of 80 millimeters (3.15 in) and weighed between 18 and 21 tonnes. The Ausf. F was armed with two 7.92-millimeter MG-34s. Thirty were produced in 1940, and a second order of 100 was later canceled. In order to compensate for the increased weight, a new 150 horsepower (110 kW) Maybach HL45 Otto engine was used, allowing a maximum road speed

A Panzer I crew of the Condor Legion.

of 25 kilometers per hour (15.5 mph). Eight of the thirty tanks produced were sent to the 1 Panzer Division in 1943 and saw combat at the Battle of Kursk. The rest were given to several army schools for training and evaluation purposes.

Combat history

SPANISH CIVIL WAR

On 18 July 1936, war broke out on the Iberian Peninsula as Spain dissolved into a state of civil war. After the chaos of the initial uprising, two sides coalesced and began to consolidate their position—the Popular front (the Republicans) and the Spanish Nationalist front. In an early example of a proxy war, both sides quickly received support from other countries, most notably the Soviet Union and Germany, who wanted to test their tactics and equipment. The first shipment of foreign tanks, fifty Soviet T-26's, arrived on 15 October. The shipment was under the surveillance of the German Navy and Germany immediately responded by sending forty-one Panzer I's to Spain a few days later. This first shipment was followed by four more shipments of Panzer I Ausf. B's, with a total of 122 vehicles.

The first shipment of Panzer I's was brought under the command of Lieutenant Colonel Wilhelm Ritter von Thoma in Gruppe Thoma (also referred to as Panzergruppe Drohne). Gruppe Thoma formed part of Gruppe Imker, the ground formations of the German Condor Legion, who fought on the side of Franco's Nationalists. Between July and October, a rapid Nationalist advance from Seville to Toledo placed them in position to take the Spanish capital, Madrid. The Nationalist advance and the fall of the town of Illescas to Nationalist armies on 18 October 1936 caused the government of the Popular Front's Second Republic, including President Manuel Azaña, to flee to Barcelona and Valencia. In an attempt to stem the Nationalist tide and gain crucial time for Madrid's defence, Soviet armor was deployed south of the city under the command of Colonel Krivoshein before the end of October. At this time, several T-26 tanks under the command of Captain Paul Arman were thrown into a Republican counterattack directed towards the town of Torrejon de Velasco in an attempt to cut off the Nationalist advance north. This was the first tank battle in the Spanish Civil War. Despite initial success, poor communication between the Soviet Republican armor and Spanish Republican infantry caused the isolation of Captain Arman's force and the subsequent destruction of a number of tanks. This battle also marked the first use of the molotov cocktail against tanks. Ritter von Thoma's Panzer Is fought for the Nationalists only days later on 30 October, and immediately experienced problems. As the Nationalist armor advanced, it was engaged by the Commune de Paris battalion, equipped with Soviet BA-10 armored cars. The 45-millimeter (1.7 in) gun in the BA-10 was more than sufficient to knock out the poorly armored Panzer I at ranges of over 500 meters (550 yd).

Although the Panzer I would participate in almost every major Nationalist offensive of the war, the Nationalist army began to deploy more and more captured T-26 tanks to offset their disadvantage in protection and firepower. At one point, von Thoma offered up to 500 pesetas for each T-26 captured. Although the Panzer I was initially able to knock out the T-26 at close range—150 meters (165 yd) or less—using an armor-piercing 7.92 millimeter bullet, the Republican tanks began to engage at ranges where they were immune to the machine guns of the Panzer I.

The Panzer I was upgraded in order to increase its lethality. On 8 August 1937, Major General García Pallasar received a note from Generalísimo Francisco Franco which expressed the need for a Panzer I (or negrillo, as their Spanish crews called them) with a 20-millimeter gun. Ultimately, the piece chosen was the Breda Model 1935, due to the simplicity of the design over competitors such as the German Flak 30. Furthermore, the 20 mm Breda was capable of perforating 40 millimeters of armor at 250 meters (1.57 in at 275 yd), which was more than sufficient to penetrate the frontal armor of the T-26. Although originally forty Italian CV.35 light tanks were ordered with the Breda in place of their original armament, this order was subsequently canceled after it was thought adaptation of the same gun to the Panzer I would yield better results. Prototypes were ready by

COMPARISON OF LIGHT TANKS IN THE SPANISH CIVIL WAR				
	T-26	Panzer I	CV.33	CV.35
Weight	9.4 t	5.4 t	3.15 t	2.3 t
Gun	45 mm cannon	2 × 7.92 mm MG 13	6.5 mm or 8 mm machine gun	8 mm Breda machine gun
Ammunition	122 rounds	2,250 rounds	3,200 8mm or 3,800 6.5mm	3,200
Road range	175 km	200 km	125 km	125 km
Armor	7–16 mm	7–13 mm	5–15 mm	5–13.5 mm

PANZER I DELIVERIES TO SPAIN (1936–1939)	
Date	Number of Vehicles
October 1936*	41
Dec-36	21
Aug-37	30
End of 1937	10
Jan-39	30
Total:	122

Formed part of the Condor Legion

September 1937 and an order was placed after successful results. The mounting of the Breda in the Panzer I required the original turret to be opened at the top and then extended by a vertical supplement. Four of these tanks were finished at the Armament Factory of Seville, but further production was canceled as it was decided sufficient numbers of Republican T-26 tanks had been captured to fulfill the Nationalist leadership's request for more lethal tanks. The Breda modification was not particularly liked by German crews, as the unprotected gap in the turret, designed to allow the tank's commander to aim, was found to be a dangerous weak point.

In late 1938, another Panzer I was sent to the Armament Factory of Seville in order to mount a 45 mm gun, captured from a Soviet tank (a T-26 or BT-5). A second was sent sometime later in order to exchange the original armament for a 37-millimeter Maklen anti-tank gun, which had been deployed to Asturias in late 1936 on the Soviet ship A. Andreiev. It remains unknown to what extent these trials and adaptations were completed, although it is safe to assume neither adaptation was successful beyond the drawing board.

SECOND WORLD WAR

During the initial campaigns of the Second World War, Germany's light tanks, including the Panzer I, formed the bulk of its armored strength. In March 1938, the German Army

A Panzer I Ausf B on the streets of Calais, France in May 1940, while rounding up British prisoners of war.

marched into Austria, experiencing a mechanical breakdown rate of up to thirty percent. However, the experience revealed to Guderian several faults within the German Panzerkorps and he subsequently improved logistical support. In October 1938, Germany occupied Czechoslovakia's Sudetenland, and the remainder of the country in March 1939. The capture of Czechoslovakia allowed several Czech tank designs, such as the Panzer 38(t), and their subsequent variants and production, to be incorporated into the German Army's strength. It also prepared German forces for the invasion of Poland.

POLAND AND THE CAMPAIGN IN THE WEST

On 1 September 1939, Germany invaded Poland using seventy-two divisions (including 16 reserve infantry divisions in OKH reserves), including seven panzer divisions (1., 2., 3., 4., 5., 10., "Kempf") and four light divisions (1., 2., 3., 4.). Three days later, France and Britain declared war on Germany. The seven panzer and four light divisions were arrayed in five armies, forming two army groups. The battalion strength of the 1 Panzer Division included no less than fourteen Panzer Is, while the other six divisions included thirty-four. A total of about 2,700 tanks were available for the invasion of Poland, but only 310 of the heavier Panzer III and IV tanks were available. Furthermore, 350 were of Czech design—the rest were either Panzer Is or Panzer IIs. The invasion was swift and the last Polish pockets of resistance surrendered on 6 October. The entire campaign had lasted five weeks (with help of the Soviet forces which attacked on 17 September), and the success of Germany's tanks in the campaign was summed up in response to Hitler on 5 September: when asked if it had been the dive bombers who destroyed a Polish artillery regiment, Guderian replied, "No, our panzers!"

The Poles suffered almost 190,000 casualties (including around 66,300 killed) in the campaign, the Germans around 55,000 (including around 35,000 wounded. However, some 832 tanks (including 320 PzI, 259 PzII, 40 Pz III, 76 PzIV, 77 Pz35(t), 13 PzBef III, 7 PzBef 38(t), 34 other PzBef and some Pz38(t)) were lost during the campaign, approximately 341 of which were never to return to service. This represented about a third of Germany's armor deployed for the Polish campaign. During the campaign no less than a half of Germany's tanks were unavailable due to maintenance issues or enemy action, and of all tanks, the Panzer I proved the most vulnerable to Polish anti-tank weapons.

Furthermore, it was found that handling of armored forces during the campaign left much to be desired. During the beginning of Guderian's attack in northern Poland, his corps was held back to coordinate with infantry for quite a while, preventing a faster advance. It was only after Army Group South had its attention taken from Warsaw at the Battle of Bzura that Guderian's armor was fully unleashed. There were still lingering tendencies to reserve Germany's armor, even if in independent divisions, to cover an infantry advance or the flanks of advancing infantry armies. Although tank production was increased to 125 tanks per month after the Polish Campaign, losses forced the Germans to draw further strength from Czech tank designs, and light tanks continued to form the majority of Germany's armored strength.

Months later, Panzer Is participated in Operation Weserübung—the invasion of Denmark and Norway.

Despite its obsolescence, the Panzer I was also used in the invasion of France in May 1940. Of 2,574 tanks available for the campaign, no fewer than 523 were Panzer Is. Furthermore, there were only 627 Panzer IIIs and IVs. At least a fifth of Germany's armor was composed of Panzer Is, while almost four-fifths was light tanks of one type or another, including 955 Panzer II, 106 Czech Panzer 35(t), and 228 Panzer 38(t). For their defense, the French boasted up to 4,000 tanks, including 300 Char B1, armed with a 47-millimeter (1.7 in) gun in the turret and a larger 75-millimeter (2.95 in) low-velocity gun in the hull. The French also had around 250 Somua S-35, widely regarded as one of the best tanks of the period, armed with the same 47 millimeter main gun and protected by almost 55 millimeters (2.17 in) of armor at its thickest point. Nevertheless, the French also deployed over 3,000 light tanks, including about 500 World War I-vintage FT-17s. The two main advantages German armor enjoyed were radios allowing them to coordinate faster than their British or French counterparts and superior tactical doctrine.

NORTH AFRICA AND CAMPAIGNS IN THE EAST

Italian setbacks in Egypt and their colony of Libya caused Hitler to dispatch aircraft to Sicily, and a blocking force to North Africa. This blocking force was put under the command of Lieutenant General Erwin Rommel and included the motorized 5th Light Division and the 15th Panzer Division. This force

Panzer I Ausf. A in combat during the German invasion of Norway.

landed at Tunis on 12 February 1941. Upon arrival, Rommel had around 150 tanks, about half Panzer III and IV. The rest were Panzer I's and IIs, although the Panzer I was soon replaced. On 6 April 1941, Germany attacked both Yugoslavia and Greece, with fourteen divisions invading Greece from neighboring Bulgaria, which by then had joined the Tripartite Pact. The invasion of Yugoslavia included no less than six panzer divisions, which still fielded the Panzer I. Yugoslavia surrendered 17 April 1941, and Greece fell on 30 April 1941.

The final major campaign in which the Panzer I formed a large portion of the armored strength was Operation Barbarossa, 22 June 1941. The 3,300 German tanks included about 410 Panzer I's. By the end of the month, a large portion of the Red Army found itself trapped in the Minsk pocket, and by 21 September Kiev had fallen, thereby allowing the Germans to concentrate on their ultimate objective, Moscow. Despite the success of Germany's armor in the Soviet Union, between June and September most German officers were shocked to find their tanks were inferior to newer Soviet models, the T-34 and Kliment Voroshilov (KV)

Panzerbefehlswagen in Russia.

series. Army Group North quickly realized that none of the tank guns currently in use by German armor could penetrate the thick armor of the KV-1. The performance of the Red Army during the Battle of Moscow and the growing numbers of new Soviet tanks made it obvious the Panzer I was not suitable for this front. Some less battle-worthy Panzer I's were tasked with towing lorries through mud to alleviate logistics problems at the front.

FOREIGN SERVICE

After Germany, Spain fielded the largest number of Panzer I tanks. A total of 122 were exported to Spain during the Spanish Civil War, and, as late as 1945, Spain's Brunete Armored Division fielded 93. The Panzer I remained in use in Spain until aid arrived from the United States in 1954 when they were replaced by the relatively modern M47 Patton. Between 1935 and 1936, an export version of the Panzer I Ausf. B, named the L.K.B. (Leichte Kampfwagen B), was designed for export to Bulgaria. Modifications included up-gunning to a 20-millimeter gun and fitting a Krupp M 311 V-8 gasoline engine. Although three examples were built, none were exported to Bulgaria, although a single Panzer I Ausf. A had previously been sold. In 1937, around ten Ausf. As were sold to China during a period of Sino-German cooperation, which were used in the Battle of Nanjing by the 3rd Armored Battalion. A final order was supplied to Hungary in 1942, totalling eight Ausf. B's and six command versions. These were incorporated into the 1st Armored Division and saw combat in late 1942.

Variants

Between 1934 and the mid 1940s several variants of the Panzer I were designed, especially during the later years of its combat history. Because they were obsolescent from their introduction, incapable of defeating foreign armor, and outclassed by newer German tanks, the Panzer I chassis were increasingly repurposed as tank destroyers and other variants. One of the most well known variants was the kleiner Panzerbefehlswagen ("small armored command vehicle"), built on the Ausf. A and Ausf. B chassis—200 of these were manufactured. The Panzer I Ausf. B chassis was also used to build the German Army's first tracked tank destroyer, the Panzerjäger I. This vehicle was armed with a Czech 47-millimeter (1.85 in) anti-tank gun.

THE PANZER II

The Panzer II was the common name for a family of German tanks used in World War II. The official German designation was Panzerkampfwagen II (abbreviated PzKpfw II). Although the vehicle had originally been designed as a stopgap while more advanced tanks were developed, it nonetheless went on to play an important role in the early years of World War II, during the Polish and French campaigns. By the end of 1942 it had been largely removed from front line service, and production of the tank itself ceased by 1943. Its chassis remained in use as the basis of several other armored vehicles.

History

In 1934, delays in the design and production of the Panzer III and Panzer IV tanks were becoming apparent. Designs for a stopgap tank were solicited from Krupp, MAN, Henschel, and Daimler-Benz. The final design was based on the Panzer I,

The Panzer II

but larger, and with a turret mounting a 20 mm anti-tank gun. Production began in 1935, but it took another eighteen months for the first combat-ready tank to be delivered.

The Panzer II was the most numerous tank in the German Panzer divisions beginning with the invasion of France, until it was supplemented by the Panzer III and IV in 1940/41. Afterwards, it was used to great effect as a reconnaissance tank.

The Panzer II was used in the German campaigns in Poland, France, the Low Countries, Denmark, Norway, North Africa and the Eastern Front. After being removed from front-line duty, it was used for training and on secondary fronts. The chassis was used for a number of self-propelled guns including the Wespe and Marder II.

Design

ARMOR

The Panzer II was designed before the experience of the Spanish Civil War of 1936-39 showed that shell-proof armor was required for tanks to survive on a modern battlefield. Prior to that, armor was designed to stop machine gun fire and High Explosive shell fragments.

The Panzer II A, B, and C had 14 mm of slightly sloped homogenous steel armor on the sides, front, and back, with 10 mm of armor on the top and bottom. Many IIC were given increased armor in the front. Starting with the D model, the front armor was increased to 30 mm. The Model F had 35 mm front armour and 20 mm side armor. This armor could be penetrated by towed antitank weapons such as the Soviet 45mm and French canon de 25 and canon de 47.

ARMAMENT

Most tank versions of the Panzer II were armed with a 2 cm KwK 30 55 calibers long cannon. Some later versions used

The Marder III was a highly effective tank killer created from the chassis of the Panzer II.

the 2 cm KwK 38 L/55 which was similar. This cannon was based on the 2 cm FlaK 30 anti-aircraft gun, and was capable of firing at a rate of 600 rounds per minute (280 rounds per minute sustained). The Panzer II also had a 7.92 mm Maschinengewehr 34 machine gun mounted coaxially with the main gun.

The 2 cm cannon proved to be ineffective against many Allied tanks, and experiments were made towards replacing it with a 37 mm cannon, but nothing came of this. Prototypes were built with a 50 mm tank gun, but by then the Panzer II had outlived its usefulness as a tank regardless of armament. Greater success was had by replacing the standard armor-piercing explosive ammunition with tungsten cored solid ammunition, but due to material shortages this ammunition was in chronically short supply.

Later development into a self-propelled gun carriage saw the mounting of a 5 cm PaK 38 antitank gun, but this was seen as insufficient for the time, and the larger 7.62 cm PaK 36(r) was installed as an effective stop-gap. The main production antitank version was fitted with a 7.5 cm PaK 40 which was very effective. Artillery mounting began with a few 15 cm sIG 33 heavy infantry guns, but most effective was the 10.5 cm leFH 18, for which the Panzer II chassis became the primary carriage for the war. Most of these versions retained a pintle mounted 7.92 mm MG34 machine gun for defense against infantry and air attack.

MOBILITY

All production versions of the Panzer II were fitted with a 140 PS, gasoline-fuelled six-cylinder Maybach HL 62 TRM engine and ZF transmissions. Models A, B, and C had a top speed of 40 km/h (25 mph). Models D and E had a Christie suspension and a better transmission, giving a top road speed of 55 km/h (33 mph) but the cross country speed was much lower than previous models, so the Model F reverted back to the previous leaf spring type suspension. All versions had a range of 200 km (120 mi).

CREW

The Panzer II had a crew of three men. The driver sat in the forward hull. The commander sat in a seat in the turret, and was responsible for aiming and firing the guns, while a loader/radio operator stood on the floor of the tank under the turret.

Variants

DEVELOPMENT AND LIMITED PRODUCTION MODELS
Panzer II Ausf. a (PzKpfw IIa)

Not to be confused with the later Ausf. A (the sole difference being the capitalization of the letter A), the Ausf. a was the first limited production version of the Panzer II to be built, and was subdivided into three sub-variants. The Ausf. a/1 was initially built with a cast idler wheel with rubber tire, but this was replaced after ten production examples with a welded part. The Ausf. a/2 improved engine access issues. The Ausf. a/3 included improved suspension and engine cooling. In general, the specifications for the Ausf. a models was similar, and a total of 75 were produced from May 1936 to February 1937 by Daimler-Benz and MAN. The Ausf. a was considered the 1 Serie under the LaS 100 name.

Specifications
- Crew: 3
- Engine: Maybach HL57TR with 6 gear transmission plus reverse
- Weight: 7.6 tonnes
- Dimensions: 4.38 m(l) x 2.14 m(w) x 1.95 m(h)
- Speed: 40 km/h
- Range: 200 km
- Communications: FuG5 radio
- Primary armament: 2 cm KwK 30 L/55 gun with TZF4 gun sight, turret mounted
- Secondary armament: MG34 7.92 mm machine gun, coaxially mounted
- Ammunition: 180 20 mm and 2,250 7.92 mm carried
- Turret: 360° hand traverse with elevation of +20° and depression to -9.5°
- Armour: 13 mm front, side, and rear; 8 mm top; 5 mm bottom

Panzer II Ausf. b (PzKpfw IIb)

Again, not to be confused with the later Ausf. B, the Ausf. b was a second limited production series embodying further developments, primarily a heavy reworking of suspension components resulting in a wider track and a longer hull. Length was increased to 4.76 m but width and height were unchanged. Additionally, a Maybach HL62TR engine was used with new drivetrain components to match. Deck armor for the superstructure and turret roof was increased to 10–12 mm. Total weight increased to 7.9 tonnes. Twenty-five were built by Daimler-Benz and MAN in February and March 1937.

A Panzer II with a Panzer I following, on the Western Front, 1940

Panzer II Ausf. c (PzKpfw IIc)

As the last of the developmental limited production series of Panzer IIs, the Ausf. c came very close to matching the mass production configuration, with a major change to the suspension with the replacement of the six small road wheels with five larger independently sprung road wheels and an additional return roller bringing that total to four. The tracks were further modified and the fenders widened. Total length was increased to 4.81 m and width to 2.22 m, while height was still about 1.99 m. At least 25 of this model were produced from March through July 1937.

Panzer II Ausf. A (PzKpfw IIA)

The first true production model, the Ausf. A included an armor upgrade to 14.5 mm on all sides, as well as a 14.5 mm floor plate, and an improved transmission. The Ausf. A entered production in July 1937.

Panzer II Ausf. B (PzKpfw IIB)

Introducing only minimal changes to the Ausf. A, the Ausf. B superseded it in production from December 1937.

A Panzer II rolls into Austria during the Anschluss.

Panzer II Ausf. C (PzKpfw IIC)

Few minor changes were made in the Ausf. C version, which became the standard production model from June 1938 through April 1940. A total of 1,113 examples of Ausf. c, A, B, and C tanks were built from March 1937 through April 1940 by Alkett, FAMO, Daimler-Benz, Henschel, MAN, MIAG, and Wegmann. These models were almost identical and were used in service interchangeably. This was the most widespread tank version of the Panzer II and performed the majority of the tank's service in the Panzer units during the war. Earlier versions of Ausf. C have rounded hull front, but many vehicles of Ausf. C were up-armored to fight in France. These have extra armors bolted on the turret front and super structure front. Also up-armored versions have angled front hull like that of Ausf.F. Some were also retro-fitted with commander's cupolas.

Panzer II Ausf. F (PzKpfw IIF)

Continuing the conventional design of the Ausf. C, the Ausf. F was designed as a reconnaissance tank and served in the same role as the earlier models. The superstructure front was made from a single piece armor plate with a redesigned visor. Also a dummy visor was placed next to it to reduce anti-tank rifle bullets hitting the real visor. The hull was redesigned with a flat 35 mm plate on its front, and armor of the superstructure and turret were built up to 30 mm on the front with 15 mm to the sides and rear. There was some minor alteration of the suspension and a new commander's cupola as well. Weight was increased to 9.5 tonnes. 524 were built from March 1941 to December 1942 as the final major tank version of the Panzer II series.

Panzer II Ausf. D (PzKpfw IID)

With a completely new Christie suspension with four road wheels, the Ausf. D was developed as a cavalry tank for use in the pursuit and reconnaissance roles. Only the turret was the same as the Ausf. C model, with a new hull and superstructure design and the use of a Maybach HL62TRM engine driving a seven-gear transmission (plus reverse). The design was shorter (4.65 m) but wider (2.3 m) and taller (2.06 m) than the Ausf. C. Speed was increased to 55 km/h. A total of 143 Ausf. D and

PzKpfw II Ausf. C at the Musée des Blindés

A Panzer II Ausf F lies knocked out in the Western Desert.

Ausf. E tanks were built from May 1938 through August 1939 by MAN, and they served in Poland. They were withdrawn in March 1940 for conversion to other types after proving to have poor off road performance.

Panzer II Ausf. E (PzKpfw IIE)

Similar to the Ausf. D, the Ausf. E improved some small items of the suspension, but was otherwise similar and served alongside the Ausf. D.

Panzer II Ausf. J (PzKpfw IIJ)

Continued development of the reconnaissance tank concept led to the much up-armored Ausf. J, which used the same concept as the PzKpfw IF of the same period, under the experimental designation VK1601. Heavier armor was added, bringing protection up to 80 mm on the front and 50 mm to the sides and rear, with 25 mm roof and floor plates, increasing total weight to 18 tonnes. Equipped with the same Maybach HL45P as the PzKpfw IF, top speed was reduced to 31 km/h. Primary armament was the 2 cm KwK 38 L/55 gun. 22 were produced by MAN between April and December 1942, and seven were issued to the 12th Panzer Division on the Eastern Front.

Panzerkampfwagen II ohne Aufbau

One use for obsolete Panzer II tanks which had their turrets removed for use in fortifications was as utility carriers. A number of chassis not used for conversion to self-propelled guns were instead handed over to the Engineers for use as personnel and equipment carriers.

Panzer II Flamm

Based on the same suspension as the Ausf. D and Ausf. E tank versions, the Flamm (also known as "Flamingo") used a new turret mounting a single MG34 machine gun, and two remotely controlled flamethrowers mounted in small turrets at each front corner of the vehicle. Each flamethrower could cover the front 180° arc, while the turret traversed 360°.

The flamethrowers were supplied with 320 litres of fuel and four tanks of compressed nitrogen. The nitrogen tanks were built into armored boxes along each side of the superstructure. Armor was 30 mm to the front and 14.5 mm to the side and rear, although the turret was increased to 20 mm at the sides and rear.

Total weight was 12 tonnes and dimensions were increased to a length of 4.9 m and width of 2.4 m although it was a bit shorter at 1.85 m tall. A FuG2 radio was carried. Two sub-variants existed: the Ausf. A and Ausf. B which differed only in minor suspension components. One hundred and fifty-five Flamm vehicles were built from January 1940 through March 1942. These were mostly on new chassis but 43 were on used Ausf. D and Ausf. E chassis. The Flamm was deployed in the USSR but was not very successful due to its limited armor, and survivors were soon withdrawn for conversion in December 1941.

5 cm PaK 38 auf Fahrgestell Panzerkampfwagen II

Conceived along the same lines as the Marder II, the 5 cm PaK 38 was an expedient solution to mount the 50 mm antitank gun on the Panzer II chassis. However, the much greater effectiveness of the 75 mm antitank gun made this option less desirable and it is not known how many field modifications were made to this effect.

7.62 cm PaK 36(r) auf Fahrgestell Panzerkampfwagen II Ausf. D (Sd.Kfz. 132)

After a lack of success with conventional and flame tank variants on the Christie chassis, it was decided to use the remaining chassis to mount captured Soviet antitank guns. The hull and suspension was unmodified from the earlier models, but the superstructure was built up to provide a large fighting compartment on top of which was mounted a Soviet 76.2 mm antitank gun, which, while not turreted, did have significant traverse. Only developed as an interim solution, the vehicle was clearly too tall and poorly protected, but had a powerful weapon and was better than what the Germans had at the time.

7.5 cm PaK 40 auf Fahrgestell Panzerkampfwagen II (Marder II) (Sd.Kfz. 131)

While the 7.62 cm PaK 36(r) was a good stopgap measure, the 7.5 cm PaK 40 mounted on the tank chassis of the Ausf. F resulted in a better overall fighting machine. New production amounted to 576 examples from June 1942 to June 1943 as well as the conversion of 75 tanks after new production had stopped. The work was done by Daimler-Benz, FAMO, and MAN. A much improved superstructure for the 7.62 cm mounting was built giving a lower profile. The Marder II became a key piece of equipment and served with the Germans on all fronts through the end of the war.

Leichte Feldhaubitze 18 auf Fahrgestell Panzerkampfwagen II (Wespe)

After the development of the Fahrgestell Panzerkampfwagen II for mounting the sIG 33, Alkett designed a version mounting a 10.5 cm leichte Feldhaubitze 18/2 field howitzer in a built-up

Panzer II Ausf. L in the Musée des Blindés, Saumur.

superstructure. The Panzer II proved an efficient chassis for this weapon and it became the only widely produced self-propelled 105 mm howitzer for Germany. Between February 1943 and June 1944, 676 were built by FAMO and it served with German forces on all major fronts.

Munitions Selbstfahrlafette auf Fahrgestell Panzerkampfwagen II

To support the Wespe in operation, a number of Wespe chassis were completed without installation of the howitzer, instead functioning as ammunition carriers. They carried 90 rounds of 105 mm caliber. 159 were produced alongside the Wespe. These could be converted by installation of the leFH 18 in the field if needed.

Panzerkampfwagen II mit Schwimmkörper

One of Germany's first attempts at developing an amphibious tank, the Schwimmkörper was a device built by Gebr Sachsenberg which consisted of two large pontoons that attached to either side of a Panzer II tank. The tanks were specially sealed and some modification to the engine exhaust and cooling was needed. The pontoons were detachable. The modified tanks were issued to the 18th Panzer Regiment which was formed in 1940. However, with cancellation of Operation Sealion, the plan to invade England, the tanks were used in the conventional manner by the regiment on the Eastern Front.

Panzer II Ausf. L (PzKpfw IIL) "Luchs"

A light reconnaissance tank, the Ausf. L was the only Panzer II design with the overlapping/interleaved road wheels and "slack track" configuration to enter series production, with 100 being built from September 1943 to January 1944 in addition to conversion of the four Ausf. M tanks. Originally given the experimental designation VK 1303, it was adopted under the alternate name Panzerspähwagen II and given the popular name Luchs (Lynx). The Lynx was larger than the Ausf. G in most dimensions (length 4.63 m; height 2.21 m; width 2.48 m). It was equipped with a six speed transmission (plus reverse), and could reach a speed of 60 km/h with a range of 290 km. The FuG 12 and FuG Spr a radios were installed, while 330 rounds of 20 mm and 2,250 rounds of 7.92 mm ammunition were carried. Total vehicle weight was 11.8 tonnes.

LIMITED PRODUCTION, EXPERIMENTS AND PROTOTYPES
Panzer II Ausf. G (PzKpfw IIG)

The fourth and final suspension configuration used for the Panzer II tanks was the five overlapping road wheel configuration termed Schachtellaufwerk by the Germans. This was used as the basis for the redesign of the Panzer II into a reconnaissance tank with high speed and good off-road performance. The Ausf. G was the first Panzer II to use this configuration, and was developed with the experimental designation VK901. There is no record of the Ausf. G being issued to combat units, and only twelve full vehicles were built from April 1941 to February 1942 by MAN. The turrets were subsequently issued for use in fortifications.

Specifications
- Crew: 3
- Engine: Maybach HL66P driving a five speed transmission (plus reverse)
- Weight: 10.5 tonnes
- Dimensions: length 4.24 m; width 2.38 m; height 2.05 m
- Performance: speed 50 km/h; range 200 km
- Main armament: 7.92x94 mm MG141 automatic rifle, turret mounted with TZF10 sight
- Secondary armament: 7.92 mm MG34 machine gun, coaxially mounted
- Turret: 360° hand traverse
- Armor: 30 mm front, 15 mm sides and rear

Panzer II Ausf. H (PzKpfw IIH)

Given experimental designation VK903, the Ausf. H was intended as the production model of the Ausf. G, with armor for the sides and rear increased to 20 mm and a new four speed transmission (plus reverse) similar to that of the PzKpfw 38(t) nA. Only prototypes were ever completed by the time of cancellation in September 1942.

5 cm PaK 38 auf Panzerkampfwagen II

Planned as a light tank destroyer, the first two prototypes were delivered in 1942 but by then their 50 mm gun was not sufficient and the program was canceled in favor of 75 mm weapons.

Brückenleger auf Panzerkampfwagen II

After failed attempts to use the Panzer I as a chassis for a bridge layer, work moved to the Panzer II, led by Magirus. It is not known how many of these conversions were made, but four were known to have been in service with the 7th Panzer Division in May 1940.

15 cm sIG 33 auf Fahrgestell Panzerkampfwagen II (Sf)

One of the first gun mount variants of the Panzer II design

was to emplace a 15 cm sIG 33 heavy infantry gun on a turretless Panzer II chassis. The prototype utilized an Ausf. B tank chassis, but it was quickly realized that it was not sufficient for the mounting. A new, longer chassis incorporating an extra road wheel was designed and built, named the Fahrgestell Panzerkampfwagen II. An open-topped 15 mm thick armored superstructure sufficient against small arms and shrapnel was provided around the gun. This was not high enough to give full protection for the crew while manning the gun, although they were still covered directly to the front by the tall gun shield. Only 12 were built in November and December 1941. These served with the 707th and 708th Heavy Infantry Gun Companies in North Africa until their destruction in 1943.

Bergepanzerwagen auf Panzerkampfwagen II Ausf. J

A single example of an Ausf. J with a jib in place of its turret was found operating as an armored recovery vehicle. There is no record of an official program for this vehicle.

Panzer Selbstfahrlafette 1c

Developed in prototype form only, this was one of three abortive attempts to use the Panzer II chassis for mounting a 5 cm PaK 38 gun, this time on the chassis of the Ausf. G. Two examples were produced which had similar weight to the tank version, and both were put in front-line service, but production was not undertaken as priority was given to heavier armed models.

Panzer II Ausf. M (PzKpfw IIM)

Using the same chassis as the Ausf. H, the Ausf. M replaced the turret with a larger, open-topped turret containing a 5 cm KwK 39/1 gun. Four were built by MAN in August 1942, but did not see service.

VK1602 Leopard

The VK1602 was intended as a 5 cm KwK39-armed replacement for the Ausf. L, with a Maybach HL157P engine driving an eight speed transmission (plus reverse). While the hull was based on that of the PzKpfw IIJ, it was redesigned after the PzKpfw V Panther, most noticeably with the introduction of fully sloped frontal armor. Two versions were initially planned, a lighter, faster 18 ton variant and a slower, 26 ton vehicle; the former was abandoned at an early stage. Subsequently, work on the first prototype was abandoned when it was determined that the vehicle was under-armed for its weight, and versions of the PzKpfw IV and -V could serve just as well in the reconnaissance role while being more capable of defending themselves. This vehicle never received an official Panzerkampfwagen title, but it would have been called the "Leopard" had it entered production. Its turret design was adopted for the SdKfz 234/2 Puma.

Legion Condor

The Condor Legion (German: Legion Condor) was a unit composed of volunteers from the German Air Force (Luftwaffe) and from the German Army (Wehrmacht Heer) which served with the Nationalists during the Spanish Civil War of July 1936 to March 1939. The Condor Legion developed methods of terror bombing which were used widely in the Second World War shortly afterwards. The bombing of Guernica was the most infamous operation carried out by the Condor Legion during this period. Hugo Sperrle commanded the aircraft units of the Condor Legion and Wilhelm Ritter von Thoma commanded the ground units.

HISTORY OF MILITARY AID TO SPAIN
Following the military coup in Spain at the start of the Spanish Civil War, the Spanish Second Republic turned to the Soviet

He-111E of the Condor Legion, 1939

Union and France for support, and the nationalists requested the support of Hitler's Germany and fascist Italy. The first request for German aircraft was made on 22 July, with an order for 10 transport aircraft. Hitler decided to support the nationalists on 25 or 26 July, but was wary of provoking a Europe-wide war. The Reich Air Travel Ministry concluded that nationalist forces would need at least 20 Ju 52s, flown by Luft Hansa pilots, to carry the Army of Africa from Spanish Morocco to Spain. This mission became known as Operation Magic Fire (German: Feuerzauber). The joint Spanish-German "Spanish-Moroccan Transport Company" (Spanish: Companía Hispano-Marroquí de Transporte, HISMA) and an entirely German company, the Raw Materials and Good Purchasing Company (German: Rohstoffe-und-Waren-Einkaufsgesellschaft, ROWAK) were established. This involvement was kept covert, hidden from both foreign and economic ministries, and funded with three million Reichmarks.

The organisation and recruitment of German volunteers was

also kept secret. The first contingent of 86 men left on 1 August, unaware of where they were going. They were accompanied with six biplane fighters, anti-aircraft guns and about 100 tons of other supplies. They were placed at Tablada airfield near Seville, and accompanied by German Air transport began the airlift of Franco's troops to Spain. Germany's involvement grew in September to encompass the Wehrmacht's other branches; Operation Magic Fire was renamed Operation Guido in November. A wide belief was that the soldiers would train Spanish nationalists, and not engage. The head of the Kriegsmarine provided submarines from 24 October. The German navy also provided various surface ships and coordinated movement of German supplies to Spain. German U-Boats were dispatched to Spanish waters under the codename Ursula.

In the two weeks following 27 July, German transport moved nearly 2,500 troops of the Army of Africa to Spain. By 11 October, the mission's official end, 13,500 troops, 127 machine guns and 36 field guns had been carried into Spain from Morocco. Over this period there was a movement from training and supply missions of overt combat. The operation leader, Alexander von Scheele, was replaced by Walter Warlimont. In September, 86 tons of bombs, 40 Panzer PzKpfw I tanks and 122 personnel had been landed in Spain; they were accompanied with 108 aircraft in the July–October period, split between aircraft for the Nationalist faction itself and planes for German volunteers in Spain.

German air crews supported the Nationalist advance on Madrid, and the successful relief of the Siege of the Alcázar. Ultimately, this phase of the Siege of Madrid would be unsuccessful. Soviet air support for the Republican was growing, particularly through the supply of Polikarpov aircraft. Warlimont appealed to Nazi Germany to step up support. Following German recognition of Franco's government on 30 September, German efforts in Spain were reorganised and expanded. The existing command structure was replaced with the Winterübung Rügen, and the military units already in Spain were formed into a new legion, which was briefly called the Iron Rations (German: Eiserne Rationen) and the Iron Legion (German: Eiserne Legion) before Göring renamed it the Condor Legion (German: Legion Condor). The first German chargé to Franco's government, General Wilhelm von Faupel, arrived in November, but was told not to interfere in military matters.

Its debut (combat test) was during Spanish Civil War (1936-38). First 32 PzKpfw I along with single Kleiner Panzer Befehlswagen I arrived in October of 1936. Only 106 tanks, (102 Ausf A, Ausf B and 4 Kleiner Panzer Befehlswagen I) saw service with "Condor Legion" (Major Ritter von Thoma's Panzer Abteilung 88 also known as Abteilung Drohne) and General Franco's "Nationalists". Pz.Abt.88 with its 3 companies was based at Cubas near Toledo, where German instructors trained future Spanish crews, while the unit was used for training duties and combat (e.g. assault on Madrid). Panzerkampfwagen I tanks proved to be outclassed by Soviet T-26 and BT-5 provided to "The Republicans".

Some Panzerkampfwagen I captured by "The Republicans" were rearmed with French Hotchkiss 25mm Model 1934 or 1937 anti-tank guns mounted in a modified turret (PzKpfw I Ausf.

Dornier Do 17 E-1 of the Condor Legion

Ju 52 plane undergoing maintenance

A mit 20mm Flak L/65 Breda Model 1935). During Spanish Civil War, PzKpfw I Ausf B was experimentally armed with Italian 20mm Breda Modello (model) 1935 light anti-aircraft gun mounted in a modified turret, in order to increase its combat potential. Some sources state that three tanks were converted that way.

PzKpfw Is equipped two Nationalist tank battalions (Agrupacion de Carros) - 1st and 2nd Tank Battalion. German High Command used the opportunity of the Spanish Civil War to test their new weapons and tactics of Blitzkrieg. Its very thin armor offered only protection against small firearms and its twin MGs were no match for anything other than infantry units and proved completly useless in combat.

The following information is provided on Gruppe Imker - the codename of the German Ground Contingent of the Condor Legion:
- 1 Pz.Kp (from the 1 Battalion of Panzer Regiment 6 (Neuruppin))
- 2 Pz.Kp.(from the II Battalion of Panzer Regiment 6 (Neuruppin))

- Transport Kp
- Tansport Kp
- Nachrichtenzug (Signals Platoon)
- Werkstatts-Kp (Workshop Company)
- 1 Pak. Kdo. (Antitank Gun Command)

Upon the completion of training, the Spanish tank companies retained their German Pz.Kpfw.1s and accompanied them to the front. The German training companies would then receive another supply of tanks to be used for the next training session. Army ground personnel in Spain never exceeded 600 men at any time. Gruppe Imker (Group Beekeeper) had a staff, under the command of oberstleutenant von Thoma, which coordinated and maintained all direct communications to Germany. Imker's Panzer units were codenamed Gruppe "Drohne" or Group "Drone".

Each company had 11 Pz-Is with 3 companies to a Battalion (Agrupacion) and a T-26 company added later (captured tanks).

Overleaf is a collection of documents to Cpl Eugene Alexejen of Legion Condor, awarded Spanish cross in silver. He was in the Condor Legion with Panzer Regiment 6 "Neuruppin" of the third Panzer Division.

In Spain in early October 1936 General der Panzertruppe Wilhelm Josef Ritter von Thoma was sent by the German high command to Spain as the commander of the group "Imker" (Beekeeper), the ground contingent of the German Condor Legion. Tasked with training Franco's Spanish Nationalist officers and men in tanks, infantry tactics and artillery and signals employment. Cpl Eugene Alexsejen would have been part of this and would have helped in the front line in combat.

MOTIVATION

In the years following the Spanish Civil War, Hitler gave several possible motives for German involvement. Among these were the distraction it provided from German re-militarisation;

A back view of a Panzer I from the Condor Legion in Spain.

the prevention of the spread of communism to Western Europe; the creation of a state friendly to Germany to disrupt Britain and France; and the possibilities for economic expansion. Although the offensive on Madrid was abandoned in March 1937, a series of attacks on weaker Republican-controlled areas was supported by Germany; despite prolonging the Civil War, it would help to distract the other western powers from Hitler's ambitions in central Europe. The offensive on Vizcaya, a mining and industrial centre, would help fuel German industry. On 27 June 1937, Hitler (in a speech at Wurzburg) declared he supported Franco to gain control of Spanish ore.

Discussions over German objectives for intervention occurred in January 1937. Germany was keen to avoid prompting a Europe-wide war, which at the time they felt committing further resources to Spain would do. Contradictory views were held by German officials: Ernst von Weizsäcker suggested it was merely a matter of graceful withdrawal; Hermann Göring stated that Germany would never recognise a "red Spain". A joint Italian–German decision, that the last shipments would be made by the

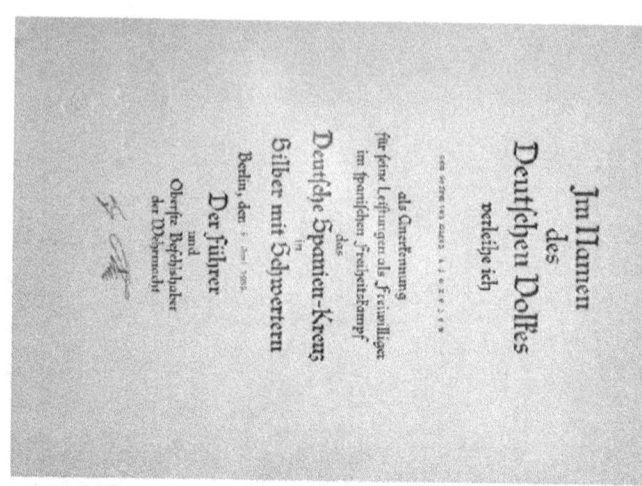
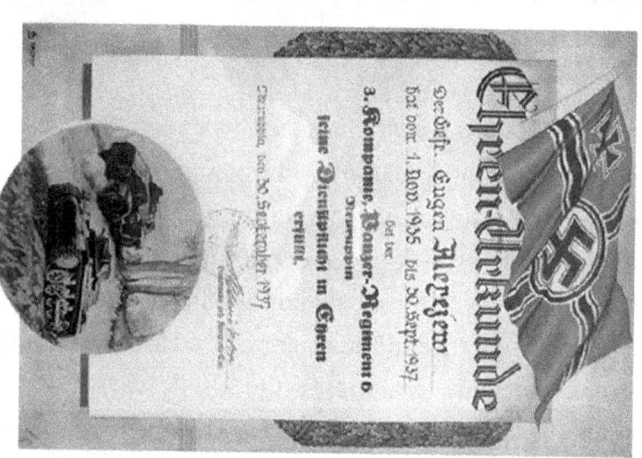

start of February, was agreed.

It has been speculated that Hitler used the Spanish Civil War issue to distract Mussolini from Hitler's own designs on and plans for union (Anschluss) with Austria. The authoritarian Catholic, anti-Nazi Vaterländische Front government of autonomous Austria had been in alliance with Mussolini, and in 1934 the assassination of Austria's authoritarian president Engelbert Dollfuss had already successfully invoked Italian military assistance in case of a German invasion.

A communique in December 1936, from German ambassador in Rome Ulrich von Hassell illustrates another point:

The role played by the Spanish conflict as regards Italy's relations with France and England could be similar to that of the Abyssinian conflict, bringing out clearly the actual, opposing interests of the powers and thus preventing Italy from being drawn into the net of the Western powers and used for their machinations. All the more clearly will Italy recognize the advisability of confronting the Western powers shoulder to shoulder with Germany.

Certificates opposite: The left-hand document roughly translates to: In the name of the German people I give Corporal Eugene Alexejen as recognition for fine service as a volunteer in the Spanish War of Independence the German Spanish Cross in Silver with Swords, Berlin the 6 June 1939. The Fuhrer and Supreme Commander of the Wehrmacht. Centre is an "Honor Deed" showing his service with the regiment between 1935 and 1937. Roughly translated it reads: Honor Deed of Cpl Eugene Alexejen has from 1 Nov 1935-30 Sept 1937 in Third Company, Panzer Regiment 6 "Neuruppin" fulfilled his compulsory service with honor. "Neuruppin" the 30 September 1937. Signed Captain and Company commander
On the right is an award document for the Spanish Red Cross of Military Merit. The text for the Spanish campaign award shown above translates roughly as follows: Spanish army: on the meritorious service in operations during the war—Sergent Eugene Alexejen—S.E. the chief of state and generalissimo of the Nationalist Army has seen fit to give the Campaign Medal and for the record and to the satisfaction of the applicant, issued on behalf of "SE". Burgos to 1st December 1938, III triumphant year—The Minister of National Defence

OPERATIONAL RECORD

The Condor Legion, upon establishment, consisted of the Kampfgruppe 88, with three squadrons of Ju 52 bombers and the Jagdgruppe 88 with three squadrons of Heinkel He 51 fighters, the reconnaissance Aufklärungsgruppe 88 (supplemented by the Aufklärungsgruppe See 88), an anti-aircraft group, the Flakbteilung 88, and a signals group, the Nachrichtenabteilung 88. Overall command was given to Hugo Sperrle, with Alexander Holle as chief of staff. Scheele was transferred to become a military attaché in Salamanca. Two armoured units under the command of Wilhelm Ritter von Thoma, with four tanks each, were also operational.

The Nationalists were supported by German and Italian units and materials at the Battle of Madrid. However, the military situation in Madrid remained poor for the nationalists, and both German and Italian aircraft (under Franco's direction) began bombing raids on the city as a whole. The Germans were keen to observe the effects of civilian bombings and deliberate burning of the city. Offensives involving German aircraft, as well as the bombings, were unsuccessful. Increasing Republican air superiority became apparent, particularly the strength of the Soviet Polikarpov I-15 and I-16 aircraft. Historian Hugh Thomas describes their armaments as "primitive". Faupel, in November–December, urged the creation of a single German unit of 15,000–30,000, believing it would be enough to turn the tide of the war to the Nationalists. Hans-Heinrich Dieckhoff argued this would insufficient, and that larger measures could provoke the wrath of the Spanish.Between late 1936 and early 1937, new aircraft were sent to the Condor Legion, including Henschel Hs 123 dive bombers, and prototypes of the Heinkel He 112 and Messerschmitt Bf 109, with the last proving the most successful. The Heinkel He 111 was added to the bomber fleet, along with the Dornier Do 17 (E and F types). Older aircraft were passed onto the Nationalists. By the end of 1936, 7,000 Germans were in Spain.

German forces also operated in the Battle of Jarama, which began with a Nationalist offensive on 6 February 1937. It included German-supplied ground forces, including two batteries of machine guns, a tank division, and the Condor Legion's anti-aircraft guns. Bombing by both Republican and Nationalist aircraft, including Ju 52s from the Legion, helped ensure a stalemate. It showed up the inadequacy of the Legion's aircraft, faced with superior Soviet-made fighters. Von Thorma requested Irish nationalist support for a tank advance at one point, never to be replicated. Use of He 51 and Ju 52s, and the Legion's anti-aircraft guns used in ground roles, only partly mitigated what was a significant defeat for the Nationalists at the Battle of Guadalajara during March. A joint Italian-German general had been set up in January 1937 to advise Franco on war planning. The defeat of a significant Italian force and the growing Soviet superiority in tanks and aircraft led the Germans to support a plan to abandon the offensive on Madrid and instead concentrate a series of attacks on weaker Republican-controlled areas. Whilst many countries believed motorised troops to have been proven less effective than first thought, it was the inadequacy of the Italians as a fighting force that dominated German thought.

THE VIZCAYA CAMPAIGN

The isolated area of Vizcaya, a predominantly Basque part of northern Spain, was the most immediate target, in what was called the War in the North. It was largely a Nationalist and Italian offensive, but was supported by a consistently re-equipping Condor Legion. The terrain was favourable, with the planes coming over a range of mountains to the south, masking their entrance. Sperrle remained in Salamanca; Wolfram von Richthofen replaced Holle in January as deputy and in actual command. Since the Basque air force was very limited, even fighters were used in ground-attack roles. The Legion's air force initially attacked the towns of Ochandiano and Durango. Durango had no anti-aircraft defence, and only minor other defences. According to the Basques, 250 civilians died on the 31 March, including the priest, nuns and congregation of a church ceremony. The Germans, with their air raids, were hated. The Basque ground forces were in full retreat towards Bilbao, through the town of Guernica, which was attacked on 26 April in one of the most controversial attacks of the Spanish Civil War.

GUERNICA

In Operation Rügen, waves of Ju 52 and He 51 planes bombed and strafed targets in Guernica. The number of casualties is a matter of controversy, with perhaps 200–300 people killed; the number reported dead by the Basques was 1,654 dead and 889 wounded. Several explanations were put forward by the Nationalists, including blaming the attack on the Republicans, that the attack on the town had been a prolonged offensive, or that the Rentería bridge, outside Guernica, was the true target. However, the nature of the operation itself, including the formation and armaments used, makes this seem unlikely. Guernica was a clear target of the Condor Legion, rather than the Nationalists as a whole. The offensive on Bilbao, when it eventually came on 11 July, was supported by ground units of the Condor Legion, and extensive air operations. It proved the worth of the Condor Legion to the Nationalist cause.

The first English-language media reports of the destruction in Guernica appeared two days later. George Steer, a reporter for The Times, who was covering the Spanish Civil War from inside the country, authored the first full account of events. Steer's reporting set the tone for much of the subsequent reportage. Steer pointed out the clear German complicity in the action. The

Ruins of Guernica (1937)

evidence of three small bomb cases stamped with the German Imperial Eagle made clear that the official German position of neutrality in the Civil War and the signing of a Non-Intervention Pact was a sham. Steer's report was syndicated to the New York Times and then worldwide, generating widespread shock, outrage, and fear.

FURTHER CAMPAIGNS

The Condor Legion also took part in the Battle of Brunete, designed as a Republican offensive to take the pressure off northern Spain, where fighting was ongoing. The Legion was sent from the north to reinforce the broken line. There were repeated raids on Republican armoured vehicles and later defensive positions by both bombers and fighters based at Salamanca. Republican aircraft were ineffective, despite Nationalist fears, compared with German aircraft; the Messerschmitt Bf 109 was shown to be superior to the I-15 and I-16 models used by Republican forces. The Legion lost 8 aircraft, but claimed

18 victories. German tactics were also improved with the experience of Brunete, particularly the en masse use of tanks by the Nationalists.

The Nationalists returned to focus on the capture of northern Spain. German test aircraft, with latest models, faced an outdated Basque air force, although it did have some Russian planes. Heavy aerial bombardment from 200 Nationalist, German and Italian planes was used far behind Basque lines in August 1937, leading to the fall of Santander after the Battle of Santander on 1 September. The formal battle in Asturias ended with the fall of Gijón on 21 October. A large amount of ammunitions had been used by the Legion, including a million machine gun rounds and 2,500 tonnes of bombs. Germany immediately began to ship industrial production back to Germany. Sperrle argued repeatedly with Faupel, and against HISMA's monopoly. Faupel was replaced by Franco, through Sperrle. Sperrle also returned to Germany and was replaced by Helmuth Volkmann; following disagreements with Volkmann, Von Richthofen would be replaced with Hermann Plocher in early 1938.

Whilst the next major campaign – Madrid or Barcelona – was discussed, the Condor Legion was moved to Soria and began a week of strikes against Republican airfields, halted by the Republican advance on Teruel and the ensuing Battle of Teruel. Both the Legion's land and air forces were used, and the Legion moved to Bronchales. Poor weather resulted in few flights, and the town fell to Republican forces on 6 January. Up to 100 sorties a day were launched during the Nationalist's counter-offensive through the Alfambra valley. The Junkers Ju 87A was used for the first time on the advance on Teruel, which was retaken on 22 February. The continued Nationalist offensive on Aragon in April–June 1937, including the Battle of Belchite, involved bombing raids and the use of the Legion's ground forces. The Legion was switched to focus in the north, towards the Segre river, before moving south again following Nationalist successes. The Legion moved its main headquarters to Benicarlo; single-engined planes operated from airfields nearby, and twin-engined planes from Zaragoza. Hitler's words to his colleagues belied a change in attitude about the war in Germany – that a quick victory in the war was not desirable, a mere continuation of the war would be preferable. German policy would be to prevent a Republican defeat. However, casualties were beginning to mount for the Legion and, combined with a resurgence in Republican air activity, the Nationalist advance stalled. This was, perhaps, because of the reluctance of commanders in Germany to supply reinforcements, with the Czechoslovakia crisis mounting. Arguments over the bill to the Germans – now rising at 10 million Reichmarks a month – continued, unresolved. The Legion's materiel had been exhausted.

On 24–25 July, Republican forces launched the last major offensive of the war, the Battle of the Ebro. Reconnaissance units of the Condor Legion had noticed a troop build-up, and warned Nationalists forces. The warning went unheeded. Although the Republic gained ground, Republican forces failed to gain control of Ganesa, with 422 sorties by the Legion (with around 70 aircraft operational) having considerable effect. The rest of the battle saw a series of attacks using artillery or air strikes, followed by a Nationalist ground advance. However, tensions in Czechoslovakia and a shortage of pilots in Germany led to the return of 250 pilots from the Legion, around half of them being bomber crews. Although trained Spaniards made up some of the shortfall, Volkmann complained to central command in Berlin, which would lead to his recall in September. During the battle, which saw 113 days of fighting, only 10 aircraft were lost (some by accident) and 14 were badly damaged; the Legion claimed around 100 Republican aircraft, a third of those lost. Only 5 aircrew had been killed, and 6 captured. Aid from Germany temporarily halted in mid-September. Germany and Nationalist Spain settled the issue of German interests in Spanish mines.

The Legion took a short break from active duty to receive new aircraft, including Bf 109Es, He 111Es and Js, and Hs 126As, bringing its strength to 96 aircraft, around a fifth of the Nationalist's force as a whole. Von Richthofen returned to Spain in overall command, with Hans Seidemann as chief of staff. This reinforcement may have been the single most important intervention by a foreign side in the war, enabling a counterattack after the Battle of the Ebro. It mainly took part in operations against the remaining Republican air force during January–February 1939, with considerable success. After it took part in parades in Barcelona and elsewhere, and minor duties over Madrid, it was rapidly dissolved. The men returned on 26 May; the best aircraft were returned to Germany and the rest of the equipment bought by the new Spanish regime.

The Condor Legion claimed to have destroyed 320 Republican planes using aircraft (either shot down or bombed on the ground), and shot down another 52 using anti-aircraft guns. They also claimed to have destroyed 60 ships. They lost 72 aircraft due to hostile action, and another 160 to accidents.

MARITIME OPERATIONS

The Maritime Reconnaissance Staffel 88 (German: Aufklärungsstaffel See 88) was the Condor Legion's maritime unit under the command of Karl Heinz Wolff. Operating independently of the land-based division, it acted against enemy shipping, ports, coastal communications and occasionally inland targets such as bridges. It used floatplanes, starting with the Heinkel He 60, which began operating at Cadiz in October 1936. Missions started as reconnaissance but, following the move from Cadiz to Mellila in Spanish Morocco in December 1936, the focus shifted to attacks on shipping. It was again moved in

February 1937 to Málaga, newly captured, and then to Majorca when Málaga proved unsuitable. Beginning in June, operations were expanded to allow attacks on all Republican ports, so long as no British ships were present. 10 ships were attacked in the second half of 1937; however, the Norwegian torpedoes being used proved ineffective, and strafing or bombing targets was used instead.

The arrival of Martin Harlinghausen (known as "Iron Gustav") saw operations expand, and operations targeted Alicante, Almeria, Barcelona and Cartegena. As naval activity declined, inland targets became more numerous, and night missions began. Activities in support of ground forces became the main focus of the unit until the end of hostilities. Both Wolff and Harlinghausen received the Spanish Cross in Gold with Swords and Diamonds. In total, eleven men were killed in action, and five others died due to accident or illness.

OTHER OPERATIONS

Overtly, the Kriegsmarine was part of force enforcing the Non-Intervention Agreement from interfering in the Civil War. However, this agreement was clearly broken by Germany. As a result, the German pocket battleship Deutschland stood guard over Ceuta to prevent interference from Republican ships while Franco transported troops to the Spanish mainland. By mid-October, the German North Sea Group around Spain consisted of the pocket battleships Deutschland and Admiral Scheer, the light cruiser Köln and four torpedo boats. After the Germans claimed that Leipzig had been attacked by an unidentified submarine, it did formally withdraw from international patrols.

Operation Ursula (named after the daughter of Karl Dönitz) saw a group of German U-boats active around Spain. It began on 20 November 1936, with the movement of the U-33 and U-34 from Wilhelmshaven. Any identification marks were obscured, and the whole mission was kept secret. Difficulties in identifying legitimate targets and concerns about discovery limited their operations. During their return to Wilhelmshaven in December, the Republican submarine C-3 was sunk; the Germans claimed this was due to a torpedo fired from U-34, although the Republican's enquiry claimed its loss was due to an internal explosion. Their return marked the official end of Operation Ursula. However, it does seem that further submarines were sent in mid-1937, but details of the operation are not known; six are believed to have been involved.

ABWEHR

The German Intelligence service, the Abwehr, working independently of the Legion Condor was secretly involved in Operation Bodden. This was to later play a part in the detection of the Operation Torch invasion fleet.

MILITARY ADVANTAGES GAINED
Training

It is known that the leaders of the Army were hesitant about becoming involved in the conflict, and resisted a call made by the Italian government for a dual transfer of ground troops to fight in Spain. The involvement of the Luftwaffe, however, was not entirely restricted and a commonly held viewpoint is that the involvement of the Luftwaffe in the Civil War constituted a proving ground for troops employed later during World War II. This view is supported by the testimony of Hermann Göring, later Reichsmarschall of the Luftwaffe, when on trial at the International Military Tribunal in Nürnberg. When asked about the decision to use the Luftwaffe, Göring states:

When the Civil War broke out in Spain, Franco sent a call for help to Germany and asked for support, particularly in the air. One should not forget that Franco with his troops was stationed in Africa and that he could not get the troops across, as the fleet was in the hands of the Communists, or, as they called themselves at the time, the competent Revolutionary

"Condor Legion" infantry training school in Ávila, Spain.

Government in Spain. The decisive factor was, first of all, to get his troops over to Spain. The Fuehrer thought the matter over. I urged him to give support [to Franco] under all circumstances, firstly, in order to prevent the further spread of communism in that theater and, secondly, to test my young Luftwaffe at this opportunity in this or that technical respect.

This was also a view put forth in western media following the disengagement of German forces from Spain.

Dozens of Messerschmitt Bf 109 fighters and Heinkel He 111 medium bombers, and from December 1937, at least three Junkers Ju 87 Stuka dive-bombers, first saw active service in the Condor Legion against Soviet-supplied aircraft. The Stuka's first mission flown in Spain was February 1938. Each of these aircraft played a major role during the early years of the Second World War. The Germans also quickly realized that the days of the biplane fighter were finished. The Heinkel He 51 fighter, after suffering many losses during the first 12 months of the conflict, was switched to a ground attack role and later saw service as a trainer.

Bf 109 C-1, Jagdgruppe 88, Legion Condor

OTHER UNITS

The Condor Legion also included non-aircraft units. Panzer crews operating Panzerkampfwagen I light tanks were commanded by Wilhelm Ritter von Thoma. The Germans also tested their 88 mm heavy anti-aircraft artillery which they used to destroy Republican tanks and fortifications using direct fire, as well as enemy aircraft in their designed role.

German involvement in Spain also saw the development of the first air ambulance service for evacuation of wounded combatants.

TECHNICAL ADVANCES

One important factor in World War II which is thought to have directly resulted from the conflict is the technical development of the Messerschmitt Bf 109. The V3 – V6 types entered service in Spain directly from operational trials around January 1937. In the spring of 1938 these were joined by type C aircraft with type Es being first fielded in December 1938.

As a result of combat in Spain improvements were also made to the 88 mm gun.

TACTICS

Alongside the potential for gains in combat experience it is also thought that various strategic initiatives were first trialed as part of Luftwaffe involvement in the conflict. Theories on strategic bombing were first developed by the Luftwaffe with the first exhibition of "carpet bombing" in the September 1937 Asturias campaign. As the fighting progressed into March 1938 Italian pilots under Fieldmarshal Hugo Sperrle were involved in thirteen raids against Barcelona involving fire and gas bombs. These particular raids resulted in the deaths of thousands of civilians. It is worth noting that a subsequent commander of the Legion in Spain, Wolfram Freiherr von Richthofen was to become heavily involved in the operation of the Luftwaffe as part of Operation Barbarossa.

Tactics of combined or joint operations were a particular focus. Close air support for Nationalist troops, attack bombing of Republican troop concentrations, and strafing became features of the war. The Legion worked closely in missions which maximized the fighting ability of the Nationalist air force and troops, the Italian CTV, and pilots from the Aviazione Legionaria (Legionary Air Force). German Air ace Adolf Galland was to claim after World War II that although there was a focus on taking lessons from the conflict in Spain, he believed the wrong conclusions were drawn by the German High Command with particular respect to the Luftwaffe:

> Whatever may have been the importance of the tests of German arms in the Spanish Civil War from tactical, technical and operational points of view, they did not provide the experience that was needed nor lead to the formulation of sound strategic concepts.

REACTION TO GERMAN INVOLVEMENT

Various sympathetic writers participated in condemning the scarcely concealed interference by Germany and Italy. An example was Heinrich Mann, who appealed from exile in France with the slogan "German soldiers! A rogue sends you to Spain!" in response to the Legion's involvement.

Other states tacitly approved the fight of the German Legion against the Soviet-supplied Spanish Republican side.

TREATMENT IN NAZI GERMANY

As part of his longterm "Blumenkrieg" strategy Hitler drew parallels between the conflict in Spain and the peaceful methods he used to gain control in Germany. The regime also made use of the conflict as an opportunity for political education and aggrandizement. Highlighting of the military aspects and success story for German arms is also evident with the publication of various pulp semi-autobiographical works in 1939, most notably:

- Wir funken für Franco (literally We transmit for Franco) by Hellmut Führing,
- Als Jagdflieger in Spanien (As a fighter pilot in Spain) by Hannes Trautloft,
- Das Buch der Spanienflieger (The Spanish Pilot's Book) by Hauptmann Wulf Bley.

Each book had a high circulation; in the case of Bley the circulation was estimated at over 1 million books sold. Although accurate in part these works are now accepted by scholars on the period and conflict as laced with propaganda which emphasizes daring escapades and fails to address the realities of military combat in general.

Contemporary Documents

Reconnaissance By Light Tank Platoons
Intelligence Bulletin, May 1943

1. INTRODUCTION

In German tank organizations, a light tank platoon consisting of seven Pz. Kw. 2's is an organic part both of the regimental headquarters company and the battalion headquarters company. The regimental light tank platoon is normally used for reconnaissance purposes. German doctrine covering the reconnaissance duties of patrols drawn from these platoons is summarized below. (It assumes that superior German forces are conducting an advance.)

2. THE DOCTRINE

a. Teamwork

Teamwork, the Germans point out, is the secret of successful reconnaissance. They believe that haphazardly formed reconnaissance patrols, made up of men who have never worked together before, are of little value.

b. Reconnaissance Before H-Hour

(1) Orders.—Orders given to light tank patrols which are to perform reconnaissance before H-hour include:

(a) Information about hostile forces and the terrain.

(b) German intentions (especially those of a patrol's own and flanking units).

(c) Composition of the patrol.

(d) Time of departure.

(e) Line of advance and objectives.

(f) Method and procedure of reporting (radio or motorcycle).

(g) Position of the patrol commander, and of the commander to whom he will report.

(h) Action to be taken on completion of task, or on meeting superior opposing forces.

It is prohibited to take written orders and situation maps on reconnaissance. Special precautions are insisted upon when markings of any kind are made on maps used on reconnaissance; these markings are required to be of a kind which will not reveal German dispositions if the maps are captured.

(2) Information Needed Beforehand.—For its disposition and method of work, the German patrol depends on knowing:

(a) Up to what point contact with the opposition is unlikely. (Until reaching this point, the patrol saves time by advancing rapidly and avoiding elaborate protective measures.)

(b) At what point contact is probable. (After this, increased alertness is maintained.)

(c) At what point contact is certain. (Here the patrol is ready for action.)

The patrol commander is also given necessary particulars regarding air support and information as to the attitude of the civil population.

(3) Method of Advance.—The light tank patrol advances rapidly from one observation point to the next, making use at first of roads and paths, but later, as it approaches hostile forces, using all available cover. When approaching villages, woods, or defiles, the patrol leaves the road in sufficient time to upset the opposition's aimed antitank-fire calculations.

(4) Command.—The German patrol commander makes a rapid estimate of our position, and tries to attack and overrun us if he thinks that we are weak. If such a move does not seem advisable, he attempts to discover the type and strength of the opposition encountered, without becoming involved in combat.

"Keen, capable, and well-trained officers or noncoms must be selected to command the light tank patrol," the Germans state. "These must be constituted of quick-thinking, resourceful troops who have functioned as a unit long enough to know and have confidence in their leader."

c. Reconnaissance after H-Hour

(1) Mission.—The mission of reconnaissance after H-hour is to explore the hostile position in detail, to protect German deployment, and to discover hostile gun positions, as well as natural and artificial obstacles in the line of advance.

(2) How Performed.—The mission is carried out by light tank patrols (which may be reinforced) operating ahead or on the flanks, as in reconnaissance before H-hour. The reconnaissance tanks employed immediately ahead or to a forward flank are detailed automatically by the first wave of the attacking force. (Normally, one light tank per platoon of heavier tanks in the first wave, and always the same light tank. The remaining light tanks work behind the first wave, performing other duties.) The reconnaissance tanks advance rapidly, making for suitable high ground. They keep 300 to 500 yards ahead of the first wave, and maintain visual contact with it. The reconnaissance tanks observe from open turrets or, if fired on, through their telescopes, with turrets closed. They advance by bounds, from cover to cover, keeping the terrain ahead under continuous observation.

The tanks in the first wave, especially the Pz. Kw. 4's, cover the reconnaissance tanks as they advance.

When the reconnaissance tanks contact our infantry, they attempt to overrun us and, if they are successful, they report and continue their mission. A reconnaissance tank discovering hostile antitank weapons and artillery reports them, takes up a position, and waits for the rest of its company. While waiting, it fires on hostile antitank weapons.

Tanks are avoided, but are observed from concealed positions. The reconnaissance tanks report suitable terrain for meeting an attack by hostile tanks. As under the circumstances described in the previous paragraph, each reconnaissance tank waits for the rest of its company.

Opposition which begins to retreat is promptly attacked, the reconnaissance tanks reporting the development and continuing the pursuit.

In the event of an attack by the opposition, the reconnaissance tanks take up a position, meet the attack, report, and wait for the rest of their companies to come up.

In all these instances, the reconnaissance tanks avoid obstructing the field of fire of the heavier tanks following them. Throughout, the light tanks report by radio if it is available, by prearranged flag or smoke signals, or by significant firing or maneuvering.

Pz. Jäg. II Aus D, E für 7.62 cm Pak 36 (Sd. Kfz. 131): S.P. Antitank Gun (Russian)
Catalog of Enemy Ordnance, 1945

The Pz. Kpfw. II chassis embodying the suspension on four large bogie wheels has been used as a self-propelled mount for the German modified Russian gun 7.62 cm Pak 36 (r) as well as the Pz. Kpfw. II models utilizing five bogie wheels. These equipments are used in an antitank capacity.

The turret and superstructure of the original tank has been removed and replaced by a high box-like superstructure shield of approximately 15 mm thickness, sloping about 75° to the horizontal. Centrally located above the lower shield superstructure is a three-sided shield of approximately 10 mm thickness with a slotted front plate through which the long muzzle of the gun projects well over the front of the chassis. The original shield of the gun has been retained.

The gun, 163 1/2 inches in length including the muzzle brake,

is of monobloc construction. The breech mechanism is of the falling-wedge type. The elevating gear is operated by a handwheel located on the left side of the gun; the traversing gear is on the right. The estimated elevation of the piece is -5° to +22°; traverse 65°. Its muzzle velocities are as follows: H.E. shell, 1805 f/s; A.P.C. shell, 2430 f/s. Firing A.P.C. shell this gun will defeat 3.2 inches of homogeneous armor of 30° obliquity at 1000 yards, and 4.1 inches at normal.

Specifications
- Weight: 10.5 tons
- Length: 16 ft. (excl. gun)
- Width: 7 ft., 6 ins.
- Height: 6 ft., 9 ins.
- Ground clearance: 12 ins.
- Tread centers: 5 ft., 10 ins.
- Ground contact: 7 ft., 10 ins.
- Width of track
- Track links: 96 (est.)
- Pitch of track: Fording depth: 3 ft.
- Theoretical radius of action: Roads: 115 miles,
- Cross-country: 75 miles
- Speed: Roads: 28 m.p.h., Cross-country: 12 m.p.h.
- Armor: Front plate: 30 mm, Sides: 15 mm, Shield: 15 mm

- Armament: 7.62 cm Pak 36 (r)
- Ammunition:—
- Wt. of Projectiles: A.P.C.: 16.7 lb., H.E.: 12.6 lb.
- Engine: Maybach, 140 B.H.P.
- Transmission: 5 speeds forward, 1 reverse
- Steering: Epicyclic clutch brake
- Crew: 4 (probably)

Gw. II für 15 cm s.I.G. 33: S.P. Heavy Infantry Howitzer
Catalog of Enemy Ordnance, 1945

This vehicle consists of the 15 cm. heavy infantry howitzer mounted in the hull of a modified, turretless Pz. Kpfw. II chassis. The chassis is approximately three feet longer than that of the standard Pz Kw II tank and has six bogie wheels instead of the usual five. The sprockets, rear idlers, bogie wheels, return rollers, steering assembly, gear box and hull nose are those of the Pz. Kpfw. II; the instrument panel is that of a Pz. Kpfw. III. The front shield is in one piece extending straight across the full width of the superstructure. The driver's visor is of the double shutter type. The road performance of this equipment approximates that of the Pz. Kpfw. II tank. The gun, a standard infantry support weapon, is mounted low in the hull, projecting through a vertical slot in the shield. The gun shield is 15 mm thick and is of shallow construction. It extends about a third of the distance of the superstructure to the rear. Unlike the "Wasp" there are no protecting side plates along the entire length of the superstructure.

The gun is 64.57 inches in length, has a muzzle velocity of 790 f.s. and a maximum effective range of 5140 yards. The casting containing the recuperator and buffer, housed underneath the barrel, extends almost to the end of the barrel. The breech

mechanism is similar to the 10.5 cm. I.F.H. 18. The elevating gear is operated from the right and the traversing gear from the left. In field mounting its traverse is 11°, its elevation 0° to +73°.

Two types of ammunition are fired, the 15 cm. I. Gr. 33 and the 15 cm. I. Gr. 38. The H.E. capacity is high, 21.8%. The only other shell that the weapon is known to fire is a smoke shell, the 15 cm. I. Gr. 38 Nb. The same percussion fuze, s. I. Gr. Z. 23, which weighs 75 lbs., is used in each case.

Specifications
- Weight: (approx.) 12 tons
- Length: (approx.) 18 ft.
- Width: 7 ft., 4 ins.
- Height (approx.): 5 ft., 6 ins.
- Ground clearance: 13 ins.
- Tread centers: 6 ft., 2 ins.
- Ground contact: Width of track: 11 1/8 ins.,
- Pitch of track: 3 5/8 ins.
- Track links
- Fording depth: 3 ft.
- Theoretical radius of action: Roads: 118 miles,
- Cross-country: 78 miles
- Speed: Roads: 25 m.p.h., Cross-country: 15 m.p.h.
- Armor: Front plate: 15 + 20 mm, Sides: 15 mm

- Gun shield: 15 mm
- Armament: 15 cm. s.I.G. 33
- Ammunition (rds.)
- Engine: 140 B.H.P. Maybach, HL 62 TRM
- Transmission: 6 forward speeds, 1 reverse
- Steering: Epicyclic clutch brake
- Crew: Probably 4

Gw. II (Wespe) für 10.5 cm le. F. H. 18/2 (Sd. Kfz. 124): S.P. Light Howitzer (Wasp)
Catalog of Enemy Ordnance, 1945

This equipment, known as the "Wasp," consists of the 10.5 cm. light field howitzer mounted on a chassis which, with the exception that there are only three return rollers, is that of a normal Pz. Kpfw. II tank, Models A-C, with five bogie wheels. Its road performance approximates that of the Pz. Kpfw. II tank.

The gun is the 10.5 cm. 1.F.H. 18 M with muzzle brake. It is mounted at the rear of the chassis within an open top box type shield which is 10 mm thick, its muzzle brake being almost flush with the front of the chassis. Its recuperator and buffer mechanisms, mounted on the bottom and top of the barrel, respectively, are clearly visible beyond the shield. Overlapping the gun shield and sloping back to the rear of the superstructure are side plates, also 10 mm thick. The fighting compartment is open at the top and rear. Its silhouette is high.

The piece has a normal-charge muzzle velocity of 1542 f.s. and a maximum range of 11,650 yards. Firing the long range charge (Fern-ladung) the gun has a muzzle velocity of 1772 f.s. and a maximum range of 13,500 yards. All charges, except the long range, can be fired without the muzzle brake. It has a traverse of 32° and an elevation of -5° to +42°. It is reported to fire four types of ammunition, the 32.6 lb. HE (F. H. Gr.—Feldhaubitze Granate—field howitzer shell), the cast steel HE (F. H. Gr. Stg.—Stahlring—steelring), the 25.9 lb. hollow charge (10 cm. Gr. 39 rot Rohl Ladung—red hollow charge), and a 32.5 lb. smoke shell.

Specifications
- Weight: 12 tons
- Length: 15 ft., 9 ins.
- Width: 7 ft., 4 ins.
- Height: 7 ft., 10 1/2 ins.
- Ground clearance: 13 ins.
- Tread centers: 6 ft., 2 ins.
- Ground contact: 7 ft., 10 ins.
- Width of track: 11 1/8 ins.
- Pitch of track: 3 5/8 ins.
- Track links
- Fording depth: 3 ft.
- Theoretical radius of action: Roads: 125 miles,
- Cross-country: 70 miles
- Speed: Roads: 24 m.p.h., Cross-country: —

- Armor: Front plate: —, Sides: —
- Armament: 10.5 cm. l.F.H. 18 (M)
- Ammunition (rds.): —
- Engine: Maybach HL 62 TR, 140 h.p.
- Transmission: 6 speeds forward, 1 reverse
- Steering: Epicyclic clutch brake
- Crew: —

Pz. Kpfw. II Aus. F (Sd. Kfz. 121): Light Tanks
Catalog of Enemy Ordnance, 1945

Produced in 1941. This is the latest type of Pz. Kpfw. II tank identified in action. The major modifications appearing in this model are (1) increased thickness of the basic frontal armor, (2) new design of hull nose, (3) use of uninterrupted length of plate for front vertical superstructure plate, (4) use of dummy visor mounted alongside the driver's visor.

The single skin nose of the Model F hull is constructed, of flat plates 35 mm thick with a Brinell hardness of 426 and is nearer vertical than the superimposed nose plate in the earlier reinforced models. This modification to the nose of the hull has shortened its length by approximately five inches.

The turret front and mantlet remain unaltered except for the omission of the additional plates and a corresponding thickening of the basic armor to 30 mm. Model F is equipped with a new driver's visor of the double shutter type. A dummy visor, a one-piece aluminum casting, is mounted alongside the driver's visor on the right, presumably to draw fire from the latter.

The suspension arrangement of five bogie wheels and four return rollers is the same as that utilized in the previous models A, B and C. The power plant consists of the HL 62 TR Maybach, a 6-cylinder, water-cooled gasoline engine rating 140 B.H.P. at 2600 r.p.m.

The transmission is of normal synchromesh, manual control type, providing six forward speeds and one reverse, and the steering system utilizes the epicyclic clutch and brake principle.

Armament comprises one 2.0 cm KwK 30 gun with coaxial 7.92 M.G. 34 in turret.

Models G and J have been mentioned in an official German document but there are no details available.

Specifications
- Weight: 10.5 tons
- Length: 14 ft., 9 ins.
- Width: 7 ft., 4 ins.
- Height: 6 ft., 6 ins.
- Ground clearance: 13 ins.
- Tread centers: 6 ft., 2 ins.
- Ground contact: 7 ft., 10 ins.
- Width of track: 11 1/8 ins.
- Pitch of track: 3 5/8 ins.
- Track links: 106
- Fording depth: 3 ft.
- Theoretical radius of action: Roads: 125 miles,
- Cross-country: 85 miles
- Speed: Roads: 30 m.p.h., Cross-country: 15 m.p.h.
- Armor: Front plate: 35 mm, Sides: 20 mm

- Armament: One 2.0 cm KwK 30, One 7.92 mm M.G. 34
- Ammunition (rds.): 2 cm gun 180 M.G. 2550
- Engine: 140 B.H.P. Maybach HL 62 TRM
- Transmission: 6 forward speeds, 1 reverse
- Steering: Epicyclic clutch brake
- Crew: 3

Pz. Kpfw. II (F) (Sd. Kfz. 122): Flamethrower Tank
Catalog of Enemy Ordnance, 1945

The flamethrower tank, Pz. Kpfw. II (F) is a conversion of Pz. Kpfw. II, Models D and E, which employed the four bogie wheel suspension, and should not be confused with the Model F, which utilizes the five bogie wheel type of suspension. The road performance of the flamethrower tank approximates that of Models D and E.

The flamethrower projectors, having a range of about 35 yards, are mounted in small turrets set well forward on each trackguard. The turrets have 180° traverse while the projectors themselves have a limited elevation. Fuel is supplied from two tanks, provided with armored shields, which are mounted externally on the trackguards, and by compressed nitrogen from the four nitrogen cylinders located inside, below the turret. The tanks have a capacity of 35 gals. each. Two small cylinders mounted just behind the projector turrets contain acetylene, which is used for fuel ignition. The flamethrower is controlled electrically from panels in the turret.

Since this equipment is essentially a close-combat weapon, the tank is liberally fitted for smoke production to screen its movements. Not only is the normal smoke generator rack fitted at the rear, but there is on each trackguard a triple smoke generator discharger, aimed to fire forward, and bowden cable

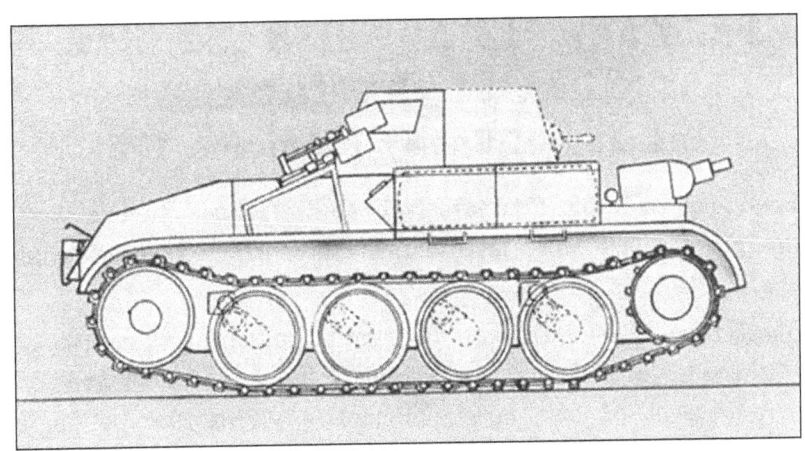

controlled from the turret. Armament also includes a machine gun on a ball mounting in the turret.

Specifications
- Weight: 11 tons
- Length: 16 ft.
- Width: 7 ft., 6 ins.
- Height: 6 ft., 9 ins.
- Ground clearance: 12 ins.
- Tread centers: 5 ft., 10 ins.
- Ground contact: 7 ft., 10 ins.
- Width of track: 11 1/8 ins.
- Pitch of track: 6 3/4 ins.
- Track links: 55
- Fording depth: 3 ft.
- Theoretical radius of action: Roads: 125 miles, Cross-country: 85 miles
- Speed: Roads: 30 m.p.h., Cross-country: 12 m.p.h.
- Armor: Front plate: 30 mm, Sides: 15 mm
- Armament: Two independent flamethrowers, One M.G.
- Ammunition: Flamethrower—70 gals., M.G. 1800 rds.
- Engine: 140 B.H.P. Maybach, HL 62 TRM
- Transmission: 6 speeds forward, 1 reverse
- Steering: Epicyclic clutch brake
- Crew: 3

Pz. Kpfw. II Aus D, E (Sd. Kfz. 121): Light Tanks
Catalog of Enemy Ordnance, 1945

Produced in 1939. Comparatively few of these models were made and these were later converted to flamethrower tanks (Pz. Kpfw. II, Aus. (F)).

Model D—Although the hull, turret, and superstructure of this model are similar to preceding models, its suspension arrangement of four large, rubber-tired, Christie-type bogie wheels which touch the top and bottom of the track make it easy to recognize. Models D and E are the only Pz. Kpfw. II tanks with this type of suspension. The bogie wheels are large enough to eliminate return rollers. The front drive sprocket, rear idler, and the dry-pin, center-guide track complete the suspension assembly. The track can be fitted with snow spuds. These are inserted in the outer web members and held by a split cotter-pin.

The power plant is the Maybach HL 62 TR, six-cylinder, water-cooled engine rated at 140 B.H.P. The transmission provides five forward speeds and one reverse. The steering system embodies the epicyclic clutch and brake principle.

The normal Pz. Kpfw. II armament of one 2 cm Kw.K. 30

with one coaxial 7.92 mm M.G. 34 is mounted. Armor plate thicknesses range from 30 mm front to 15 mm sides.

Model E—Same as Model D.

Specifications

- Weight: 10 tons
- Length: 16 ft.
- Width: 7 ft., 6 ins.
- Height: 6 ft., 9 ins.
- Ground clearance: 12 ins.
- Tread centers: 5 ft., 10 ins.
- Ground contact: 7 ft., 10 ins.
- Width of track:—
- Pitch of track:—
- Track links: 96 (est.)
- Fording depth: 3 ft.
- Theoretical radius of action, Roads: 125 miles, Cross-country: 85 miles
- Speed: Roads: 30 m.p.h., Cross-country: 12 m.p.h.
- Armor: Front plate: 30 mm, Sides: 15 mm
- Armament: 1—2.0 cm Kw.K. 30, 1—7.92 M.G. 34
- Ammunition:—
- Engine: Maybach 140 B.H.P.
- Transmission: Synchromesh, 5 speeds forward, 1 reverse
- Steering: Epicyclic clutch brake
- Crew: 3

Pz. Kpfw. II Aus A, B, C (Sd. Kfz. 121): Light Tanks
Catalog of Enemy Ordnance, 1945

Model A was produced in 1937, followed by B and C in 1938. It is not known whether there are any important differences between these models. All had a suspension consisting of five equally spaced rubber-tired bogie wheels on each side mounted independently on suspension arms pivoted on hull and provided with quarter elliptic leaf springs. There are four 8 in. diameter return rollers on each side, a 2 ft., 7 in. diameter sprocket, and a 2 ft., 1 in. diameter idler.

The frontal armor of this series was originally only 15 mm thick and the hull had a rounded nose formed by the bending of a single plate which also incorporated the glacis and nose plate. At some time after the battle of France (1940) the armor of these models was reinforced by bolting 20 mm armor plates on the front of the tank. The additional armor on the front of the hull consisted of flat nose and glacis plates which entirely altered the appearance of the hull and nose and gave the effect of spaced armor in front of the rounded part of the basic plate. The gun mantlet armor was thickened by the addition of a 15 mm plate.

The Maybach, HL 62 TR, 6-cylinder gasoline engine, which comprises the power plant, has a rating of 140 h.p.

The armament consists of a 2.0 cm gun which is fired by a trigger on the elevating handwheel, and a coaxial 7.92 mm M.G. 34 which is fired by a trigger on the traversing handwheel.

These models are often converted for use as mounts for heavy anti-tank guns such as the 7.5 cm Pak 40 and the 7.62 cm Pak 36 (r), as well as the 10.5 cm l.F.H. 18 M, known as the Wasp, and the 15 cm s.I.G. 33; the suspension for the latter having a sixth bogie wheel.

Specifications

- Weight: 10 tons
- Length: 15 ft., 2 3/4 ins.
- Width (overall): 7 ft., 4 ins.
- Height: 6 ft., 5 3/4 ins.
- Ground clearance: 13 ins.
- Tread centers: 6 ft., 2 ins.
- Ground contact: 7 ft., 10 ins.
- Width of track: 11 1/8 ins.
- Pitch of track: 3 5/8 ins.
- Track links: 105
- Fording depth: 3 ft.
- Theoretical radius of action: Roads: 125 miles,
- Cross-country: 85 miles
- Speed: Roads: 30 m.p.h., Cross-country: 15 m.p.h.
- Armor: Front plate: 15 + 20 mm, Sides: 15 mm
- Armament: One 2.0 cm KwK 30, One 7.92 mm M.G. 34
- Ammunition: 2.0 cm gun 180, M.G. 1425
- Engine: 140 h.p. Maybach HL 62 TRM
- Transmission: Crash-type gear box, 6 fwd. speeds, 1 reverse
- Steering: Epicyclic clutch brake
- Crew: 3

Pz. Kpfw. II Aus a1, a2, a3, b, c: Light Tanks
Catalog of Enemy Ordnance, 1945

The early development of the Pz. Kpfw. II is indicated by five models, a1, a2, a3, b and c. They were considered as prototype tanks.

Model a1—Had a suspension arrangement of six small bogie wheels, each side mounted on three hull pivots connected by an outside girder. There were four return rollers, sprocket, and a cast rear idler. It weighed about 8¼ tons, was manned by a crew of three and mounted one 2 cm KwK 30 and a coaxial 7.92 mm M.G. 34 in the turret. It was powered by a six-cylinder Maybach (HL 57 TR) gasoline engine and was fitted with epicyclic and brake steering without a final reduction gear. The frontal armor was 20 mm in thickness, the sides 15 mm.

Model a2—Same as Model a1 except for variation in construction of engine compartment and welded rear idler instead of cast.

Model a3—Same as Model a1 except for minor modifications in the suspension arrangement and cooling system.

Model b—Incorporated an improved Maybach (HL 62 TR) engine, as well as a new track with wider driving sprockets, bogie wheels and return rollers. A final reduction gear was also introduced, which necessitated slight alterations in the structure of the front of the hull. The model weighed 9 tons.

Model c—An entirely new suspension comprising five independently sprung bogie wheels on each side made its appearance in this model. It is believed that the torsion bar system of bogie wheel suspension originated in this tank. Modifications to the driving sprocket, rear idler, and return rollers, the latter of which now numbered four, were made. Improved epicyclic and steering brakes were also introduced, the latter being equipped with automatic take-up to compensate for wear. Model c weighed 9 1/2 tons.

Specifications

- Weight: 8 1/2 to 9 1/2 tons
- Length: 15 ft., 2 ins.
- Width: 7 ft., 4 ins.
- Height: 6 ft., 5 ins.
- Ground clearance: 13 ins.
- Tread centers: 6 ft., 2 ins.
- Ground contact: 7 ft., 10 ins.
- Width of track: 11 1/8 ins.
- Pitch of rack: 3 5/8 ins.
- Track links: 106
- Fording depth: 3 ft.
- Theoretical radius of action: Roads: 102 miles,
- Cross-country: 60 miles
- Speed: Roads: 30 m.p.h., Cross-country: 15 m.p.h.
- Armor: Front plate: 20 mm, Sides: 15 mm
- Armament: One 2 cm KwK 30, One M.G. 34
- Ammunition (rds.): 2 cm gun 180, M.G. 2550
- Engine: HL 57 TR or HL TRM 62
- Maybach: 140 B.H.P.
- Transmission: 6 speeds forward, 1 reverse
- Steering: Epicyclic clutch brake
- Crew: 3

Pz. Jäg. II Aus. A–E u.F für 7.5 cm Pak 40 (Sd. Kfz. 131): S.P. Antitank Gun
Catalog of Enemy Ordnance, 1945

Produced in 1942. This antitank equipment was encountered in the battle of Tunisia. It is composed of the 7.5 cm antitank gun mounted on a Pz. Kpfw. II chassis and its road performance will closely follow that of the Pz. Kpfw. II tank.

The gun, which retains its original shield, recoil system, traversing and elevating gears, is mounted on a platform high on the hull and fires forward. A protective shield 10 mm thick, which slopes away to the rear of the chassis, has been provided. The shield is nearly rectangular except for a projecting portion in front of the gun mounting itself and the top and back are apparently open. The traverse of the gun is limited due to the gun shield fouling the protective shield. A barrel support for travelling is fitted in front of the hull.

The piece, 134 inches in length, is a monobloc type, semi-automatic, with horizontal sliding breech. It consists of barrel

with shoes; breech ring with locking ring; breech block with firing mechanism; semi-automatic gear and muzzle brake. The recoil mechanism is comprised of a buffer cylinder, filled with a mixture of glycerine and distilled water, mounted in the cradle and secured by a nut to the front end plate. The piston rod, which is connected to the gun lug, is hollow, and is fitted with a bronze piston head. Ports are drilled in the conical part of the piston. A tapered rod is screwed into the front plug of the cylinder and projects into the hollow piston rod. During recoil the piston moves to the rear and the oil is forced from the buffer cylinder through the ports in the piston and hence through the annular space between the tapered rod and a bushing fitted in the piston. Recoil control is effected by a brass control plunger screwed to the end of the tapered rod. The recuperator is hydro-pneumatic.

Specifications

- Weight: 10 tons
- Length: 15 ft., 2 3/4 ins.
- Width: 7 ft., 4 ins.
- Height: 6 ft., 5 3/4 ins.
- Ground clearance: 13 ins.
- Tread centers: 6 ft., 2 ins.
- Ground contact: 7 ft., 10 ins.
- Width of track: 11 1/8 ins.
- Pitch of track: 3 5/8 ins.
- Track links: 105
- Fording depth: 3 ft.
- Theoretical radius of action: Roads: 118 miles,
- Cross-country: 78 miles
- Speed: Roads: 25 m.p.h., Cross-country: 12 m.p.h.
- Armor: Front plate: 15 + 20 mm, Sides: 15 mm
- Armament: 7.5 cm Pak 40 A.T. gun.
- Max. effective range: 3200 yards. M.V. (Wt. 12.6 lb.): H.E. 1800 f.s. M.V. (Wt. 15 lb.): A.P.C. 2525 f.s.
- Elevation: -5° to +22°. Traverse: 65°: :

- Penetration of homogeneous armor—A.P.C.B.C. shell
    - 500 yds.: 4.0" at 30°, 4.8" normal
    - 1000 yds.: 3.6" at 30°, 4.3" normal
    - 1500 yds.: 3.2" at 30°, 3.9" normal
    - 2000 yds.: 2.8" at 30°, 34" normal
    - 2500 yds.: 2.5" at 30°, 3.0" normal
- Ammunition:—
- Engine: Maybach HL 62 TRM, 140 h.p.
- Transmission: Crash-type gear box, 6 fwd. speeds, 1 reverse
- Steering: Epicyclic clutch brake
- Crew: Probably 4

THE PANZER III

Germany's Medium Tank

The Panzer III was the common name of a medium tank that was developed in the 1930s by Germany and was used extensively in World War II. The official German designation was Panzerkampfwagen III Sd Kfz. 141 (abbreviated to PzKpfw III) translating as "armored fighting vehicle number three".

The Panzer III was purpose designed to create a breakthrough on the battlefield and also to fight other armored fighting vehicles. The performance of the Panzer III was adequate in the early years of the war; however as the Germans came to face faced the formidable T-34 and KV-1 in Russia, it was immediately obvious that a stronger main gun with a considerably enhanced anti-tank capability was now needed. The Panzer IV had a bigger

A good study of the Panzer III Ausf.E. Note the two machine guns in the turret.

turret ring and was capable of mounting a larger main weapon, the traditional roles were therefore reversed. The Panzer IV mounted the long barreled 7.5 cm KwK 40 gun was detailed to fight in tank-to-tank battles, the Panzer III became obsolete in this role and for most purposes was supplanted by the Panzer IV. From 1942, the last version of Panzer III, Ausf. N, mounted the 7.5 cm KwK 37 L/24 short barelled howitzer better suited for infantry support. Production of the Panzer III ended in 1943. However, the Panzer III's capable chassis provided hulls for the Sturmgeschütz III until the end of the war.

The constantly changing role of the Mark III required close scrutiny from Allied intelligence services in order to keep the front line troops up to speed on the variants which they faced in the field.

This wartime military intelligence report on the German Panzer III was originally published in the US intelligence magazine Tactical and Technical Trends, No. 10, October 22nd, 1942.

MARK III TANK – THREE BASIC DESIGNS
Tactical and Technical Trends, No. 10, October 22nd, 1942.

Close examination of a considerable number of photographs of Mark III tanks, together with those available for examination in the Western Desert, indicates that the Mark III fighting-type tank is found in three basic designs.

Of these, the first has an armor basis of 30 mm (1.18 in) all around. The front sprocket has eight spokes, and the rear idler, though having eight spokes, is almost solid. This type is known originally to have been produced mounting a 37-mm gun and either one or two machine guns coaxially in the turret, with one machine gun firing forward in the hull. Later, however, the 50-mm was substituted for the original principal armament, and this mounting has only one machine gun mounted coaxially in the turret, the hull machine gun being retained. Of the actual specimens examined, all mounted the 50-mm gun (many are now mounting the long-barrelled type), and in these there has invariably been a Variorex gearbox, the steering being hydraulically operated. This basic type, irrespective of armament, has not been found to carry any additional armor, improvised or otherwise.

The second type has an armor basis of 30 mm all around with additional 30-mm plates bolted on. This type has a six-spoke front sprocket, and the rear idler, although having eight spokes, is more open than the first type. An ordinary six-speed gear box and hydraulically operated steering gear are fitted. Neither photographs nor specimens of this type have shown any principal armament other than the 50-mm gun with one coaxial machine gun. Moreover, every individual tank of this type has had similar additional 30-mm plates on the front and rear, this additional armor not having been found on any other type of Mark III fighting tank. The inference is, therefore, that this additional armor is actually part of the design of the tank and probably incorporated during manufacture. There have been no indications that this type originally mounted a 37-mm gun, although this remains a possibility.

The third type has 50-mm armor on the front and rear, with 30-mm armor on the sides. No additional armor has been found on any tanks of this type, and the armament has always been found to be the 50-mm gun with a coaxial machine gun and one machine gun in the hull. The front sprocket and rear idler are similar to those in the second type, and an ordinary six-speed gear box is fitted, the steering being operated by mechanical linkage. The driver's and hull gunner's entrance doors have been changed from the former double doors to single doors hinged at the forward edge. In place of the normal mantlet

A Pz.Kpfw.III Ausf.G captured by the British in North Africa, 1942.

protecting the hull machine gun, a more hemispherical mantlet is fitted.

The following minor differences of design between these three basic types have also been noted. Originally on the first type the armor protecting the driver's visor consisted of two plates, one being raised, and the other lowered, to give protection. The third type, and probably the second type as well, have had a single hinged piece of armor which can be lowered to give protection. The third type has also had a slightly different design of the two shields protecting the exhausts from the steering tracks. In the first and second types the air filters were located between the rear bulkhead of the fighting compartment and the engine, air being drawn from the fighting compartment. These filters were believed to be an oil-soaked gauze type. On the third type this arrangement superseded by four oil bath filters, installed over the top of the engine blocks.

The suspension on all these types has been the same, the familiar six small bogie wheels with three return rollers, a front sprocket, and a rear idler. Two early types, however, are known to have had respectively five large bogie wheels and eight small bogie wheels. Both these types mounted a 37-mm gun. Nothing has been heard of either type over a considerable period, and it is probable that they were prototypes only and not produced in significant numbers.

It is known that Mark III fighting tanks have been produced in at least five models designated 'E', 'F', 'G', 'H', and 'J'. These models have consecutive chassis number blocks, and it is logical to assume that they are successive developments. There should therefore be a link with the development shown above, but so far it is not possible definitely to say what each model designation represents. It is, however, known that the first type described above has included Model 'G' tanks, and the third type has included Model 'J' tanks. All three types are known to have been in existence early in 1941, the third type probably being at that time a very new production.

It should be specially noted that, in describing German armor thickness, round numbers are almost invariably given. Careful measurement, has shown that these figures are frequently incorrect. 30-mm, for example, should almost invariably be up to 32-mm.

* * *

The vulnerability of German Tanks was an obvious area for investigation by intelligence gathering services. This article, also taken from Tactical and Technical Trends, provides an interesting contemporary intelligence report on vulnerability of

German tanks to short-range attacks with incendiary grenades. It was originally published in Tactical and Technical Trends, No. 11, November 5th, 1942.

VULNERABILITY OF GERMAN TANKS
Tactical and Technical Trends, No. II, November 5th, 1942.

When enemy armored force vehicles are attacked at close quarters with incendiary grenades, the air louvres are very vulnerable. It is therefore important that differentiation be made between "inlet" and "outlet "ducts, since obviously a grenade thrown against an exhaust opening will be less effective than one aimed at an inlet, which will draw the inflammable liquid into the vehicle. If the engine is not running, all openings are equally vulnerable.

In general, it may be said that in the Pz Kw II and III tanks the best targets are the flat top-plates of the rear superstructures, since the air intakes are located there. The side louvres in these tanks are invariably protected by a vertical baffle. On the Pz Kw IV, the left side ports are intake and thus more vulnerable than the right-hand exhaust ports.

* * *

The following report on the new armament of the up-gunned German Pz.Kw. III originally appeared in Tactical and Technical Trends, No. 20, on 11th March 1943. This is how Allied troops were informed of the fact that the Panzer III was now operating in a more efficient form. American reports from the period invariably refer to the German tanks using Arabic rather than Roman numerals.

NEW ARMAMENT OF GERMAN PZ.KW. 3

Tactical and Technical Trends, No. 20, IIth March 1943

Pz. Kw. 3

As previously reported in Tactical and Technical Trends (No. 4, p. 15) recent models of two German tanks, the Pz.Kw. 3 and 4, have been fitted with more powerful armament, as shown in the accompanying sketches. These sketches are based on photographs of German tanks captured by the British in North Africa.

Pz.Kw. 3.

The principal armament of this tank is a long-barrelled 50-mm gun. It is reported that this gun bears considerable similarity to the 5-cm Pak 38 (50-mm antitank gun), except that there is no muzzle brake and that the mounting is, of course, different. The over-all length from the breech opening to the muzzle is 9 feet, 4 inches. The barrel overhangs the front of the tank by about 3 feet. The ammunition used is that of the 50-mm antitank gun with no adaptation or alteration apart from the fitting of an electric primer, the tank gun being electrically fired. The muzzle velocity of this tank gun has been estimated as a little over 3,000 feet per second. It has been reported that the performance of the tank gun should not be very different from that of the antitank gun, the estimated penetration figures for which are as follows:

- 79-mm (3.1 in) homogeneous armor at 300 yds at 30°
- 71-mm (2.8 in) homogeneous armor at 600 yds at 30°
- 63-mm (2.5 in) homogeneous armor at 850 yds at 30°

* * *

Advice on how to combat the Panzer III was required and the following article, from Tactical and Technical Trends, No. 22, April 8th, 1943, describes areas on German tanks vulnerable to attack with incendiary grenades or Molotov cocktails.

VULNERABLE SPOTS FOR INCENDIARY GRENADES ON GERMAN TANKS

In attacking enemy tanks at close quarters with Molotov cocktails or incendiaries, the air intakes are among the most vulnerable points. It is important, therefore, that the location of these intakes and outlets be known, as the flame and fumes of a grenade thrown against an intake while the engine is running will be sucked inside, but if the grenade lands on an outlet, they will be blown clear of the tank.

The best targets are the flat top-plates behind the turret. Side intakes are invariably protected by a vertical baffle. The accompanying sketches show the "soft spots" on German tanks Pz.Kw.3

* * *

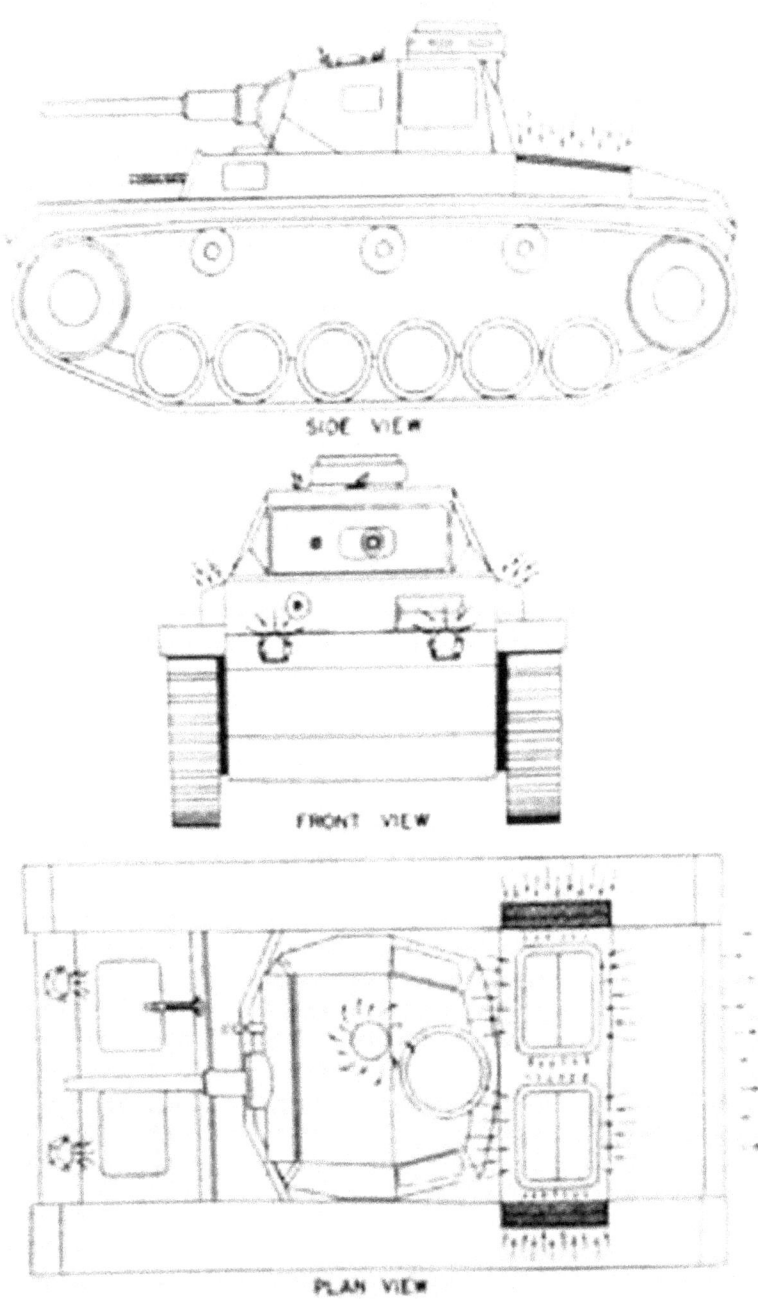

Pz. Kw. 3

The response to these and other threats was to increase protection on the Panzer III. This U.S. intelligence report on the Panzer III and its increasing armor specification originally appeared in Tactical and Technical Trends, No. 25, May 20th, 1943.

INCREASED PROTECTION ON PZKW 3
Tactical and Technical Trends, No. 25, May 20th, 1943.

The history of the changes in the light medium PzKw 3 demonstrates how fortunate the Germans were in having a basic tank design that could be improved as battle experience indicated, for a basic design can be improved and still remain familiar to the users. Furthermore, the problems of maintenance and supply of parts are greatly reduced and these problems are a major factor in keeping tanks ready for operational use.

(1) General

The Germans seem to be making a gradual increase in thickness of armor-plate as the guns used against it increase in hitting power and range. The PzKw 3 medium tank is illustrative of this trend in tank armor and design, and affords a remarkable example of what can be done to improve the armor protection and fighting efficiency of a tank without changing its basic design. The key of this basic design is the welded main structure which allows heavier plates to be used when desired. Also, operating components of the tank are not hung on the plates, likely to be changed to thicker ones.

(2) Pre-War

The early model PzKw 3 (produced in 1936-38) had basic armor of .59-inch homogeneous plate. At this time there were only 5 bogie wheels on a side instead of the present 6. There is a gap in the formation until 1939, when the tank appeared with 1.18-inch face-hardened armor on the turret and front. This

A Panzer III packed with fifteen or more grenadiers conveys the impression of just how sturdy these machines were.

model had 6 bogie wheels on the side. The side armor which forms a great part of the chassis was of softer, machineable-quality plate, due both to necessities of manufacture and to the undesirable weakening effect on hardened plate of the necessary suspension and bracket holes. The model also had improved aperture protection in the form of an external moving mantlet, additional armor around the machine-gun port, and an improved double-flap driver's visor. It appears that these features were added with the modification of but 2 plates on the tank.

(3) 1941 Changes.

In 1941, as more powerful guns were being used against tanks, 1.20 inches of additional armor plate was bolted against the plates on the front of the superstructure and on the upper and lower nose-plates. The 1.18-in. basic plates were face-hardened to a Brinell hardness of 600 to 800 and 1.20-in additional plates were the same. About a year later, in January 1942, the tank appeared with a basic armor of 1.96 inches on the front and back, the side-armor thickness remaining unchanged at 1.20 inches. This armor was face-hardened and performed well against monobloc shot, but once the face-hardening was pierced, the shell fragments penetrated the remainder with ease.

(4) 1942.

Therefore, in June 1942, a .79-inch additional plate was bolted on the gun mantlet and front superstructure as a means to defeat a shot with a piercing cap. Between this plate and the basic armor was an air gap or space, varying from 4 to 8 inches. The plate conformed roughly to the shape of the section covered. The spaced armor seems to have been a field expedient, resulting undoubtedly from the demonstrated fact that the spare section of track carried on the front of German tanks gave additional protection. This method of adding armor was officially recognized, as later models had brackets fitted for installing spaced armor when desirable.

* * *

Four photographs of German Panzer III tanks captured in North Africa were exhibited in Tactical and Technical Trends, No. 32, August 26th, 1943.

GERMAN PzKw 3
Tactical and Technical Trends, No. 32, August 26th, 1943

FIG. 1

FIG. 2

FIG. 3

FIG. 4

The accompanying photographs show four views of the German medium tank PzKw 3. Figures 2, 3 and 4 is the PzKw 3 with the long-barreled 50-mm gun. Figure 1 is essentially the same tank except that it is equipped with a short-barreled 50-mm gun.

***

The intelligence report on the German Panzer III Flammpanzer, entitled "German Flame Thrower on Pz Kw 3 Chassis" was originally published in Tactical and Technical Trends, No. 45, April 1st, 1944. As we have seen some 100 Panzer III were converted to perform this role. The initial report contained some errors and a later report in the July 1944 issue corrected some of the details given in this article.

GERMAN FLAME THROWER ON PZ KW 3 CHASSIS
Tactical and Technical Trends, No. 45, April 1st, 1944

a. THE TANK

German flame-throwing tanks were noted in Tactical and Technical Trends, No. 19, p. 9, and in No. 39, p. 9, a Pz Kw 2 tank was described, mounted with two small flame throwers on the front end of the track guards. At that time, it seemed odd that

Fig.1: Flame-thrower tank

a more powerful projector should not be installed in the turret. Such a tank has now appeared. Flame-thrower Pz Kw 3 tanks were taken on the Italian front, some in good condition. A front view of this tank is shown in figure 1.

(1) External Appearance.

The flame-throwing tank has a special type of flame thrower mounted on some available chassis. Reports indicate that flame-throwing apparatus is designed to be adaptable to any model of tanks, light as well as heavy. The tank here described is a standard Pz Kw 3 with six bogies and three return rollers. The chassis, hull and turret are identical with the ordinary tank. An additional armor plate 1.18 inch thick has been welded to the front of the chassis and another of like thickness forms the curved shield protecting the front of the turret and the flame gun. This shield is pierced for one coaxially mounted machine gun, and another is mounted in the usual position in the right front of the hull, opposite the driver's vision slit. Smoke projectors of three tubes each are mounted on each side of the front edge of the turret. For comparison see figures 2 and 3. The markings are the standard black-and-white German crosses on the right rear of the chassis, and a little in front of the center roller. Organizational numbers appear on the two sides of the turret directly above the black-and-white cross. Two tanks captured in good condition were marked respectively, F. 23 and F. 24.

(2) Flame Gun.

At first sight, the flame gun which projects 5.28 feet beyond the curved shield of the turret, has the identical appearance of the usual 50-mm tank cannon. Even the short reinforcing jacket is simulated. However, the barrel has no taper whatever, and if seen from the muzzle end, is thin-walled, like a shotgun barrel. This "gun" is actually the cover for the flame-projector tube. The muzzle end of the gun is detachable, forming a flame shield designed to facilitate the burning of the flame-oil by having four openings cut in the sides, 4 inch wide and 4.9 inches long,

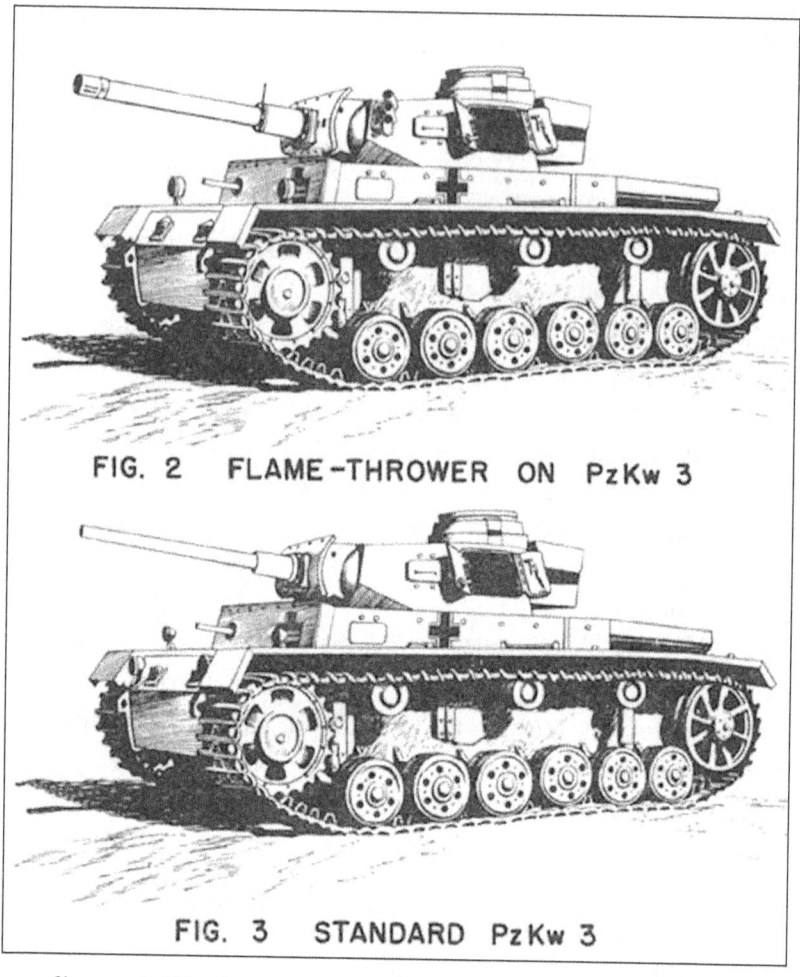

FIG. 2 FLAME-THROWER ON PzKw 3

FIG. 3 STANDARD PzKw 3

see figure 4. The top and side openings are shielded to prevent the dropping of unburned flame oil on the top of the tank.

Within the turret, a counter-balance weight is attached to the breech of the gun for ease in vertical alignment. Elevation and traverse are controlled by the tank commander through two hand wheels — the right controlling elevation, the left the swing of the turret. The maximum elevation of the flame gun is about 530 mils (30 degrees); the depression, 180 mils (10 degrees). The indicated horizontal traverse is approximately 800 mils (44 degrees) right and left of center. An indicator with a dial numbered clockwise from 1 to 12 to indicate the position of

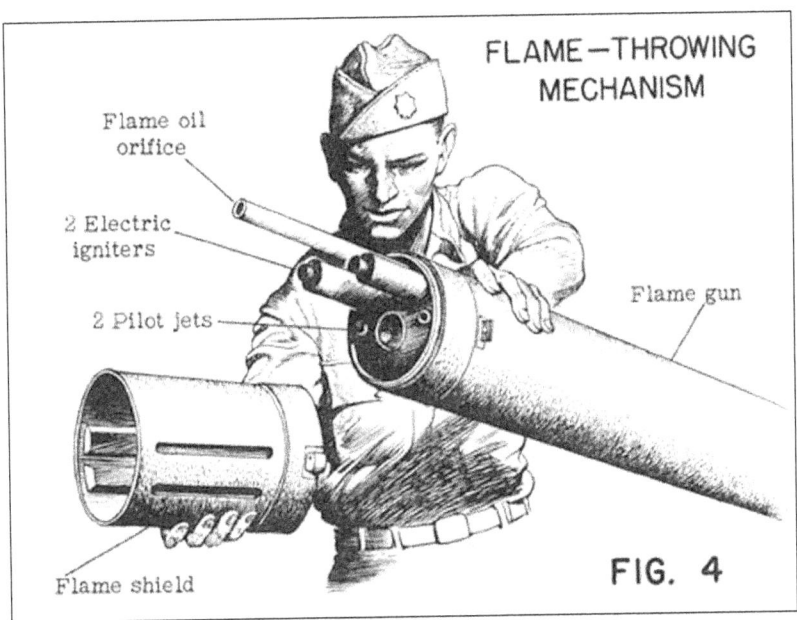

FLAME—THROWING MECHANISM

Flame oil orifice
2 Electric igniters
2 Pilot jets
Flame shield
Flame gun

FIG. 4

the turret with reference to the forward motion of the tank is placed near the hand wheels.

Comment: The turret does NOT have an all-round traverse and no machine gun fires rearward. This flame-thrower tank therefore appears to be more vulnerable to attacks of tank-destroyer squads than the gun-carrying model.

(3) Mechanical Operation.

Pressure for the flame-thrower fluid is obtained by the operation of an auxiliary two-cylinder motor driving a rotary pump located in the left rear of the tank. Flame-oil pressure is indicated by a pressure gage directly in front of the tank commander, graduated from 0 to 250 units. The flame-oil release is obtained by the dual operation of a right-foot pedal and an electric control mounted above and behind the pressure gage. At the muzzle of the flame gun are two pilot jets; two electric, ground-return igniters, and one opening .394 inch in diameter for the ejection of the flame fluid.

(4) Sighting.

Aiming is accomplished by the tank commander sighting through

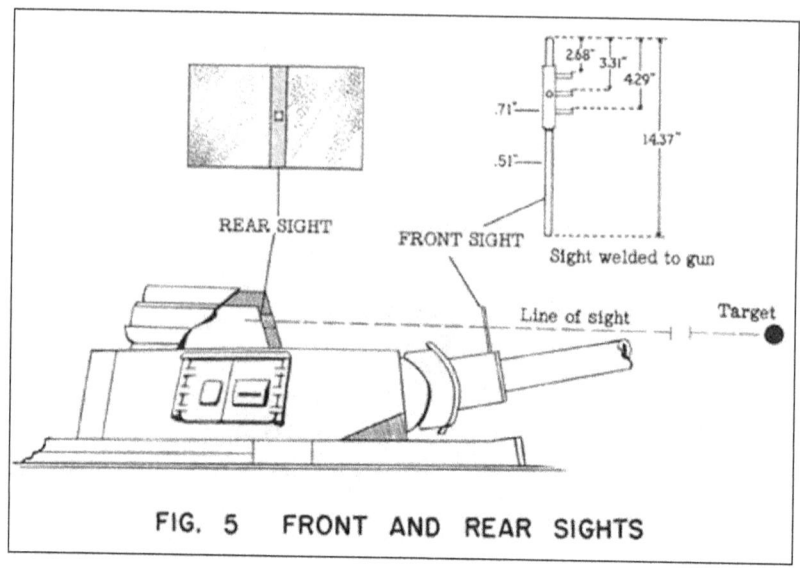

FIG. 5   FRONT AND REAR SIGHTS

an improvised rear sight, two mm (.08 inch) square and mounted in the turret directly in the rear of the shatter-proof-glass vision slit, and aligning the target with an improvised front sighting device mounted on top of the exterior base of the flame gun (see figure 5). The elevation for estimated target range is obtained by elevating the flame gun so that the line of sight passes over the selected one of three metal horizontal projections, attached to the vertical bar of the front sight. Elevated to range, the gun is kept trained on the target as the tank approaches. As the sights are aligned, the commander presses the electric control and the right-foot pedal. In short bursts the flaming oil is sprayed upon the target, the liquid sticking and burning with intense heat upon the object it touches. The range is normally from 55 to 65 yards; maximum, 84.

(5) Fuel Tanks and Flame Oil

The flame-oil fuel tanks consist of two welded metal containers of approximately 40 to 50 gallons each, mounted beside the tank commander on the right and left of the chassis, set low enough to allow free rotation of the turret, and fitted with meter gages.

The fuel is a thin, black, sticky oil smelling strongly of creosote, which showed upon analysis the following composition by volume:

- Light oils up to 170° - 39.0 percent
- Medium or carbolic oils from 170 to 230° -17.4 percent
- Heavy oils or creosote from 230 to 270° - 4.2 percent
- Medium oils or (coal tar?) oils, 270° - 21.5 percent
- Residual difference at 100 - 17.9 percent

(6) Accessories.

(a) Smoke Projectors

Two three-barreled smoke projectors are bolted to the forward sides of the turret and with the center barrel approximately aligned with it, all having an elevation of about 44 degrees. The two outer barrels fire laterally right and left from the center barrel at approximately 20 degrees. These are fired electrically from a lid-covered firing box on the inside of the turret. Each button of the box set is connected with one barrel of the projector. The projectile used is the standard smokepot weighing about five or six pounds, which can be projected an estimated distance of from 150 to 200 yards. The pot produces an opaque, light-gray cloud for about two minutes.

(b) Radio

A pair of radio head sets for intertank or interior communication are supplied to the driver and commander for listening, and connected parallel with the radio operator for inner-phone communication.

(c) Demolition Charge

For the destruction of the tank in case of imminent capture, a demolition charge is provided. The one examined weighed about 8.5 pounds, and was 15 inches long, 3.54 inches in diameter, containing a dense, white solid — perhaps nitro-starch. A fuze screwed into a booster, and a soft, gray-iron hanging strap for fastening the charge to an object were attached. The charge fitted snugly into a metal carrying case.

(d) Very Pistol

A Very pistol was carried on the right side of the turret behind the commander's right shoulder, with two boxes of 12 colored flares each, one in the rear of the commander's seat, the other beside the turret machine gun. Red, blue or violet, green and white cartridges were provided. Their signal meaning is changed by order of the commanding officer, but it is believed the following apply:

- Red - Enemy attacking
- Blue or violet - Attack by tanks
- Green - Help
- White - We are here
- Flares fired into the enemy's lines - We are withdrawing

(e) Miscellaneous Accessories

Spare multi-layer vision-slit glasses for the commander and driver, totalling 3.34 inches in thickness, were stored in racks. There were also three fire extinguishers, standard gas masks for the crew, and a spare smokepot. In one tank a rack of black egg-grenades 3 inches long by 2 inches in diameter were found. Racks for four fire extinguishers were provided on Pz Kw 3 flame-throwing tanks, two for the tank commander, one for the tank driver and one mounted on the outside of the tank.

(7) Crew.

The crew apparently consists of four — commander, driver, radio operator, and turret machine gunner.

b. TACTICAL USE.

(1) Tank Attack.

Two Pz Kw 4's and a Pz Kw 3 flame thrower attacked a platoon position unsupported by AT guns in the following manner: the two Pz Kw 4's opened fire at 400 yards with machine guns from a hull-down position. Still firing, they advanced to about 200 yards where they remained, continuously firing their machine guns.

At the same time, the flame thrower advanced between the two, actually reached the platoon in spite of machine- and Bren-gun fire, and sprayed the men at close range.

Other data indicates that the flame-throwers are usually

A Flammpanzer III demonstrates the effectiveness of it main armament.

attached to units of Pz Kw 4 tanks in the ratio of two or three flame throwers to 20 or 25 standard tanks. Their greatest value comes into play when darkness, smoke, or weather conditions make possible a close approach. Against woods, trenches, blockhouses or buildings, flame thrower tanks force defenders into the open where they can be attacked with small-arms fire. Buildings up to four stories in height can be successfully attacked. The Pz Kw 3 was extensively employed at the siege of Stalingrad.

(2) Target Area.

The most vulnerable target areas are the vision slits of the tank commander and driver, the area of the center roller on the side, and the right side of the rear end of the chassis. This is also the best target for Molotov cocktails.

Development History

On January 11, 1934, following specifications laid down by Heinz Guderian, the Army Weapons Department drew up plans for a medium tank with a maximum weight of 24,000 kg and a top speed of 35 kilometres per hour (21.75 mph). It was intended as the main tank of the German Panzer divisions, capable of engaging and destroying opposing tank forces.

Daimler-Benz, Krupp, MAN, and Rheinmetall all produced prototypes. Testing of the prototypes took place in 1936 and 1937, leading to the Daimler-Benz design being chosen for production. The first model of the Panzer III, the Ausf. A, came off the assembly line in May 1937, and a total of ten, two of which were unarmed, were produced in 1937. Mass production of the Ausf. F version began in 1939.

Between 1937 and 1940, attempts were made to standardize parts between Krupp's Panzer IV and Daimler-Benz's Panzer III.

Much of the early development work on the Panzer III was a quest for a suitable suspension. Several varieties of leaf-spring suspensions were tried on Ausf. A through Ausf. D before the torsion-bar suspension of the Ausf. E was standardized. The Panzer III, along with the Soviet KV heavy tank, was one of the first tanks to use this suspension design.

A distinct feature of Panzer III, influenced by British Vickers tanks, was a three-man turret. This meant that commander was not distracted with either loader's or gunner's tasks and could fully concentrate on maintaining situational awareness. Other tanks of the time did not have this capability, providing the Panzer III with a potential combat advantage. For example the French Somua S-35, had only one-man turret crew, and the Soviet T-34 (originally) had two-men. The practical importance of this feature is signified by the fact that not only all the further

An early 1941 image of the North Africa campaign - the crew are wearing the original tropical issue pith helmets.

German tank designs inherited it, but also later into the war, most of the Allied tanks' designs either quickly switched to the three-man turret, or were abandoned as obsolete.

The Panzer III, as opposed to Panzer IV, had no turret basket, merely a foot rest platform for the gunner.

The Panzer III was intended as the primary battle tank of the German forces. However, when it initially met the KV and T-34 tanks it proved to be inferior in both armor and gun power. To meet the growing need to counter these tanks, the Panzer III was up-gunned with a longer, more powerful 50-mm (1.97 in) cannon and received more armor although this failed to effectively address the problem caused by the KV tank designs. As a result, production of self-propelled guns, as well as the up-gunning of the Panzer IV was initiated.

In 1942, the final version of the Panzer III, the Ausf. N, was created with a 75-mm (2.95 in) KwK 37 L/24 cannon, a low-velocity gun designed for anti-infantry and close-support work. For defensive purposes, the Ausf. N was equipped with rounds of hollow charge ammunition which could penetrate 70 to 100 mms (2.76 to 3.94 in) of armor depending on the round's variant but these were strictly used for self-defense.

The emergence of the Panzer III with 75-mm Gun signalled the fact that the Panzer IV had finally usurped the role of main battle tank relegating the Panzer III to its former role as an infantry support tank. By 1943 with Germany on the defensive there was always the possibility that the Panzer III would meet other tanks with better armor and a far better main armament. The Panzer III Ausf.N was not a success on the battlefield, technology had moved on and production ended early in 1943.

The following intelligence report on the German Panzer III Ausf. N armed with the short 75-mm gun was published in Tactical and Technical Trends, No. 21, March 25, 1943.

PZ. KW. 3 WITH 75-MM GUN
Tactical and Technical Trends, No. 21, March 25, 1943

Among enemy tanks recently examined in the Middle East was a Pz. Kw. 3 mounting a short-barreled 75-mm gun (7.5-cm KwK 38), identical with the short-barreled gun mounted on the Pz. Kw. 4. [Recently Pz. Kw. 4's with a long-barreled 75-mm gun have been encountered by Allied forces (see Tactical and Technical Trends, No. 20, p. 10).] The tank had been demolished, but it appeared that the only alteration, apart from the substitution of the 75-mm gun for the normal 50-mm gun, was the fitting of the armored barrel-sleeve into the front plate of the recoil mechanism belonging to the 75-mm. (Compare accompanying sketch with sketch of Pz. Kw. 3 armed with the long-barreled 50-mm gun, appearing in Tactical and Technical Trends, No. 20, p. 11.)

The German nomenclature for this tank is not known, but recently the Germans have referred to an Einheitspanzer. This is said to be a new standard tank combining the best features

Pz. Kw. 3
WITH 75-MM GUN

of both Pz. Kw. 3 and 4, and to consist of a Pz. Kw. 3 chassis with a short-barreled 75-mm gun mounted in the turret. If this is true, the tank examined may be an Einheitspanzer.

Another Pz. Kw. 3 with the short-barreled 75-mm gun has been captured in Tunisia. Presumably this is the same model tank as that examined in the Middle East.

***

THE EVOLUTION ON THE PANZER III

Trials and tests of new prototypes took place from 1936 to 1937 on testing grounds in Kummersdorf and Ulm. They resulted in the Daimler-Benz design being chosen for full-scale production and in early 1937, Waffenamt ordered Daimler-Benz to produce the first series (0-Series) of their design.

Krupp's ZW prototype, designated as MKA, featured leafsprings and bogie wheel mountings type of a suspension. In turn, many features of this vehicle were used in the design of Panzerkampfwagen IV, which was designed by Krupp.

The PzKpfw III design was composed of four sections - hull, turret, and front superstructure with the opening for the turret and rear superstructure with the engine deck. Each section was of a welded construction and all four were bolted together.

A Panzer III advances along a railway line during the early stages of Operation Barbarossa, July 1941.

The hull was divided into two main compartments divided by a bulkhead. The front compartment housed the gearbox and steering mechanism, and the rear one both the fighting and engine compartment. Basic hull, turret, superstructure and crew layout remained unchanged throughout the production life of Panzerkampfwagen III series.

After modifications, the first Panzerkampfwagen III Ausf A (1-Serie) was produced in May of 1937 by Daimler-Benz, with total of 10 produced until the end of 1937 (chassis numbers 60101-60110). Some sources state that as many as 15 were manufactured. Only eight Ausf As were armed (and equipped units of 1st, 2nd and 3rd Panzer Division and took part in the Anschluss, the take-over of Sudetenland and the Polish Campaign) and other unarmed Ausf As were used for further testing.

In 1937, the Ausf B (2-Serie) was produced by Daimler-Benz with total of 15 produced (chassis numbers 60201-60215). A number of Ausf Bs saw service during the Polish Campaign. In

October of 1940, five Ausf B tanks were modified and used as prototypes of Sturmgeschutz III series.

In June of 1937, the next variant Ausf C (3a-Serie) was produced by Daimler-Benz and its production ended in January of 1938, again with total of 15 produced (chassis numbers 60301-60315). A number of Ausf Cs saw service during the Polish Campaign.

In January of 1938, the next variant Ausf D (3b-Serie) was produced by Daimler-Benz and its production ended in 1939 with total of 55 produced (chassis numbers 60221-60225 and 60316-60340). Only 30 Ausf Ds produced in two groups of 15 were armed, and another 25 unarmed Ausf Ds were used for further testing. A number of Ausf Ds saw service during the Polish Campaign and in Norway.

The early models of Panzer III (Ausf A, B, C and D) were pre-prototypes of the entire series produced exclusively by Daimler-Benz. All were unsuitable for large-scale production but each new model was considered an improved version of the previous one. Each model featured different type of suspension e.g. Ausf A - individual coil springs, Ausf B - two sets of leaf springs, Ausf C - three sets of leaf springs and Ausf D - angled leaf springs.

Ausf A, B, C and D were powered by 250hp petrol Maybach HL 108 TR engines with a 5 or 6 speed Zahnradfabrik gearbox. All early models were armed with 37mm KwK 35/36 L/46.5 gun and three 7.92mm MG 34 machine guns (two mounted co-axially beside the main armament in the turret and one in the hull). Their armor protection ranged from 5 to 15mm, offering protection only against anti-tank rifles and machine gun fire. The reason behind the inadequate armor protection was a result of Daimler-Benz keeping the vehicle in its designated weight range of 15 tons. Some of early models were up-armored and had their maximum armor protection increased to 30mm.

Ausf A, B, C had simple drum shaped "dustbin" commander's cupolas, while Ausf D had cast cupolas similar to that of the PzKpfw IV Ausf B.

A few of the early Panzer IIIs saw actual combat (with units of 1st, 2nd and 3rd Panzer Division) during the Polish Campaign, others were troop tested (1937-February 1940). In February of 1940, existing number of early Panzer IIIs was handed over to NSKK for training purposes. Afterwards, only a few Ausf D saw service with PzAbt zbV 40 (along with PzKpfw NbFz VI) during fighting in Norway in April/May of 1940, followed by service with PzAbt zbV 40 in Finland, 1941/42.

Raw Materials Used in Production of PzKpfw III:
- Steel: 39000.00kg
- Tin: 1.40kg
- Copper: 60.10kg
- Aluminium: 90.40kg
- Lead: 71.10kg
- Zinc: 49.10kg
- Rubber: 125.00kg

In December of 1938, the Ausf E (4-serie) entered production, and 96 were produced by Daimler-Benz, Henschel and MAN when production ended in October of 1939 (chassis numbers 60401-60496). It was the first PzKpfw III that was produced in any significant number. The basic design remained unchanged from its predecessor, but it featured a new independent torsion bar suspension, designed by Ferdinand Porsche for the automotive industry in 1930s. It was composed of six roadwheels and three return rollers. The Ausf E was armed with a 37mm KwK 35/36 L/46.5 gun and three 7.92mm MG 34 machine guns (two in the turret and one in the hull). Its armor protection ranged from 12 to 30mm. During production, escape hatches were installed on both sides of the hull and a vision port was added on the superstructure side for the radio-operator. The driver's visor was provided with an upper and lower sliding shutter, which could be closed together. Also two-piece side hatches were installed in the turret. Unlike its predecessors, the Ausf E was powered by new 300hp petrol Maybach HL120TR engine with a new Maybach Variorex 10 speed gearbox. It was also heavier than all previous models, which were in the 16 ton range but Ausf E weighted 19.5 tons. From August 1940 until 1942, all Ausf E tanks were rearmed with a 50mm KwK 38 L/42 gun mounted in an external mantlet also housing one MG. At the same time, armor protection was increased by the installation of 30mm armor plates to the hull, front and rear, as well as the superstructure front. During service, the number of Ausf E tanks was also reworked to Ausf F standard.

In September 1939, another new variant, the Ausf F (5-serie) entered production. Until July 1940, 435 were produced by Daimler-Benz, Henschel, MAN, Alkett and FAMO (chassis numbers 61001-61650). It was a refined version of the Ausf E and it did not feature any significant modifications or changes other than an improved Maybach HL120TRM engine and modified upper hull nose (with air intakes). The first 335 Ausf F tanks were armed with a 37mm KwK 35/36 L/46.5 gun and three 7.92mm MG 34 machine guns (two in the turret and one in the hull). The last 100 tanks were factory armed with a 50mm KwK 38 L/42 gun mounted in an external mantlet housing one MG. Ausf F vehicles were fitted with a hull rear mounted rack of five smoke generators remotely released from the turret. Some vehicles were also mounted with a stowage box at the rear of the turret. From August 1940 until 1942, all 37mm Ausf F, just as Ausf E tanks, were rearmed with 50mm KwK 38 L/42 guns. They also had their armor protection improved at the same time as Ausf E tanks. Only 40 Ausf F tanks with 50mm KwK 38 L/42 guns were rushed into service before the end of the French Campaign and saw little or no combat. There is still controversy

A Panzer III Ausf L with schurzen in Russia, 1943.

surrounding this as it is reported that the first PzKpfw III armed with 50mm guns entered production in July of 1940. The first production of Sturmgeschutz III assault guns / tank destroyers were based on the Panzerkampfwagen III Ausf F chassis and components. In 1942/43, a number of Ausf F tanks were rearmed with a 50mm KwK 39 L/60 gun. Rearmed and up-armored Ausf F tanks remained in service as late as June of 1944 (e.g. 116th Panzer Division in Normandy).

An interesting fact is that the study report of the captured PzKpfw III Ausf F made by the British in 1942, was then sent to United States Army Ordnance Department where it was decided to utilize a copy of German torsion bar suspension system in future American tanks (e.g. M18 Gun Motor Carriage, M24 Chaffee, M26 Pershing etc.).

In 1940/41, attempts were made to standardize the production of Panzer III and Panzer IV. A few prototypes based on the Panzer III Ausf G/H with new large overlapping roadwheels and FAMO suspension were produced - PzKpfw III Ausf G/H mit Schachtellaufwerk. Since 1940, prototypes were used for testing and training purposes. Further development was halted and in 1943/44, prototypes were fitted with dozers and were used to clean up the streets of bombed cities. This suspension was later adopted in Tiger and Panther.

From April 1940 to February 1941, 600 new Ausf G (6-serie) tanks were produced by Daimler-Benz, Henschel, MAN, Alkett, Wegmann, MNH and FAMO (chassis numbers 65001-65950). The Ausf G was a slight improvement over previous Ausf E and Ausf F tanks. Some 50 Ausf G tanks were armed with 37mm KwK 35/36 L/46.5 guns mounted in an internal mantlet, while the rest were armed with a 50mm KwK 38 L/42 gun mounted in an external mantlet. Both 37mm and 50mm tanks had additional two MG 34 machine guns, one in the turret and another in the hull. Armor protection ranged from 12mm to 30mm, although the majority of the protection ranged from 21mm to 30mm. Also a new pivoting visor for the driver (Fahrersehklappe 30) was installed. The turret was modified and mounted on the roof with a fan exhaust and one signal port was eliminated. Mid-production vehicles were mounted with the new type of commander's cupola as used in the PzKpfw IV Ausf E, F and G, which became standard on all later models of PzKpfw III. Late production vehicles had wider 400mm tracks instead of standard 360mm tracks. The Ausf G was the first to be mounted with the "Rommelkiste" (Rommelbox) - turret mounted storage bin (Gepack Kasten), which then became the standard on all PzKpfw IIIs. From August 1940 until 1942, all 37mm Ausf G tanks just as Ausf E and F tanks were rearmed with the 50mm KwK 38 L/42 gun. Vehicles sent to North Africa were equipped with additional air filters and a different cooling fan reduction ratio. They were designated Ausf G(Tp), Tp being short for Tropisch / Trop / Tropen - tropical. A small number of Ausf G tanks remained in service as late as September 1944.

In October 1940, the Ausf H (7-serie) entered production. It was produced by MAN, Alkett, Henschel, Wegmann, MNH and MIAG until April of 1941 with 308 produced (chassis numbers 66001-66650). The Ausf H featured a newly designed turret to mount a 50mm gun with a single 30mm armor rear plate. Armor protection ranged from 10mm to 30mm, but hull, front and rear, as well as the superstructure front had 30mm armor plates bolted on to them increasing the protection. The increase in armor protection in the Ausf H neutralized the threat of British 2pdr, Soviet 45mm and American 37mm anti-tank guns. The new six speed Maybach SSG 77 gearbox replaced the previously used Variorex. In addition, the suspension system was slightly modified and new sprocket and idler wheels were used in the Ausf H. Consequently, because of the weight gain to 21.8 tons, due to the increase in armor protection, torsion bars were strenghtenedd. Originally, the Ausf H was armed with a 50mm KwK 38 L/42 gun and two MG 34 machine guns, but in 1942/43, they were rearmed with a50mm KwK 39 L/60 gun.

Ausf E, F, G and H were designated as Panzerkampfwagen III Ausf E, F, G and H / Sd.Kfz.141.

As of May 10th 1940, the Panzertruppe had only 381 Panzer III models in service, but 135 were lost during the Blitzkrieg in the west.

In March 1941, the last Sd.Kfz.141 and the first Sd.Kfz.141/1 Panzerkampfwagen III tank - Ausf J (8-serie) entered production. It was produced by Daimler-Benz, MAN, Alkett, Henschel, Wegmann, MNH and MIAG until July 1942 with 2616 produced (chassis numbers 68001-69100 and 72001-74100). The Ausf J had its armor protection significantly improved and it ranged from 10mm to 50mm. The increase in armor was accompanied by the installation of the new driver's visor (Fahrersehklappe 50) and a ballmount (Kugelblende 50) for a 7.92mm MG 34 machine gun in the hull. A new type of front access hatch was installed along with new air intakes on

A Panzer III in action during the Demjansk pocket battle.

the hull front. From April 1942, 20mm spaced armor was added to the gun mantlet and/or superstructure front. 1549 vehicles produced from March 1941 to July 1942 were armed with a 50mm KwK 38 L/42 gun and two MG 34 machine guns. Those vehicles were designated as PzKpfw III Ausf J / Sd.Kfz.141. 1067 vehicles produced from December 1941 to July 1942, were armed with 50mm KwK 39 L/60 and two MG 34 machine guns. Those vehicles were designated as PzKpfw III Ausf J / Sd.Kfz.141/1. The only difference between these models was the main armament and ammunition stowage for 84 rounds in contrast to the previous 99 rounds. When encountered in North Africa, the British nicknamed the 50mm L/60 Ausf J the "Mark III Special". The 50mm L/60 gun was a significant improvement over the original 37mm gun, although it was still inadequate to deal with American M4 Sherman and Soviet T-34/76 tanks. In 1941/42, there was an unsuccessful attempt by Krupp to mount the Ausf J with Panzerkampfwagen IV Ausf G's turret to create a new Panzerkampfwagen III variant designated Ausf K.

From August to November 1942, 81 Ausf J tanks were

produced as command tanks - Panzerbefehlswagen III mit 5cm KwK L/42 / Sd.Kfz.141. From March to September 1943, an additional 104 Ausf J were converted as well. The vehicle was the basic Ausf J tank but it lacked a hull machine gun and carried less ammunition (75 rounds). It was fitted with additional radio equipment and periscope.

In June 1942, the Ausf L tank entered production. 653 were produced by Daimler-Benz, MAN, Alkett, Henschel, Wegmann, MNH and MIAG until December 1942 (chassis numbers 74101-75500). The Ausf L was armed with a 50mm KwK 39 L/60 gun and two 7.92mm MG 34 machine guns. Externally it was almost identical to the late model Ausf J as it was developed by modifying it. The main difference was the new torsion bar gun counter balance, which replaced the original coil spring gun recoil mechanism. Armor protection of the front turret was increased from 30mm to 57mm and 20mm spaced armor was installed on the superstructure front, and in many cases on the gun mantlet. The design of the vehicle was simplified as the rear deck was modified (air-intakes and hatches) and early in production the hull escape hatches, the loader's vision port on the mantlet and turret side ports were removed. The Ausf L was also mounted with a new special system to transfer heated engine coolant from one vehicle to another. A single Ausf L was mounted with an experimental 75/55mm tapered-bore KwK0725 gun and was designated as PzKpfw III Ausf L mit Waffe 0725. Vehicles send to North Africa were equipped with additional air filters, modified oil filters, a different cooling fan reduction ratio and were designated as Ausf L(Tp). The Ausf L was also first to be mounted with an anti-aircraft machine gun mount (Fliegerbeschussgerat 41/42) on the commander's cupola. This became standard on all new PzKpfw III tanks and was mounted on older models during service. Many were mounted with 5mm hull and turret armor skirts (Schurzen).

From October 1942 to February 1943, 250 new Ausf M (10-serie) tanks were produced by Wegmann, MIAG, MAN and MNH (chassis numbers 76101-77800). The Ausf M was a late production model Ausf L mounted with new wading equipment allowing wading up to depth of approximately 1.3m, in contrast to the previous 0.8-0.9m. This led to all air inlets and outlets as well as other openings and joints being sealed, while a modified muffler with closure-valve was installed high on the hull rear. The new system was developed and a modified version was used in Tauchpanzer III submersible wading tanks. The hull rear mounted rack of five smoke generators was replaced by three 90mm NbK dischargers mounted forward on both sides of the turret. The Ausf M just as the Ausf L was armed with a 50mm KwK 39 L/60 gun and two 7.92mm MG 34 machine guns. Vehicles produced in 1943 were factory mounted with 5mm hull and turret armor skirts (Schurzen). Large number of Ausf M were converted to either Sturmgeschütz III or Ausf N.

**

A report on mounting of 50-mm tank gun in German Panzer III tanks, from Tactical and Technical Trends, No. 33, September 9, 1943.

MOUNTING OF 50-MM KW.K 39 TANK GUN
Tactical and Technical Trends, No. 33, September 9, 1943

A preliminary examination in the United Kingdom of a captured PzKw 3 Model L (Tp)* has disclosed that the long-barreled 50-mm tank gun, 50-mm Kw. K 39, is balanced by means of a torsion-bar compensator.

As shown in the sketch overleaf, the torsion bar is mounted on the inside of the turret roof parallel to the trunnion axis and is

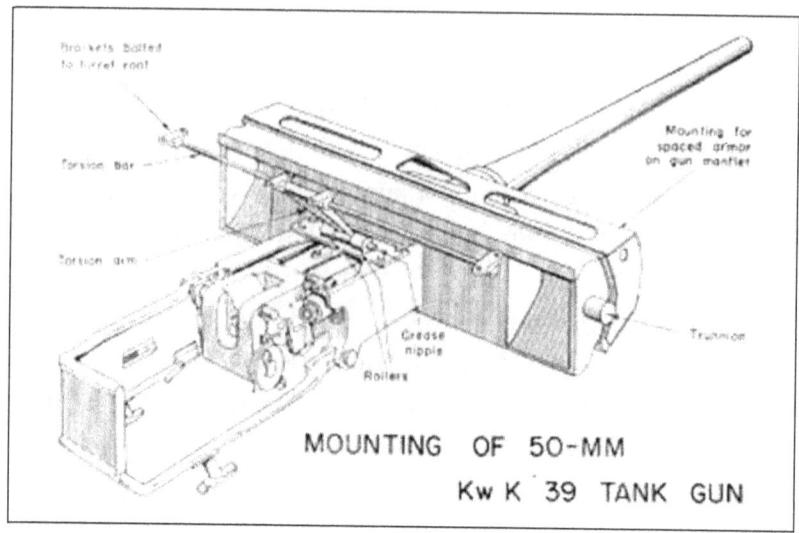

MOUNTING OF 50-MM KwK 39 TANK GUN

anchored at each end. An arm is attached to the center of the bar which carries at its free end a pair of rollers. The bar is pre-set so that the rollers exert a downward force on a flat plate bolted to the gun cradle a few inches from the trunnion axis.

It will be seen from the sketch that, as this plate is fairly close to the trunnion axis, the maximum twist of the bar (from full depression to full elevation) is quite small.

The short tank gun, 50-mm Kw. K, in a captured PzKw 3 Model J previously examined was balanced by a coil spring in compression on the right of the mounting.

*The abbreviation Tp (Tropmunition) following the model-letter of the tank indicates that this tank is adapted for use in the tropics.

***

From February 1943 to April 1943, 100 Ausf M tanks produced by MIAG in Braunsweig (chassis numbers 77609-77708) were converted by Wegmann in Kassel to Flammpanzer - flame-thrower tanks. These new vehicles were designated as PzKpfw III (Fl) / Sd.Kfz 141/3. They were also commonly known as Flammpanzer III or Panzerflammwagen III. It was an unmodified Ausf M tank with an additional 30mm to 50mm armor plates welded on for protection to the hull front. This was done because Flammpanzer III tanks had to get closer to their targets and were more vulnerable to enemy fire. In contrast to regular tanks, it was operated by a three men crew composed of commander/flame gunner, radio operator/hull gunner and driver. The main gun and internal ammunition stowage were replaced with the flame-thrower and fuel tanks. This vehicle was armed with a 14mm Flammenwerfer flame-thrower and two 7.92mm MG 34 machine guns. The flame-thrower was mounted in place of the original 50mm gun and concealed in a thick 1.5m long pipe made to appear as standard armament. The flame-thrower could be lowered 8 degrees and raised 20 degrees. Each vehicle carried some 1020 liters of inflammable oil (Flammol) in two tanks inside the vehicle. Oil was pumped into the pipe by a Koebe pump driven by a two-stroke DKW

Panzerkampfwagen III Ausf E/F in Russian village.

engine, and was ignited by an electric charge (Smitskerzen). The supply of oil allowed some 125 one second or some 80 to 81 two to three seconds long bursts. The maximum range of the flame-thrower was 60m using ignited oil and 50m using cold oil. The range also depended on the weather conditions.

The Flammpanzer III was designed in mind with fighting in the urban areas such as Stalingrad, but it was never to reach its destination. Eventually, the Flammpanzer III equipped the Panzer Regiment's (Panzer Abteilung) Flame-thrower Platoons (Panzer-Flamm-Zug), each with seven vehicles. A report dated May 5th 1941 gives the following distribution of the vehicles, along with a single vehicle to Schule Wunsdorf:

Division	No. of Vehicles
Panzer Division Grossdeutschland	28
6th Panzer Division	15
1st Panzer Division	14
24th Panzer Division	14
16th Panzer Division	7

A report from 1943, states that from March to December, Flammpanzer III tanks were serving with the following Panzer Divisions: 1st, 6th, 11th, 14th, 24th and Grossdeutschland in Russia and the 16th and 26th in Italy. In July 1943, 41 flame-thrower tanks were reported in service with the 6th, 10th and Grossdeutschland Panzer Divisions in preparation for the attack on Kursk. The Flammpanzer III's design proved to be unsuccessful and vehicles returned for repair were rebuilt into standard combat tanks or Sturmgeschutz III assault guns / tank destroyers. In November 1944, only 10 out of original 100 were repaired and issued to Panzer-Flamm-Kompanie 351, which saw service as late as April of 1945 with Heeres Gruppe Sud. Today, a Panzerkampfwagen III (Fl) (chassis number 77651) captured in Italy can be seen in Koblenz Museum in Germany

Panzerkampfwagen III Ausf L

after being transferred to the museum from Aberdeen Proving Grounds in U.S.A.

In June 1942, the last PzKpfw III model entered production. A new model Ausf N was produced until August 1943 by Henschel, Wegmann, MNH, MIAG and MAN (chassis numbers 73851-77800). Ausf N tanks were produced on Ausf J (3), L (447) and M (213) chassis with total of 663 produced. 37 additional Ausf N tanks were converted from rebuilt older PzKpfw III tanks. The PzKpfw III Ausf N was also known as Sturmpanzer III. The Ausf N was the same as Ausf J, L and M with the main difference being its main armament. It was armed with short 75mm KwK 37 L/24, originally used in PzKpfw IV Ausf A to F1 tanks, which then rearmed with longer 75mm guns. Additional armament consisted of the standard two MG 34 machine guns. The internal ammunition stowage was modified and 56 (based on Ausf L chassis) or 64 (based on Ausf M chassis) rounds were carried. The Ausf N did not have spaced armor as previous models because of the weight of the new 75mm gun. Late production vehicles were fitted with modified type of commander's cupola with single hatch instead of two-piece one, as well as one-piece side turret hatches. A number of late vehicles were mounted

PzKpfw III Ausf N / (Sturmpanzer III) / Sd.Kfz. 141/2

with the commander's cupola used in PzKpfw IV Ausf G tanks. Vehicles produced from March 1943 were factory mounted with 5mm hull and turret armor skirts (Schurzen). In addition, vehicles produced from early 1943 were factory applied with Zimmerit - anti-magentic paste. PzKpfw III Ausf N tanks were used for close support role. They were either assigned to Tiger Battalions (sPzAbt/sSSPzAbt) as a way to protect them from enemy infantry or to Panzer-Grenadier Divisions. Some sources also state that a variant designated Ausf O existed, although there is no proof of its existence.

The interesting fact is that in 1938, work began on the vehicles which were to replace newly introduced Panzerkampfwagen III and Panzerkampfwagen IV. Daimler-Benz was awarded the contract for a new tank, which was to replace Panzerkampfwagen III - VK 2001 (III). It was a completely new design with new chassis and hull layout. It was also designated as GBK - Kampfwagen des Generalbevollmaechtigen (Battle Tank for the Commission for Standardization of Automotive Designs). The work on this tank stopped in December of 1941 and all efforts were focused on the development of a heavier tank - the Panther.

Some of the later Panzer III variants were fitted with turret mounted storage bins (Gepack Kasten). The canister racks mounted on the turret and/or at the rear of the hull were very common. During the early stages of Operation Barbarossa in 1941, Panzer IIIs were equipped with single-axle trailers carrying extra fuel in order to increase their radius of operation. During production, the PzKpfw III's design underwent many changes including various modifications made on the turret (e.g. cupola, gun mantlet, vision slots, hatches, armor skirts) and hull (e.g. escape hatch, armor skirts) and superstructure (e.g. air intakes, spaced armor, headlights arrangement) components. Since mid 1943, Panzer IIIs were mounted with Schurzen - 5mm armor skirts. During service and repairs, many Panzer III tanks were up-armored, rearmed and re-equipped with new equipment and components creating completely non-standard variants. Vehicles send to North Africa were equipped with additional air filters and different cooling fan reduction ratio. They were designated as (Tp), Tp being short for Tropisch / Trop / Tropen - tropical.

Panzerkampfwagen III saw action in small numbers during the invasion of Poland in September of 1939. The Panzer III was designed as platoon commander's vehicle (Zugfuhrerwagen) and was Germany's first true main/medium battle tank. The design of Panzer III came from lessons learned from the combat tested Panzer I and Panzer II. The Panzer III formed the bulk of the Panzer Divisions' strength during early years of war. By October 1943, only five Panzer Divisions on the Eastern Front had one or more Panzer Company equipped with Panzer IIIs. By late 1944, only 79 Panzer IIIs were in service with frontline units on the Eastern Front. A number of PzKpfw IIIs remained in service until the end of the war in places like Norway and Holland.

The Panzerkampfwagen III's production was slow and ceased in August of 1943. In the early years, gaps were filled with the Czech PzKpfw 35(t) and PzKpfw 38(t), which possessed a similar combat value. Its design was also a great help in the development of its bigger brother Panzerkampfwagen IV and shared many common parts with it.

Types Ausf A-J(early) (1936-1941) of Panzer III were called "Short" and types Ausf J(late)-N (1941-1943) were called "Long". Overall around 6000 Panzerkampfwagen IIIs (long and short) were produced. The majority of PzKpfw IIIs were produced by Alkett along with Daimler-Benz, FAMO, Henschel & Sohn, MAN, MIAG, Waggonfabrik Wegmann and MNH.

Sd.Kfz.141 (Short)		
Ausf A	1937	37mm L/45
Ausf B	1937	37mm L/45
Ausf C	1937/38	37mm L/45
Ausf D	1938	37mm L/45
Ausf E	1938/39	37mm L/45 (early) / 50mm L/42 (late)
Ausf F	1939/40	37mm L/45 (early) / 50mm L/42 (late)
Ausf G	1940/41	37mm L/45 (early) / 50mm L/42 (late)
Ausf H	1940/41	50mm L/42 (early) / 50mm L/60 (late)
Ausf J	1941/42	50mm L/42 (early)
Sd.Kfz.141/1 (Long)		
Ausf J	1941/42	50mm L/60 (late)
Ausf L	1942	50mm L/60
Ausf M	1942/43	50mm L/60
Sd.Kfz.141/2 (Long)		
Ausf N / (Sturmpanzer III)	1942/43	75mm L/24
Sd.Kfz.141/3 (Long)		
Ausf M / (Flamm)	1943	14mm Flammenwerfer

Panzer III saw an extensive service on all fronts until late 1943, when it was totally replaced by Panzerkampfwagen IV. As a common practice, the Panzer III's chassis/components became a base for a few conversions and prototypes. By 1943 standards,

Minenraumpanzer III / Minenraumgerat mit PzKpfw Antrieb.

the Panzer III was obsolete and lost its combat effectiveness which resulted in many being converted to perform various functions.

From February 1942 to April 1944, 262 Panzerkampfwagen III Ausf E/F/Gs were up-armored and converted into Artillerie Panzerbeobachtungswagen III (Sd.Kfz.143) - observation vehicles which served with Wespe and Hummel batteries until the end of the war. Panzerbeobachtungswagen III had a dummy gun mounted and in the place of original gun, Kugelblende (ballmount) for a 7.92mm MG34 machine gun was installed. The Sd.Kfz.143 had a crew of five and was equipped with powerful radio equipment.

In 1943, some Ausf L and Ms were converted into turretless Pionierpanzerwagen III - engineer tanks mounted with additional equipment. In mid 1944, 176 Panzer IIIs (including Ausf E, F and G) were converted into Bergepanzer IIIs - recovery vehicles fitted with additional equipment. Also in 1943/44 a number of early Panzer IIIs was converted into Schlepper - artillery tractors and Munitionspanzer - ammunition carriers.

One of the most interesting prototypes based on the Panzer III's chassis was the Minenraumpanzer III - a mine clearing/mine destroyer tank developed by Krupp. It proved to be unsuccessful and never entered production.

In October of 1943, a prototype of PzKpfw III Ausf N als Schienen-Kettenfahrzeug was tested. Three Ausf Ns (mounted with railway suspension by Sauer Werke of Vienna) were converted to travel by rail at maximum speed of 100km/h. They were to be used to protect the rail network behind the frontlines in the East. Only three prototypes were produced but further development of this project was cancelled.

From June 1938 to February 1943, a number of Panzer IIIs were converted by Daimler-Benz to Panzerbefehlswagens III Ausf D1 (30), Ausf E (45) and Ausf H (175) (Sd.Kfz.266-268) command tanks equipped with extra radios and additional equipment and saw active service until the end of the war. Command tanks were mounted with a dummy gun and were armed only with a single 7.92mm MG machine gun. 185 Panzerbefehlswagen III mit 5cm KwK L/42 (based on Ausf J) and 50 Ausf K (based on Ausf L) were armed with 50mm L/42 and 50mm L/60 guns respectively.

Variant:	Production Period:	Number Produced:
Ausf A	1937	15
Ausf B	1937	15
Ausf C	1937/38	15
Ausf D	1938	30
Ausf E	1938/39	96
Ausf F	1939/40	435
Ausf G	1940/41	600
Ausf H	1940/41	308
Ausf J (early)	1941/42	1549
Ausf J (late)	1941/42	1067
Ausf L	1942	653
Ausf M	1942/43	250
Ausf N	1942/43	700

Turrets removed from PzKpfw IIIs converted to other vehicles were used in fortifications of the Atlantic Wall and Hitler's Line

PzKpfw III Ausf G and IV Ausf F1 of Lt. N.Baryshev's platoon from 107th Independent Tank Battalion, Volkhov Front, July 6th of 1942.

in Italy. In 1945, it was decided to utilize the obsolete PzKpfw III and mount it with Wirbelwind or Ostwind turrets, designated as Flakpanzer III. 90 were ordered but the end of the war terminated the production.

The most interesting field conversion was created by the field workshops of the Afrika Korps in North Africa, who converted a damaged Panzerkampfwagen III Ausf H to 150mm s.I.G.33 gun carrier by using components (such as gun itself, gun shield, superstructure sides with tool stowage and ammunition racks) from Sturmpanzer II Bison (lengthened version).

The Panzerkampfwagen III was also exported to other nations, especially Germany's Allies or pro-German states. The first country to receive the PzKpfw III was Hungary (10), followed by Romania (11 Ausf N), Bulgaria (10 Ausf N) and Slovakia (7 Ausf N). A small number of Ausf L and N tanks was also exported to Croatia. A large number (56) was ordered by Turkey but the transaction was never finalized due to the war situation, although supposedly some (20-22?) were delivered.

From 1941 to 1943, Russians captured large numbers of PzKpfw III, Sturmgeschutz III and PzKpfw IV. Some were pressed into temporary service (e.g. being used as "Trojan Horses" or as "bait"), while some were converted to assault guns designated SU-76i and SG-122A.

An interesting fact is that the Polish Tank Platoon of the Carpathian Lancers received captured PzKpfw III for training purposes, while in Egypt in August of 1942.

The most successful conversion based on the Panzerkampfwagen III's chassis was the Sturmgeschutz III - assault gun/tank destroyer series - which remained in service with the Finnish Army as late as 1967.

After the war ended, some 32 PzKpfw III were used by Norway along with Stug III Ausf Gs.

A small number of PzKpfw III tanks was also used by Czechoslovakia, including four rebuild Flammpanzer III tanks.

The Panzerkampfwagen III gained a reputation for being a highly reliable and effective vehicle, which shaped tank development plans of both German and Allied tank builders. It was the best German tank in the first part of the war, but by 1943 it was largely obsolete.

This U-Panzer belonged to the 18th Panzer Division's 18th Panzer Regiment. This photo was taken during the crossing of the River Bug at Patulin on 22nd June of 1941. During the preparation for the invasion of England - Operation Seelöwe (Sealion) - Panzer IIIs and Panzer IVs were converted into submersible tanks able to travel on the bottom of a body of water at the depths of 6 to 15 meters. From June to October of 1940, 160 Panzer III Ausf F/G/H and 8 Panzerbefehlswagen III Ausf E along with 42 Panzer IV Ausf Ds were converted into U-Panzers / Tauchpanzers. After extensive tests and modifications U-Panzer were ready for action. Since Operation Sealion was never realized, Tauchpanzer IIIs and IVs were used during Operation Barbarossa (crossing river Bug at Patulin), in service with 3rd (6th Panzer Regiment) and 18th Panzer Division. It was also planned to use U-Panzers in the aborted invasion on the island of Malta.

Specifications

Model:	Ausf H	Ausf L/M
Weight:	21800kg	22700kg
Crew:	5 men	5 men
Engine:	Maybach HL 120 TRM / 12-cylinder / 265hp	Maybach HL 120 TRM / 12-cylinder / 265hp
Speed:	Road: 40km/h	Road: 40km/h
	Cross-Country: 20km/h	Cross-Country: 20km/h
Range:	Road: 165km	Road: 155km
	Cross-Country: 105km	Cross-Country: 95km
Fuel Capacity:	320 litres	320 litres
Lenght:	5.52m (with the gun)	6.41m (with the gun)
		5.56m (w/o the gun)
Width:	2.95m	2.95m
Height:	2.50m	2.50m
Armament:	50mm KwK 38 L/42	50mm KwK 39 L/60
	2 x 7.92mm MG34	2 x 7.92mm MG34
	(1 x MG - hull)	(1 x MG - hull)
	(1 x MG - coax)	(1 x MG - coax)
Ammo:	50mm - 99 rounds	50mm - 92 rounds
	7.92mm - 2700 rounds	7.92mm - 3750 rounds
Armor (mm/angle):	Front Turret: 30/13	Front Turret: 57/15
	Front Upper Hull: 30+30/90	Front Upper Hull: 50+20/9
	Front Lower Hull: 30+30/23	Front Lower Hull: 50/21
	Side Turret: 30/25	Side Turret: 30/25
	Side Upper Hull: 30/0	Side Upper Hull: 30/0
	Side Lower Hull: 30/0	Side Lower Hull: 30/0
	Rear Turret: 30/13	Rear Turret: 30/12
	Rear Upper Hull: 30/30	Rear Upper Hull: 50/17
	Rear Lower Hull: 30+30/8	Rear Lower Hull: 50/9
	Turret Top / Bottom: 10/89	Turret Top / Bottom: 10/83
	Upper Hull Top / Bottom: 17/77	Upper Hull Top / Bottom: 18/79
	Lower Hull Top / Bottom: 16/90	Lower Hull Top / Bottom: 16/90
	Gun Mantlet: 37/0	Gun Mantlet: 50+20/0

50mm KwK 38 L/42
Penetration of Armor Plate at 30 degrees from Vertical.

Ammunition:	100m	500m	1000m	1500m	2000m
Panzergranate 39	54mm	46mm	36mm	28mm	22mm
Panzergranate 40	96mm	58mm	0mm	0mm	0mm

Pzgr.39 (APCBC) - Armor Piercing Composite Ballistic Cap
Pzgr.40 (APCR) - Armor Piercing Composite Rigid (Tungsten Core)

50mm KwK 39 L/60					
Penetration of Armor Plate at 30 degrees from Vertical.					
Ammunition:	100m	500m	1000m	1500m	2000m
Panzergranate 39	67mm	57mm	44mm	34mm	26mm
Panzergranate 40	130mm	72mm	38mm	0mm	0mm

Pzgr.39 (APCBC) - Armor Piercing Composite Ballistic Cap
Pzgr.40 (APCR) - Armor Piercing Composite Rigid (Tungsten Core)

Conversions

- PzKpfw III (Flamm) Ausf. M (Sd. Kfz. 141/3) - flame-thrower tank,
- Befehlswagen III Ausf. D1 (Sd.Kfz 267-268) - command tank,
- Befehlswagen III Ausf. E (Sd. Kfz. 266-268) - command tank,
- Befehlswagen III Ausf. H (Sd. Kfz. 266-268) - command tank,
- Befehlswagen III Ausf. K - command tank,
- Beobachtungswagen III - observation vehicle (Sd.Kfz.143),
- Bergepanzer III (Sd. Kfz. 143) - recovery vehicle,
- Sturmgeschütz III Ausf A to E (Sd.Kfz.141),
- Sturmgeschütz III (40) Ausf F/G (Sd.Kfz.141/2),
- Sturmhaubitze 42 (Sd.Kfz. 142/2) 105mm L/28 (L/30) - assault howitzer,
- Stug 33 - 150mm howitzer carrier - infantry support,
- Munitionspanzerwagen III Ausf E/F/G - ammo carrier,
- Munition Schlepper - ammo carrier for Ferdinand/Elephant units,
- Pionierpanzerwagen III - engineer's tank,
- Panzer III Ausf N Schienen-Kettenfahrzeug - rail tank,
- PzKpfw III Ausf G/H mit Schachtellaufwerk - prototype / dozer tank,
- Panzer III Ausf. E(U) (37mm gun) - submersible tank,
- Panzer III Ausf. F(U) (50mm L/42 gun) - submersible tank,
- Panzer III Ausf D1(U) - submersible command tank,
- Panzer III Ausf H(U) - submersible command tank,
- Minenraumpanzer III - mine clearing vehicle (prototype),

- Flakpanzer III (planned),
- Artillerie Schlepper - artillery tractor.

***

An engineering report on samples of German natural and artificial rubber from a Panzer III, appeared Tactical and Technical Trends, No. 33, September 9, 1943.

GERMAN TANK RUBBER ANALYSIS
Tactical and Technical Trends, No. 33, September 9, 1943

Analysis by British engineers of samples of natural and artificial rubber taken from the PzKw 3 tanks discloses some interesting points which are worth recording.

Two very similar articles, i.e. a vision forehead pad and a cupola pad of a 1940 model of this tank proved to be very different when analyzed. The former was made of natural rubber and was secured to the metal by the brass plating process. The cupola pad, on the other hand, was made from synthetic rubber and was attached to the metal by an adhesive paint. These samples confirm the previous supposition that the Germans have not yet learned how to make an efficient joint between synthetic rubber and metal.

The most interesting sample, however, was a section of a bogie wheel tire from a PzKw 3 tank (probably 1942). This sample proved to be made of synthetic rubber. This is said to be the first evidence received by the British authorities of this material being used by the Germans for solid tires. It seems to show that the Germans have made sufficient technical progress to overcome the heating difficulties previously arising when synthetic rubber was used for this type of work. The method of adhesion to the metal band was by means of an intermediate layer of hard, probably natural rubber.

***

Panzerbefehlswagen (command tank) III ausf E or F in Greece, fitted with a 37 mm gun and two coaxial machine guns (1941).

ARMOUR

The Panzer III Ausf. A through C had 15 mm (0.59 in) of homogeneous steel armor on all sides with 10 mm (0.39 in) on the top and 5 mm (0.20 in) on the bottom. This was quickly determined to be insufficient, and was upgraded to 30 mm (1.18 in) on the front, sides and rear in the Ausf. D, E, F, and G models, with the H model having a second 30 mm (1.18 in) layer of face-hardened steel applied to the front and rear hull. The Ausf. J model had a solid 50 mm (1.97 in) plate on the front and rear, while the Ausf. J[1], L, and the M models had an additional layer of 20 mm (0.79 in) of armor on the front hull and turret. This additional frontal armor gave the Panzer III frontal protection from most British and Soviet anti-tank guns at all but close ranges. The sides were still vulnerable to many enemy weapons including anti-tank rifles at close ranges

The Panzer III was intended to fight other tanks; in the initial design stage a 50-mm (1.97 in) cannon was specified.

However, the infantry at the time were being equipped with the 37-mm (1.46 in) PaK 36, and it was thought that in the interest of standardization the tanks should carry the same armament. As a compromise, the turret ring was made large enough to accommodate a 50-mm (1.97 in) cannon should a future upgrade be required. This single decision would later assure the Panzer III a prolonged life in the German Army.

The Ausf. A to early Ausf. F were equipped with a 3.7 cm KwK 36 L/46.5 which proved adequate during the campaigns of 1939 and 1940 but the later Ausf. F to Ausf. J were upgraded with the 5 cm KwK 38 L/42 and the Ausf. J[1] to M with the longer 5 cm KwK 39 L/60 cannon in response to increasingly better armed and armored opponents.

By 1942, the Panzer IV was becoming Germany's main medium tank because of its better upgrade potential. The Panzer III remained in production as a close support vehicle. The Ausf. N model mounted a low-velocity 7.5 cm KwK 37 L/24 cannon - the same used by the early Panzer IV Ausf. A to Ausf. F models. These guns had originally been fitted to older Panzer IV Ausf A to F1 models and had been placed into storage when those tanks had also been up armed to longer versions of the 75mm gun.

All early models up to and including the Ausf. F had two 7.92-mm (0.31 in) Maschinengewehr 34 machine guns mounted coaxially with the main gun, and a similar weapon in a hull mount. Models from the Ausf. G and later had a single coaxial MG34 and the hull MG34.

MOBILITY

The Panzer III Ausf. A through C were powered by a 250 metric horsepower (183.87 kW), 12-cylinder Maybach HL 108 TR engine, giving a top speed of 32 kilometres per hour (19.88 mph) and a range of 150 kilometres (93.21 mi). All later models were powered by the 300 metric horsepower (220.65 kW), 12-cylinder Maybach HL 120 TRM engine. Top speed varied, depending on the transmission and weight, but was around 40 kilometres per hour (24.85 mph). The range was generally around 155 kilometres (96.31 mi).

Combat Use

The Panzer III was used in the campaigns against Poland, France, the Soviet Union and in North Africa. A handful were still in use in Normandy, Anzio, Finland and in Operation Market Garden in 1944.

In the Polish and French campaigns, the Panzer III formed a small part of the German armored forces. Only a few hundred Ausf. A through F were available in these campaigns, most armed with the 37-mm (1.46 in) gun. They were the best medium tank available to the Germans and outclassed most of their opponents such as the Polish 7TP, French R-35 and H-35 light tanks.

The crew of a Panzer III of the 2nd SS Panzer Division Das Reich rest after heavy fighting in the Battle of Kursk.

Around the time of Operation Barbarossa, the Panzer III was numerically the most important German tank. At this time the majority of the available tanks (including re-armed Ausf. E and F, plus new Ausf. G and H models) mounted the 50-mm (1.97 in) KwK 38 L/42 cannon which also equipped the majority of the tanks in North Africa. Initially, the Panzer IIIs were outclassed and outnumbered by Soviet T-34 and KV tanks. However, the most numerous Soviet tanks were the T-26 and BT tanks. This, along with superior German tactical skill, crew training, and the good ergonomics of the Panzer III all contributed to a rough 6:1 favourable kill ratio for German tanks of all types in 1941.

With the appearance of the T-34 and KV tanks, rearming the Panzer III with a longer, more powerful 50-mm (1.97 in) cannon was prioritised. The T-34 was generally invulnerable in frontal engagements with the Panzer III until the 50 mm KwK 39 L/60 gun was introduced on the Panzer III Ausf. J[1] in the spring of 1942 (the gun was based on infantry's 50 mm Pak 38 L/60). This could penetrate the T-34 frontally at ranges under 500 metres (1,600 ft). Against the KV tanks it was a threat if armed with special high velocity tungsten rounds. In addition, to counter antitank rifles, in 1943 the Ausf. L version began the use of spaced armor skirts (schürzen) around the turret and on the hull sides. However, due to the introduction of the upgunned and uparmored Panzer IV, the Panzer III was, after the Battle of Kursk, relegated to secondary roles, such as training, and it was replaced as the main German medium tank by the Panzer IV and the Panther.

The Panzer III chassis was the basis for the turretless Sturmgeschütz III assault gun, one of the most successful self-propelled guns of the war, and the single most-produced German armored fighting vehicle design of World War II.

By the end of the war, the Pz.III had almost no frontline use and many vehicles had been returned to the factories for conversion into StuG assault guns, which were in high demand due to the defensive warfare style adopted by the German Army by then.

***

The following report written by Hauptmann Oehme, the commander of the 8.Kompanie/Panzer-Regiment 3, relates his experience in attempting to knock out T34 and KW-I tanks:

Combat Report for the Period of II through 17 August 1942

At about 1800 hours, I received the order to drive to Jelnja to support the Gruppe von Bisehoffshausen with the Panzers that had just been repaired and the four Pz.Kpfw.IV (7.5 cm Kw.K40 L/43) that had just arrived.

The Panzer-Kompanie counterattacked JeInja, which was surrounded by our Panzers and taken under heavy fire by all of the Panzers. The front elements of the Russians pulled back and most of the houses in the village went up in flames. It was observed that two T-34s drove off in reverse out of burning sheds.

As dawn broke, the Russians renewed the attack with tank and infantry forces. The tanks were immediately spotted and two T-34s on the road were knocked out at a range of about 300 meters. The rest of the tanks must have quickly retreated, as determined by the noise from their engines.

During the evening hours of 13th August, the Russians again attacked with tanks and a few infantry riding on them. In spite of night falling, a further two T34s and a KW-I were knocked out of which two enemy tanks brightly burned, upon which the rest of the tanks turned back. The attack was repulsed.

During the night, the opponent with tanks took up positions in the depression by Shulebino and at dawn attempted to break

Panzer III advancing deeper into Russia, during 1941.

through the woods by Point 208. At the same time eight to ten KW-I attacked on the road. Of these, two were knocked out in our position by the Pz.Kpfw.IV with a long gun at a range of 15 to 20 meters. The rest were convinced to turn back. It should be noted that it was necessary to use about eight Hohlraumgranaten (shaped charge shells) to set each of the KW-I on fire. At Point 208, three T34s managed to break into the position but didn't exploit the opportunity any further. The company commander of the infantry urgently requested Panzer support because these enemy tanks had hidden in the woods. One Pz.Kpfw.IV (7.5 cm Kw.K. L/24) and two Pz.Kpfw.III (5 cm Kw.K. L/42) were sent to the area where the enemy tanks had broken in.

In the afternoon, the Russians again attacked with strong tank forces. This time his attempt occurred south of the road. Several tanks landed in the swamp and remained stuck there. In the evening, these tanks were knocked out by the 5.Kompanie/Panzer-Regiment 3, while on the road four additional KW-I were knocked out by the 8.Kompanie. An 8.8 cm Flak gun had a large part in this last defensive battle. This gun was located in an alley south of the road, fell out when damaged by gun fire, and was pulled back.

On this day, several smaller Russian tanks were knocked out that had attacked separately. In addition a Pz.Kpfw.IV (7.5 cm Kw.K40 L/43) was knocked out by a KW-I. One of the crew was killed, two severely wounded, and one lightly wounded.

Another Pz.Kpfw.IV (7.5 cm Kw.K40 L/43) fought still another T34 but was itself knocked out. The Pz.Kpfw.IV immediately burned out. The commander and gunner were wounded, three of the crew were killed immediately. During these defensive actions from 11 to 17 August 1942, the 8.Kompanie knocked out 45 enemy tanks, of which 11 were T60s, and the rest T34s and KW-Is.

***

AMMUNITION STORAGE

The ammunition were laid out vertically except for those located under the seat of the gunner. The base of the round was laid out in a cavity in the floor of the rack and the point was maintained in place by a spring clip. This provision was effective in general except for certain rounds, difficult to reach. The right lower rack and two back-left racks had sliding doors (sensitive to the sand grains) then the left lower rack was equipped with an articulated door. The tanks armed with the 50mm KwK L/60 50mm laid out their ammunition in a horizontal disposition, which was easier for employment. The rounds used by L/60 were longer, which limited the number of rounds carried in the tank to 78 rounds.

For the vehicles armed with the gun of 50mm KwK L/42 the provision of the ammunition was 99 rounds stored as follows:
- 5 rounds under the seat of the gunner
- 22 rounds in a rack located in the back-right corner of the compartment
- 12 rounds in a rack located above this last
- 36 rounds in a rack located in the back-left corner of the

A Panzer III in action during the Demjansk pocket battle.

compartment
- 24 rounds in a rack located above this last.

VARIANTS
- Panzer III Ausf. A - Prototype; 10 produced in 1937, only 8 armed and saw service in Poland.
- Panzer III Ausf. B, C - Prototype; 15 of each produced in 1937, some of each saw service in Poland.
- Panzer III Ausf. D - Prototype; 55 produced in 1938, only 30 armed and saw service in Poland and Norway.
- Panzer III Ausf. E, F - Production models 1939-1940. Armed with 3.7 cm KwK 36 L/46.5 (later 5 cm KwK 38 L/42) guns. 531 produced.
- Panzer III Ausf. G - More armor on gun mantlet. Armed with 3.7 cm KwK 36 L/46.5 (later 5 cm KwK 38 L/42) gun. 600 produced in 1940-1941.
- Panzer III Ausf. H - Minor modifications. Bolt-on armor added to front and rear hull (30 mm + 30 mm plates). 308 produced in 1940-1941.

Grenadiers and Panzer III in the snow during the winter of 1942.

- Panzer III Ausf. I - Variant mentioned in Allied intelligence reports but not an actual existing vehicle.
- Panzer III Ausf. J - The hull was lengthened. Front armor increased to 50 mm plate. 482 produced in 1941.
- Panzer III Ausf. J¹ - Equipped with the longer and more powerful 5 cm KwK 39 L/60 gun. 1,067 produced in late 1941 to mid 1942.
- Panzer III Ausf. K - Panzerbefehlswagen command tank variant with a modified turret. Carried actual main armament rather than a dummy gun as found on other Panzer III command versions.
- Panzer III Ausf. L - Uparmored to 50 mm + 20 mm plates. 653 produced in 1942.
- Panzer III Ausf. M - Minor modifications such as deep-wading exhaust and schurzen. 250 produced in 1942-1943.
- Panzer III Ausf. N - Armed with a short barreled 7.5 cm KwK 37 L/24 gun, due to 7.5 cm gun's ability to fire HEAT rounds. 700 re-equipped J/L/M models in 1942-1943.

CONVERSIONS
- PzKfw III (Flamm) Ausf. M (Sd. Kfz 141/3) - flame-thrower
- Befehlswagen III Ausf. Dl (Sd. Kfz 267-268) - command tank
- Befehlswagen III Ausf. E (Sd. Kfz 267-268) - command tank
- Befehlswagen III Ausf. H (Sd. Kfz 266-268) - command tank
- Befehlswagen III Ausf. K - command tank
- Beobachtungswagen III - observation vehicle (Sd. Kfz 143)

The Tauchpanzer was developed in mid-1940 for the proposed invasion of England (Sea Lion). The Pz Kpfw III were modified and provided with a submersion kit. Air-intakes were fitted with locking covers, and the exhaust was fitted with non-return valves. The cupola, gun mantlet and hull MG were sealed with waterproof fabric covers. An inflatable rubber tube surrounded the turret ring. While submerged, the tank drew air through a pipe from a float carrying a snorkel device and radio antenna which remained on the surface. A gyro-compass was used for underwater navigation. The Tauchpanzer could operate in depths of up to 15 metres. A vessel with a hinged ramp was used to disembark the Tauchpanzer at a suitable distance from the shore. With the cancellation of 'Sea Lion', the Tauchpanzer were no longer required in quite the same form. At Milowitz near Prague, in the spring of 1941, most of the tanks were modified to make them suitable for river crossing, with a fixed snorkel pipe attached through the commander's cupola.

From July 1940, four sections of volunteers from existing Panzer regiments were trained on the Island of Sylt, and the Tauchpanzer were to be ready for operations at Putlos by 10 August. In mid-October, three of these sections were attached to the 18th Panzer Division, and the remainder went to the 6th Panzer Regiment of the 3rd Panzer Division. On 22 June 1941, the Tauchpanzer of the 18th Panzer Division crossed the River Bug at Patulin.

During September and October 1940 volunteers of the 2nd

A Panzer III with the 37mm main armament rolls past a blazing British tank North Africa, 1941.

Tank Regiment in Putlos were formed into Tank Battalion A and trained for Operation Sea Lion, the invasion of Great Britain. Two other special formations, Tank Battalions Band C, were being raised at the same time and the same place. These units later formed the 18th Tank Regiment of the 18th Panzer Division and adapted the Pz Kpfw III and IV for submerged wading. The following measures were taken. All openings, vision slits, flaps, etc, were made watertight with sealing compounds and cable tar, the turret entry ports were bolted from the inside and air intake openings for the engine completely closed. A rubber cover sheet was fixed over the mantlet, the commander's cupola and the bow machine gun. An ignition wire blew off the covering sheet upon surfacing and left the vehicle ready for action. Between the hull and the turret there was a rubber sealing ring which, when inflated, prevented the water from entering. The fresh air supply was maintained by a wire-bound rubber trunk with a diameter at about 20 cm, 18 metres long. To one end of this tube was fitted a buoy with attached antennae. The exhaust pipes were fitted with high-pressure non-return relief valves. When travelling submerged sea water was used to cool the engine and seepage was removed by a bilge pump. The maximum diving depth was 15 metres. Three metres of the air tube's 18 metre length was available as a safety measure. These submersible tanks were to be launched from barges or lighters. They slid into the water down an elongated ramp made of channel plates. Directing was achieved by radio orders from a command vessel to the submerged vehicle. Underwater navigation was carried out by means of a gyro compass and the crew was equipped with escape apparatus. The submerged machines were relatively easy to steer as buoyancy lightened them. After Operation Sea Lion was abandoned these vehicles were eventually used operationally during the Russian campaign in 1941 for the crossing of the River Bug.

***

A short intelligence report on German tanks modified for submersion, from Tactical and Technical Trends, July 29, 1943.

GERMAN SUBMERSIBLE TANKS
Tactical and Technical Trends, July 29, 1943

The delays and difficulties involved in the transport of tanks across the rivers of Eastern Europe have no doubt forced the Germans to consider very seriously all possible devices for enabling their standard tanks to cross such water obstacles under their own power.

By the summer of 1941, the weight of the PzKw 3 had already been increased by the fitting of additional armor, and it must have been clear that future developments in armor and armament would necessarily involve still further increases in the weight of this tank. While the trend towards increased weight was in many ways disadvantageous, it was definitely helpful in overcoming one of the major difficulties hitherto

Prototype development of large interleaving road wheels, using a Pz Kpfw III Ausf H (7 ZW) as the basis of the conversion. The three prototypes were built late in 1940 was used for training purposes after testing had been completed. Further development was halted and in 1943/44, prototypes were fitted with dozers and were used to clean up the streets of bombed cities. This suspension was later adopted in the Tiger and Panther.

encountered in adapting standard tanks for submersion, namely the difficulty of obtaining sufficient track adhesion.

It is therefore not surprising that the Germans, in the early stages of their campaign in Russia, were actively experimenting with standard PzKw 3's modified for submersion. These experiments met with a certain degree of success, and underwater river crossings are reported to have been made with these modified tanks under service conditions. The measures employed, according to a Russian source, included the sealing of all joints and openings in the tank with india rubber, and the fitting of a flexible air pipe, the free end of which was attached to a float. The supply of air for the crew as well as for the engine was provided for by this flexible pipe. The maximum depth of submersion was 16 feet and the time taken by trained crews to prepare the tanks was about 24 hours.

In April 1943, a PzKw 3 Model M examined in North Africa was found to be permanently modified or immersion, if not submersion. There was no mention in the report on this tank of a flexible pipe with float, but this may have been destroyed, since the tank, when examined, had been completely burnt out.

The engine air louvres were provided with cover plates having rubber sealing strips around their edges. These cover plates, which were normally held open by strong springs, could be locked in the closed position before submersion. After submersion, the springs could be released by controls from inside the tank. When submerged, air for the carburettor and for the cooling fans was apparently drawn from the fighting compartment. If, therefore, a flexible pipe were used with this tank, no doubt its purpose would be to supply air to the fighting compartment to replace that withdrawn for the carburettor and cooling fans. The two exhaust pipes led to a single silencer mounted high on the tail plate with its outlet at the top. This outlet was fitted a spring-loaded non-return valve, which during normal running could be secured in a fully open position.

***

Production history	
Designer	Daimler-Benz
Designed	1935-1937
Manufacturer	Daimler-Benz
Produced	1939–1943
Number built	5,774 (excluding StuG III)
Specifications	
Weight	23.0 tonnes (25.4 short tons)
Length	6.41 m (20 ft)
Width	2.90 m (9 ft 6 in)
Height	2.5 m (8 ft 2 in)
Crew	5 (commander, gunner, loader, driver, radio operator/bow machine-gunner)

Armor	5–70 mm (0.20–2.8 in)
Main armament	1 × 3.7 cm KwK 36 Ausf. A-F
	1 × 5 cm KwK 38 Ausf. F-J
	1 × 5 cm KwK 39 Ausf. J¹-M
	1 × 7.5 cm KwK 37 Ausf. N
Secondary armament	2-3 × 7.92 mm Maschinengewehr 34
Engine	12-cylinder Maybach HL 120 TRM 300 PS (296 hp, 220 kW)
Power/weight	12 hp/t
Suspension	Torsion-bar suspension
Operational range	155 km (96 mi)
Speed	Road: 40 km/h (25 mph)
	Off-road: 20 km/h (12 mph)

The Japanese government bought two Panzer III's from their German Allies during the war. This was for reverse engineering purposes, since Japan put more emphasis on the development of new military aircraft and naval technology and relatively little on the development of new tanks. The vehicles apparently weren't delivered until 1943 by which time much of the Panzer III's technology had arguably already become obsolete.

THE PANZER IV

The Workhorse of the Panzerwaffe

The Panzerkampfwagen IV (Pz.Kpfw. IV) Sd Kfz 161, commonly known as the Panzer IV, was a medium tank developed in Nazi Germany in the late 1930s and used extensively during the Second World War. Its ordnance inventory designation was Sd.Kfz. 161.

Designed as an infantry-support tank, the Panzer IV was not originally intended to engage enemy armor as this function was intended to be performed by the lighter Panzer III. However, by 1941, the flaws of pre-war doctrine had become apparent and in the face of the Soviet T-34 tanks, the Panzer IV soon assumed the tank-fighting role instead of the obsolete Panzer III which was too small to cope with a high velocity main armament.

A Panzer IV Ausf. E showing signs of multiple hits to the turret, including the gun barrel.

A Panzer IV Ausf.A undergoing testing during 1938.

PzKpfw IV Ausf. D

Panzer IV Ausf.H, Russia 1944

The Panzer IV chasis was robust and strong enough to accept a number of upgrades in armour and armament. As a result it was destined to become most widely manufactured and deployed German tank of the Second World War. The Panzer IV was used as the base for many other fighting vehicles, including the Sturmgeschütz IV tank destroyer, the Wirbelwind self-propelled anti-aircraft weapon, and the Brummbär self-propelled gun, amongst others.

Robust and reliable, it saw service in all combat theaters involving German forces, and has the distinction of being the only German tank to remain in continuous production throughout the war, with over 8,800 produced between 1936 and 1945. Upgrades and design modifications, often made in response to the appearance of new Allied tanks, extended its service life. Generally these involved increasing the Panzer IV's armour protection or upgrading its weapons, although during the last months of the war with Germany's pressing need for rapid replacement of losses, design changes also included retrograde measures to simplify and speed manufacture.

The following article is taken from the US wartime publication Intelligence Report. It provides a clear account of the duties of the crew from a widely used publication.

CREW AND COMMUNICATIONS OF GERMAN MARK IV TANK
Tactical and Technical Trends, No. 12, November 19th, 1942

The duties of the various crew members of the Mark IV tank are generally similar to those performed by the crews of our own medium M3 and M4 tanks. A German training pamphlet captured in Libya gives the following details on the crew duties and communications of the Mark IV.

a. DUTIES OF THE CREW

The crew consists of five men: a commander, gunner, loader, driver, and radio operator. The latter is also the hull machine-gunner.

The Commander was the most important component of the crew. He was the eyes and ears and the decision maker.

(1) Tank Commander.
The tank commander is an officer or senior NCO and is responsible for the vehicle and the crew. He indicates targets to the gunner, gives fire orders, and observes the effect. He keeps a constant watch for the enemy, observes the zone for which he is responsible, and watches for any orders from the commander's vehicle. In action, he gives his orders by intercommunication telephone to the driver and radio operator, and by speaking tube and touch signals to the gunner and loader. He receives orders by radio or flag, and reports to his commander by radio, signal pistol, or flag.

(2) Gunner.
The gunner is the assistant tank commander. He fires the turret gun, the turret machine gun, or the submachine gun as ordered by the tank commander. He assists the tank commander in observation.

(3) Loader.
This crew member loads and maintains the turret armament under the orders of the gunner. He is also responsible for care of ammunition, and when the cupola is closed, gives any necessary flag signals. He replaces the radio operator if the latter becomes a casualty.

(4) Driver.
The driver operates the vehicle under the orders of the tank commander or in accordance with orders received by radio from the commander's vehicle. So far as possible he assists in observation, reporting through the intercommunication telephone the presence of the enemy or of any obstacles in the path of the tank. He watches the gasoline consumption and is responsible to the tank commander for the care and maintenance of the vehicle.

(5) Radio Operator.
He operates the radio under the orders of the tank commander. In action, and when not actually transmitting, he always keeps

the radio set to "receive." He operates the intercommunication telephone and takes down any useful messages he may intercept. He fires the machine gun mounted in the front superstructure. If the loader becomes a casualty, the radio operator takes over his duties.

b. COMMUNICATIONS.

The following means of communication may be used:

(1) External: radio, flag, hand signals, signal pistol, and flashlight.

(2) Internal: intercommunication telephone, speaking tube, and touch signals.

For the radio, the voice range between two moving vehicles is about 3 3/4 miles and CW about 6 1/4 miles.

The flag is used for short-range communications only, and the signal pistol for prearranged signals, chiefly to other arms.

The radio set, in conjunction with the intercommunication telephone, provides the tank commander, radio operator, and driver with a means for external and internal voice communication, the same throat microphones and telephone receiver headsets being used for both radio and telephone.

When the control switch on the radio is set at EMPFANG (receive) and that on the junction box of the intercommunication telephone at BORD UND FUNK (internal and radio), the commander, radio operator, and driver hear all incoming radio signals. Any one of them can also speak to the other two, after switching his microphone into circuit by means of the switch on his chest.

For radio transmission, the switch on the set is adjusted to TELEPHONIE. The telephone switch may be left at BORD UND FUNK. Either the tank commander or the radio operator can then transmit, and they and the driver will all hear the messages transmitted. Internal communication is also possible at the same time, but such conversation will also be transmitted by the radio.

Panzer crew member and Panzer IV Ausf. B

A British Crusader passes an abandoned Panzer IV tank, Libyan desert 1941

If the radio set is disconnected or out of order, the telephone switch may be adjusted to BORD (internal). The tank commander and driver can then speak to one another, and the radio operator can speak to them, but cannot hear what they say. The same applies when a radio receiver is available but no transmitter, with the difference that incoming radio signals can then be heard by the radio operator.

The signal flags are normally carried in holders on the left of the driver's seat. When the cupola is open, flag signals are given by the tank commander, and when it is closed, the loader raises the circular flap in the left of the turret roof and signals with the appropriate flag through the port thus opened.

The signal pistol is fired either through the signal port in the turret roof, through the cupola, or through one of the vision openings in the turret wall. The signal pistol must not be cocked until the barrel is already projecting outside the tank. It is only used normally when the vehicle is stationary. Its main use is giving prearranged signals to the infantry or other troops.

When traveling by night with lights dimmed or switched off altogether, driving signals are given with the aid of a dimmed flashlight. The same method is also employed when tanks are in a position of readiness and when in bivouac.

Orders are transmitted from the tank commander to the gunner by speaking tube and by touch signals. The latter are also used for messages from the commander to the loader, and between the gunner and loader.

***

The panzer IV was vulnerable to close assault particularly in the air intakes and the Allies were quick to recognise this.

'When enemy armoured force vehicles are attacked at close quarters with incendiary grenades, the air louvres are very vulnerable. It is therefore important that differentiation be made between "inlet" and "outlet "ducts, since obviously a grenade thrown against an exhaust opening will be less effective than one aimed at an inlet, which will draw the inflammable liquid into the vehicle. If the engine is not running, all openings are equally vulnerable.

Horse drawn transport passing the wreck of a Panzer IV, Kowno, June 1941.

A Panzer IV Ausf.C still in service with the GrossDeutchsland Division in November 1943.

In general, it may be said that in the Pz Kw II and III tanks the best targets are the flat top-plates of the rear superstructures, since the air intakes are located there. The side louvres in these tanks are invariably protected by a vertical baffle. On the Pz Kw IV, the left side ports are intake and thus more vulnerable than the right-hand exhaust ports.'

Faced with these and other threats on the battlefield the German designers were quick to improve the armour on the Panzer IV, but by 1943 the Allies were aware of these developments.

INCREASED PROTECTION ON PzKw 3 AND 4
Tactical and Technical Trends, No. 25, May 20th, 1943

The history of the changes in the light medium PzKw 3 and 4 demonstrates how fortunate the Germans were in having a basic tank design that could be improved as battle experience indicated, for a basic design can be improved and still remain familiar to the users. Furthermore, the problems of maintenance and supply of parts are greatly reduced—and these problems are a major factor in keeping tanks ready for operational use.

PzKw 4

(1) Early Models

The PzKw 4, a slightly heavier tank than the 3, has passed through much the same line of development. Little is known about the models A, B, and C of this tank, but Model D was in use during the greater part of the period 1940-43. Specimens of armour cut from Model D have been examined. Of these, only the front plate of the hull appears to be face-hardened; this plate is carburized. All of the plates were high-quality, chromium-molybdenum steel, apparently made by the electric-furnace process.

The first increase in the armour of this tank was reported in 1941, when it was observed that additional plates had been

An excellent study of a group of Panzer IV Ausf.E gathered together on exercise in France during 1943. Bringing together this number of vehicles in such close proximity would not have been permitted in Russia.

Women machining tank parts in the Krupp factory.

bolted over the basic front and side armour. The additional plates on the front were 1.18 inches thick, making a total of 2.36 inches, and those on the sides were .79 inches thick, making a total of 1.57 inches. In its early stages, this addition was probably only an improvised measure for increasing the armour protection of existing PzKw 4 models in which the thickest armour was only 1.18 inches.

(2) Model E

In Model E, which had 1.96 inches of single-thickness nose plate, the fitting of additional armor on the front of the superstructure and on the sides of the fighting compartment was continued. Although the arrangement of the additional side armor on this model appears to have been standardized, that on the front superstructure was by no means uniform.

Three PzKw 4 tanks have recently been examined. In each case, extra armor had been fitted to the vertical front plate carrying the hull machine gun and driver's visor. It had also been added to the sides of the fighting compartment both above and below the track level. The extra protection above the track level extended from the front vertical plate to the end of the engine-compartment bulkhead. It was thus 110 inches long and 15 inches deep. The pieces below the track level were shaped in such a way as to clear the suspension brackets. They were 90 inches long and 30 inches deep. All this extra side protection was .97 inch in thickness.

The vertical front plate was reinforced in three different ways. On one tank, two plates were used; one over the plate carrying the hull machine gun, this additional plate being cut away to suit the gun mounting, and the other plate over the driver's front plate, cut to shape to clear his visor. On the second tank, the arrangement around the hull gun was the same, but the extra protection around the driver's visor consisted of two rectangular plates, one on each side of the visor, there being no extra plate immediately above the visor. On the third tank, the only additional front armor was the plate around the hull machine gun. No additions had been made to the driver's front plate. In all cases, the extra frontal plating was 1.18 inches thick; the nose plate was unreinforced, but it was 1.97 inches thick, and the glacis plate was .97 inch thick. The final drive

The Panzer IV Aus.F, seen here in the Army Group North sector during the summer of 1942, was the last of the short barrelled tanks to see action.

casings of PzKw 4 tanks of this period were also sometimes reinforced by .79-inch protecting rings. The additional plates on the front were face-hardened.

It is probable that the reinforced armor on the front superstructure of this model will compare closely with that on the corresponding parts of the PzKw 3 of 1941 and that the 1.96-inch nose plates will not differ substantially from those on the more recent PzKw 3's of June 1942, known as "Model J."

The reinforced (.79 inch plus .79 inch) side armor has, however, no counterpart in any PzKw 3 model. The additional plates are of homogeneous quality and have a Brinell hardness of about 370 on the front surface.

(3) Model F.

Towards the end of 1941 the Germans introduced a PzKw 4, Model F, having 1.96-inch frontal armor (gun mantlet, front superstructure and hull nose-plates) and 1.18-inch side armor. In this and many other respects, the Model F conforms more closely than its predecessors to the corresponding model of the PzKw 3 (in this case PzKw 3 Model J). So far, the armor of the PzKw 4 Model F has not been examined to ascertain its chemical and ballistic properties, but there is a strong probability that these do not differ greatly from those of the PzKw 3, Model J.

(4) Model G.

This model which mounts the long 75-mm gun, Kw.K 40, was first encountered in June 1942. It is reported from the Middle East that its armour is the same as that of Model F; namely 1.96 inches on the front, and 30 mm (1.18 inches) on the sides.

***

In addition to the increase in armor it was necessary to up-gun the tank by introducing a high velocity main armament which gave the Panzer IV its tank killing power. Not surprisingly the Allies were soon aware of this development and the intelligence was quickly spread through the regular channels.

A Panzer IV Ausf. B rolls into action during the Polish campaign, September 1939.

NOTES ON THE PzKw 4
Tactical and Technical Trends, No. 27, June 17th, 1943

The PzKw 4 is the German standard medium tank. It weighs about 22 tons. With the exception of the principal armament, the more recent models of this tank embody essentially the same features. The change in armament consists of a long-barreled 75-mm gun, the 7.5-cm Kw K. 40, being fitted in place of the short-barreled 75-mm gun (see Tactical and Technical Trends, No. 20, p. 10).

The following information on the new PzKw 4 is based on a tank captured in North Africa.

a. Suspension and Armor

The tank has eight small bogie wheels, mounted and sprung in pairs by quarter-elliptic springs, a front sprocket, a rear idler, and four return rollers on each side. The track is of steel, as is usual in German tanks.

Pz. Kw. 4

The armor probably is as follows: front, back, and turret 1.95 in.; sides 1.18 in.; back and top .39 to .79 in.[Later details indicate that the armor arrangement on current models of PzKw 4 is the same.] Sand bags were carried on top of the turret for additional protection from air attack. (German tanks often carry sand bags and additional lengths of track as added protection.)

b. Dimensions and Performance

The tank is 19 ft. 6 in. long, 9 ft. 4 in. wide, and 8 ft. 9 in. high, with a ground clearance of 16 inches. It can cross a 9-foot trench, negotiate a 2-foot step, climb a 27-degree gradient, and ford to a depth of 2 ft. 7 in. The theoretical radius of action is 130 miles on roads and 80 miles cross-country.

c. Engine

The tank is powered with a Nordbau Model V-12, four-stroke, gasoline engine, developing 320 hp. It has overhead cams, one for each bank of engines, and magneto ignition. There are two Solex down-draught carburetors, and twin radiators, with a fan for each, mounted on the right-hand side of the engine. An inertia starter is fitted. [An inertia starter is a starter equipped with its own independent fly-wheel to build up starting inertia.] The fuel capacity is 94 gallons for the engine and 20 gallons for the 2-cylinder turret-drive auxiliary engine.

d. Clutch, Brake, and Drive

The clutch is incorporated in a gear-box which is of the ordinary

Panzer V on manoeuvres in Greece during 1942.

A column of Panzer IVs at the halt during a road march through Yugoslavia.

type with 6 forward speeds and reverse. The brakes, operating on epicyclic gears, are air-cooled and hydraulically operated. The drive is through the engine, drive shaft, clutch, gear box, bevel drive, steering system, final reduction drive, and sprockets.

e. Instruments

Instruments include a revolution counter (tachometer) to 3,200 rpm with 2,600 to 3,200 in red, speedometer to 50 kph (31 mph), odometer (mileage indicator), a water temperature gauge, and two oil pressure gauges reading to 85 lbs. per sq. in. The tank is fitted to take an electric gyrocompass on the left side of the driver.

f. Armament

The tank mounts the long-barreled 75-mm gun and two model 34 machine guns, one fixed coaxially on the right side of the gun, and the other one set in the hull firing forward. While reports vary, it is thought that the gun will penetrate 2 inches of homogeneous armor at about 2,500 yards at 30 degrees. The breech is of the vertical sliding type. Firing is electric, with a safety device which prevents firing if the breech is not closed, the gun not fully run out, or the buffer not full. The traverse is by hand, or by power from a 2-cylinder, 9-hp auxiliary gasoline engine directly coupled to a generator, which supplies current to the turret traversing motor. The turret floor rotates. Eighty-three rounds of 75-mm AP or HE and smoke are carried. Five smoke candles may be carried on a rack at the rear of the tank. These candles are released from inside by a wire cable. Twenty-seven belts of 75 rounds each are carried for the machine guns.

g. Radio Equipment

Intercommunication is by radio-telephone. The aerial may be raised or lowered from inside the tank. The set is situated over the gear box on the left side of the hull gunner. Below the 75-mm gun is situated an insulated aerial guard which deflects the aerial when the turret is traversed.

h. Crew

The crew numbers five: driver, hull-gunner and radio operator, commander, gunner, and loader.

***

The tactical application of the Panzer IV was also of great interest and the Allied intelligence services were delighted by the capture of a German training manual.

COMBAT TACTICS OF GERMAN MEDIUM TANK COMPANIES
Tactical and Technical Trends, No. 26, June 3rd, 1943.

a. General

The following combat instructions for PzKw 4 units have been condensed from a German document. They give an excellent idea of recent enemy tank tactics.

b. Individual Tactics

(1) In view of the small amount of ammunition carried, the gun is normally fired at the halt in order to avoid waste. The

The crew of a Panzer IV Ausf.D on all round aerial observation, Russia spring 1942.

machine guns mounted in turret and hull may be effectively fired up to 800 yards against mass targets, such as columns, reserves, limbered guns, etc.

(2) As soon as each target has been put out of action, or as soon as the attacking German infantry are too near the target for tanks to fire with safety, the tanks move forward by bounds of

at least 200 to 300 yards. When changing position, drivers must take care to keep correct position in the tactical formation.

(3) Single tanks may be used for supporting action against prepared positions. The tank will normally move from a flank under cover of smoke. Embrasures will be engaged with AP shell. During action, it will be necessary to blind neighbouring defences by smoke. Tanks will normally fire at prepared defences from at most 400 yards' range. Assault detachments work their way forward, and once lanes have been cleared through the antitank defences, the tank will follow and engage the next target. Close cooperation between tank and assault detachment commanders is essential. Light and other signals must be prearranged. Single tanks can also be used in fighting in woods and for protection of rest and assembly areas.

c. Platoon Tactics

(1) During the attack, medium platoons move forward in support of the first wave; one half of the platoon gives covering fire while the other half advances. The whole platoon seldom moves as a body.

(2) The platoon commander directs by radio, and he can control fire by radio or by firing guiding-rounds on particular targets.

(3) Antitank weapons will normally be engaged from the halt. If the nearest antitank weapon can be dealt with by the light platoon, the medium platoon will engage more distant antitank weapons or blind them. Artillery will be attacked in the same manner as antitank weapons. Enfilading fire is particularly recommended.

(4) If friendly light tanks encounter enemy tanks in the open, the medium platoon should immediately engage them with smoke-shell in order to allow the lights to disengage and to attack the enemy from a flank.

(5) Moving targets and light weapons should be engaged with machine guns or by crushing; mass targets with HE.

(6) Against prepared defenses, the procedure is as mentioned

A group of Panzer IVs rolls forward into action during the winter of 1943.

in Paragraph b (3). When the whole platoon is employed, the advance can be made by mutual fire and smoke support. When the position is taken, the platoon covers the consolidation by smoke and fire. The platoon only moves forward again after the enemy weapons in the prepared position have been knocked out.

(7) In street fighting a medium platoon may be employed in the second echelon to give support. Nests of resistance in houses may be cleaned up with the help of the tanks' guns, and lightly built houses can be crushed.

(8) If a front-line tank formation is ordered to hold an objective until the arrival of infantry, protection will be given by the medium platoon, which will take up position on high ground with a large field of fire.

d. Company Tactics

(1) When medium platoons are attached to light companies, they work on the latter's radio frequency, and not on that of their own medium company.

(2) Reserve crews follow immediately behind the combat

echelon and move back to join the unit trains only after the beginning of an engagement. They come forward again as soon as the battle is over. Reliefs must be so arranged that drivers take over refreshed before each action, that is, on leaving the assembly area.

(3) The repair section, commanded by an NCO, travels with the combat echelon until the beginning of the battle.

(4) The company commander moves at the head of his company until the leading platoons have gone into action, when he operates from a temporary command post with unimpeded observation of the battle area. Keeping direction and contact are the responsibility of company headquarters personnel while the commander is at the head of his company.

(5) In the attack, the normal formations are a broad wedge - Breitkeil - [One platoon echeloned to the right, one to the left, and one in line to form the base of the triangle, with apex forward], or line with extended interval (geoffnete Linie). Effective fire of the whole company may be obtained if the rear

A superb study of the Panzer IV in service with the Hitler Jugend Division. Note the Zimmerit covering.

Grenadiers crammed aboard a Panzer IV, Russia February 1944.

elements give overhead fire, or if they fill up or extend the front of their company to form line.

(6) For tank-versus-tank actions, the company, where possible, should be employed as a whole. When enemy tanks appear, they must be engaged at once and other missions dropped. If time allows, the battalion commander will detach the medium platoons that have been attached to light companies and send them back to the medium company. In all situations, medium tanks should endeavor to have the sun behind them.

(7) During the pursuit, the medium company will be employed well forward in order to take full advantage of the longer range of its HE shell.

e. Miscellaneous

(1) The light tank platoon of battalion headquarters company guides the medium company on the march, and when going in to rest or assembly positions. If the medium company is moving on its own, one section of a light tank platoon may be attached to it.

(2) Parts of the antiaircraft platoon of the headquarters company may be allotted to the medium company.

(3) Tank repairmen move directly behind the combat echelons. The recovery platoon is responsible for towing away those tanks which cannot be attended to by the repair section. The recovery platoon is under the orders of the technical officer, who has under his control all equipment and spare-parts trucks of the tank companies, which may follow by separate routes as prescribed by him.

***

As the war progressed more and more intelligence became available and the methods available to combat the Panzer IV were constantly revised. An intelligence report entitled "Vulnerability of German Tank Armor" was published in Tactical and Technical Trends.

VULNERABILITY OF GERMAN TANK ARMOR
Tactical and Technical Trends, No. 8, September 24th, 1942

British forces in the Middle East have recently carried out tests with captured German tanks in order to determine the effectiveness of British and U.S. weapons against them.

The 30-mm front armor of the original German Mark III tank (see this publication No. 3, page 12) is apparently a plate of machinable-quality silico manganese. The additional 30- or 32-mm plates which have been bolted onto the basic 30-mm armor are of the face-hardened type. This total thickness of 60 to 62 mm stops the British 2-pounder (40-mm) AP ammunition at all ranges, breaking it up so that it only dents the inner plate. The U.S. 37-mm projectile, however, with its armor-piercing cap, penetrates at 200 yards at 70°. Against the 6-pounder (57-mm) AP and the 75-mm SAP, this reinforced armor breaks up the projectile down to fairly short ranges, but the armor plate itself cracks and splits fairly easily, and the bolts securing it are ready to give way after one or two hits. If 75-mm capped shot is used, however, such as the U.S. M61 round, the armor can be pierced at 1,000 yards at 70°.

Similar results may be expected against the reinforced armor of the Mark IV.

The new Mark III tank has a single thickness of 50-mm armor on the front, and this was found to be of the face-hardened type. The 2-pounder AP projectile penetrates by shattering the hardened face, but the projectile itself breaks up in the process and the fragments make a hole of about 45 mm. The 37-mm projectile does not shatter during penetration, which is secured at ranges up to 500 yards at 70°. The 50-mm plate is softer than the reinforced 32-mm plates being 530 Brinell on the face and 375 on the back. This plate is not particularly brittle and there is very little flaking.

In tests carried out against the side armor of both the old and new models of Mark III tanks, it was found that this armor showed signs of disking at the back. There is also internal petaling. This, and the condition of the front, which is flaked back at 45° for a short distance, indicates that the heat treatment makes the inner and outer skin harder than the core.

The Mark IV has only 22 mm of armor on the sides, but this is reinforced by an additional thickness of 22 mm covering the

VULNERABILITY OF GERMAN ARMOR PLATE							
	RANGES IN YARDS						
	British 2-pdr		British	U.S.	U.S. 75-mm	
	Standard	H.V.	6-pdr	37-mm	SAP	APC
Mk. III and IV: 30-mm (old type)						
Lower front plate and turret can be penetrated at	1,300	1,500	Over 2,000	1,600	Over 2,000	
Vizor plate can be penetrated at	1,400	1,600	Over 2,000	1,800	Over 2,000	
Sides can be penetrated at	1,500	1,700	Over 2,000	2,000	Over 2,000	
Mk. IV: 44-mm (reinforced plates)						
Sides can be penetrated at	1,000	1,200	2,000	1,100	Over 2,000	
Mk. III and IV: 62-mm (reinforced plates)						
Lower front plate can be penetrated at	No penetration		500	200	400	1,000
Vizor plate can be penetrated at	No penetration		600	300	500	1,000
Mk. III: 50-mm (new type)						
Lower front plate and turret front can be penetrated at	200	400	800	500	600	1,500
Vizor plate can be penetrated at	200	400	900	600	700	1,700
Sides can be penetrated at	1,500	1,800	Over 2,000	2,000	Over 2,000	

whole fighting and driving compartments. These additional plates are of the machinable type, and the hardness of this plate was found to be 370 Brinell. The bolts holding this extra armor in place are weak, and it was found that the threads stripped easily.

The table opposite shows the ranges at which the different types of German tank armor are penetrated by standard U.S. and British weapons. The angles of impact are determined by the normal slope of the armor on the tank.

Development History

THE ORIGINS OF THE PANZER IV

The Panzer IV was the brainchild of German general and innovative armored warfare theorist General Heinz Guderian. In concept, it was intended to be a support tank firing mainly high explosive for use against enemy anti-tank guns and fortifications. Ideally, the tank battalions of a panzer division were each to have three medium companies of Panzer IIIs and one heavy company of Panzer IVs.

On 11 January 1934, the German army wrote the specifications for a "medium tractor", and issued them to a number of defense companies. To support the Panzer III, which would be armed with a 37-millimetre (1.46 in) anti-tank gun, the new vehicle would have a short-barrelled 75-millimetre (2.95 in) howitzer as its main gun, and was allotted a weight limit of 24 tonnes (26.46 short tons). Development was carried out under the name Begleitwagen ("accompanying vehicle") or BW, to disguise its actual purpose, given that Germany was still theoretically bound by the Treaty of Versailles. MAN, Krupp, and Rheinmetall-Borsig each developed prototypes with Krupp's being selected

A Panzer Ausf.A rolls into the Sudetenland 1938.

for further development.

The chassis had originally been designed with a six-wheeled interleaved suspension, but the German Army amended this to a torsion bar system. Permitting greater vertical deflection of the roadwheels, this was intended to improve performance and crew comfort both on- and off-road. However, due to the urgent requirement for the new tank, neither proposal was adopted, and Krupp instead equipped it with a simple leaf spring double-bogie suspension.

The prototype required a crew of five men; the hull contained the engine bay to the rear, with the driver and radio operator, who doubled as the hull machine gunner, seated at the front-left and front-right, respectively. In the turret, the tank commander sat beneath his roof hatch, while the gunner was situated to the left of the gun breech and the loader to the right. The turret was offset 66.5 mm (2.62 in) to the left of the chassis center line, while the engine was moved 152.4 mm (6.00 in) to the right. This allowed the torque shaft to clear the rotary base junction, which provided electrical power to turn the turret, while connecting to the transmission box mounted in the hull between the driver and radio operator. Due to the asymmetric layout, the right side of the tank contained the bulk of its stowage volume, which was taken up by ready-use ammunition lockers.

Accepted into service as the Versuchskraftfahrzeug 622 (Vs. Kfz. 622), production began in 1936 at Krupp-Grusonwerke AG's factory at Magdeburg.

AUSF. A TO AUSF. F1

The first mass-produced version of the Panzer IV was the Ausführung A (abbreviated to Ausf. A, meaning "Variant A"), in 1936. It was powered by Maybach's HL 108TR, producing 250 PS (183.87 kW), and used the SGR 75 transmission with five forward gears and one reverse, achieving a maximum road speed of 31 kilometres per hour (19.26 mph). As main armament, the vehicle mounted the Kampfwagenkanone 37 L/24 (KwK 37 L/24) 75 mm (2.95 in) tank gun, which was a low-velocity gun designed to mainly fire high-explosive shells. Against armored targets, firing the Panzergranate (armor-piercing shell) at 430 metres per second (1,410 ft/s) the KwK 37

Panzer IV Ausf. C

The 300 horsepower Maybach HL 120TRM engine used in most Panzer IV production models.

could penetrate 43 millimetres (1.69 in), inclined at 30 degrees, at ranges of up to 700 metres (2,300 ft). A 7.92 mm (0.31 in) MG 34 machine gun was mounted coaxially with the main gun in the turret, while a second machine gun of the same type was mounted in the front plate of the hull. The Ausf. A was protected by 14.5 mm (0.57 in) of steel armor on the front plate of the chassis, and 20 mm (0.79 in) on the turret. This was capable only of stopping artillery fragments, small-arms fire, and light anti-tank projectiles.

After manufacturing 35 tanks of the A version, in 1937 production moved to the Ausf. B. Improvements included the replacement of the original engine with the more powerful 300 PS (220.65 kW) Maybach HL 120TR, and the transmission with the new SSG 75 transmission, with six forward gears and one reverse gear. Despite a weight increase to 16 t (18 short tons), this improved the tank's speed to 39 kilometres per hour (24 mph). The glacis plate was augmented to a maximum thickness of 30 millimetres (1.18 in), and the hull-mounted machine gun was replaced by a covered pistol port.

Forty-two Panzer IV Ausf. Bs were manufactured before the introduction of the Ausf. C in 1938. This saw the turret armor increased to 30 mm (1.18 in), which brought the tank's weight to 18.14 t (20.00 short tons).[After assembling 40 Ausf. Cs, starting with chassis number 80341 the engine was replaced with the improved HL 120TRM. The last of the 140 Ausf. Cs was produced in August 1939, and production changed to the Ausf. D; this variant, of which 248 vehicles were produced, reintroduced the hull machine gun and changed the turret's internal gun mantlet to an external one. Again protection was upgraded, this time by increasing side armor to 20 mm (0.79 in). As the German invasion of Poland in September 1939 came to an end, it was decided to scale up production of the Panzer IV,

The short-barreled Panzer IV Ausf. F1.

A good study of the main armament of the Panzer IV Ausf .F taken in 1942 in the Army Group Centre sector.

which was adopted for general use on 27 September 1939 as the Sonderkraftfahrzeug 161 (Sd.Kfz. 161).

In response to the difficulty of penetrating British Matilda Infantry tanks during the Battle of France, the Germans had tested a 50 mm (1.97 in) gun—based on the 5 cm PaK 38 L/60 anti-tank gun—on a Panzer IV Ausf. D. However, with the rapid German victory in France, the original order of 80 tanks was canceled before they entered production.

In September 1940 the Ausf. E was introduced. This had 50 millimetres (1.97 in) of armor on the bow plate, while a 30-millimetre (1.18 in) appliqué steel plate was added to the glacis as an interim measure. Finally, the commander's cupola was moved forward into the turret. Older model Panzer IV tanks were retrofitted with these features when returned to the manufacturer for servicing. Two hundred and eighty Ausf. Es were produced between December 1939 and April 1941.

In April 1941 production of the Panzer IV Ausf. F started. It featured 50 mm (1.97 in) single-plate armor on the turret and hull, as opposed to the appliqué armor added to the Ausf. E, and a further increase in side armor to 30 mm (1.18 in). The weight of the vehicle was now 22.3 tonnes (24.6 short tons), which required a corresponding modification of track width from 380 to 400 mm (14.96 to 15.75 in) to reduce ground pressure. The wider tracks also facilitated the fitting of ice sprags, and the rear idler wheel and front sprocket were modified.

The designation Ausf. F was changed in the meantime to Ausf. F1, after the distinct new model, the Ausf. F2, appeared. A total of 464 Ausf. F (later F1) tanks were produced from April 1941 to March 1942, of which 25 were converted to the F2 on the production line.

AUSF. F2 TO AUSF. J

On May 26, 1941, mere weeks before Operation Barbarossa, during a conference with Hitler, it was decided to improve the Panzer IV's main armament. Krupp was awarded the contract to integrate again the same 50 mm (1.97 in) Pak 38 L/60 gun into the turret. The first prototype was to be delivered by November 15, 1941. Within months, the shock of encountering the Soviet T-34 medium and KV-1 heavy tanks necessitated a new, much more powerful tank gun.

In November 1941, the decision to up-gun the Panzer IV to the 50-millimetre (1.97 in) gun was dropped, and instead Krupp was contracted in a joint development to modify Rheinmetall's pending 75 mm (2.95 in) anti-tank gun design, later known as 7.5 cm PaK 40 L/46. Because the recoil length was too long for the tank's turret, the recoil mechanism and chamber were shortened. This resulted in the 75-millimetre (2.95 in) KwK 40 L/43. When firing an armor-piercing shot, the gun's muzzle velocity was increased from 430 m/s (1,410 ft/s) to 990 m/s (3,250 ft/s). Initially, the gun was mounted with a single-chamber, ball-shaped muzzle brake, which provided just under 50% of the recoil system's braking ability. Firing the Panzergranate 39, the

Grenadiers crowd aboard a Panzer IV Ausf.J, Russia 1944.

KwK 40 L/43 could penetrate 77 mm (3.03 in) of steel armor at a range of 1,830 m (6,000 ft).

The 1942 Panzer IV Ausf. F2 was an upgrade of the Ausf. F, fitted with the KwK 40 L/43 anti-tank gun to counter Soviet T-34 and KV tanks.

The Ausf. F tanks that received the new, longer, KwK 40 L/43 gun were named Ausf. F2 (with the designation Sd.Kfz. 161/1). The tank increased in weight to 23.6 tonnes (26.0 short tons). One hundred and seventy-five Ausf. F2s were produced from March 1942 to July 1942. Three months after beginning production, the Panzer IV. Ausf. F2 was renamed Ausf. G. There was little to no difference between the F2 and early G models.

NEW ARMAMENT OF GERMAN PZ.KW. 4

Tactical and Technical Trends, No. 20, March IIth, 1943

As previously reported in Tactical and Technical Trends (No. 4, p. 15) recent models of two German tanks, the Pz.Kw. 3 and 4, have been fitted with more powerful armament, as shown in the accompanying sketches. These sketches are based on photographs of German tanks captured by the British in North Africa.

PZ.Kw. IV

The principal armament of this tank is a long-barrelled 75-mm gun, the 7.5-cm Kraftwagenkanone 40 (7.5-cm Kw.K. 40). It is reported that the muzzle velocity is 2,400 feet per second (also reported at 2,620 feet per second), and that 2.44 inches of armor plate can be penetrated at 2,000 yards at an angle of impact of 30 degrees. The long barrel, terminating in a muzzle brake, extends beyond the nose of the tank, and an equilibrator was provided, in the particular tank examined, to balance the consequent muzzle preponderance.

Panzer IV of the 4th Panzer Division (Panzerregiment 35)

The equilibrator is fixed to the floor of the turret and extends vertically to an attachment near the rear of the piece; it is 6 inches in diameter and 21 1/2 inches long. The gun is also provided with a traveling lock inside the turret. The traveling lock consisted of two steel bars about 1/2 inch by 2 inches and 15 inches in length. There were hardened semi-hemispherical surfaces about 1 1/2 inches in diameter projecting from each end of the steel bars, and these fitted into corresponding indentations on either side of lugs attached to the gun and to the turret roof. The steel bars were connected by two bolts; tightening the bolts provided a very positive lock.

Three types of ammunition were found with this tank: nose-fuzed HE; hollow-charge HE; and armor-piercing HE, this being an armor-piercing shell with a ballistic nose and an HE charge.

THE AUSF.G

During its production run from May 1942 to June 1943, the Panzer IV Ausf. G went through further modifications, including another armor upgrade. Given that the tank was reaching its viable limit, to avoid a corresponding weight increase, the appliqué 20-millimetre (0.79 in) steel plates were removed from its side armor, which instead had its base thickness increased to 30 millimetres (1.18 in). The weight saved was transferred to the front, which had a 30-millimetre (1.18 in) face-hardened appliqué steel plate welded (later bolted) to the glacis—in total, frontal armor was now 80 mm (3.15 in) thick. This decision to increase frontal armor was favorably received according to troop reports on November 8, 1942, despite technical problems of the driving system due to added weight. At this point, it was decided that 50% of Panzer IV productions would be fitted with 30 mm thick additional armor plates.

Production history	
Designer	Krupp
Designed	1936
Manufacturer	Krupp, Steyr-Daimler-Puch
Unit cost	~ 103,462 Reichsmarks
Produced	1936–45
Number built	9,200 (estimate)
Specifications (Pz IV Ausf H, 1943)	
Weight	25.0 tonnes (27.6 short tons; 24.6 long tons)
Length	5.92 metres (19 ft 5 in), 7.02 metres (23 ft 0 in) gun forward
Width	2.88 m (9 ft 5 in)
Height	2.68 m (8 ft 10 in)
Crew	5 (commander, gunner, loader, driver, radio operator/bow machine-gunner)
Armor	10–80 mm (0.39–3.1 in)
Main armament	7.5 cm (2.95 in) KwK 40 L/48 main gun (87 rds.)
Secondary armament	2–3 × 7.92-mm Maschinengewehr 34
Engine	12-cylinder Maybach HL 120 TRM V12, 300 PS (296 hp, 220 kW)
Power/weight	12 PS/t
Transmission	6 forward and 1 reverse ratios
Suspension	Leaf spring
Fuel capacity	470 l (120 US gal)
Operational range	200 km (120 mi)
Speed	42 km/h (26 mph) road, 16 km/h (9.9 mph) off road

ARMOR ARRANGEMENT ON GERMAN TANKS
Tactical and Technical Trends, No. 29, July 15th 1943

The accompanying sketches on the following pages show the armor arrangement on current models of the PzKw 2, 3, 4, and 6. These sketches are believed to be accurate and up-to-date. Armor thicknesses (circled figures) are given in millimeters; their equivalent in inches may be found in the article beginning on page 30. A question mark following some of these figures indicates that definite information is not available. Where two small figures appear in parentheses, it indicates that there are 2 plates at this point; in only 2 instances, namely on the PzKw 3, are the 2 plates separated to form so-called spaced armor.

The armament of these tanks is also shown.

***

Subsequently on January 5, 1943, Hitler decided to make all Panzer IV with 80 mm frontal armor. To simplify production, the vision ports on either side of the turret and on the right turret front were removed, while a rack for two spare road wheels was installed on the track guard on the left side of the hull. Complementing this, brackets for seven spare track links were added to the glacis plate. For operation in high temperatures, the engine's ventilation was improved by creating slits over the engine deck to the rear of the chassis, and cold weather performance was boosted by adding a device to heat the engine's coolant, as well as a starter fluid injector. A new light replaced the original headlight, and the signal port on the turret was removed. On March 19, 1943, the first Panzer IV with Schürzen skirts on its sides and turret was exhibited. The double hatch for the commander's cupola was replaced by a single round hatch from very late model Ausf. G. and the cupola was up-armored as

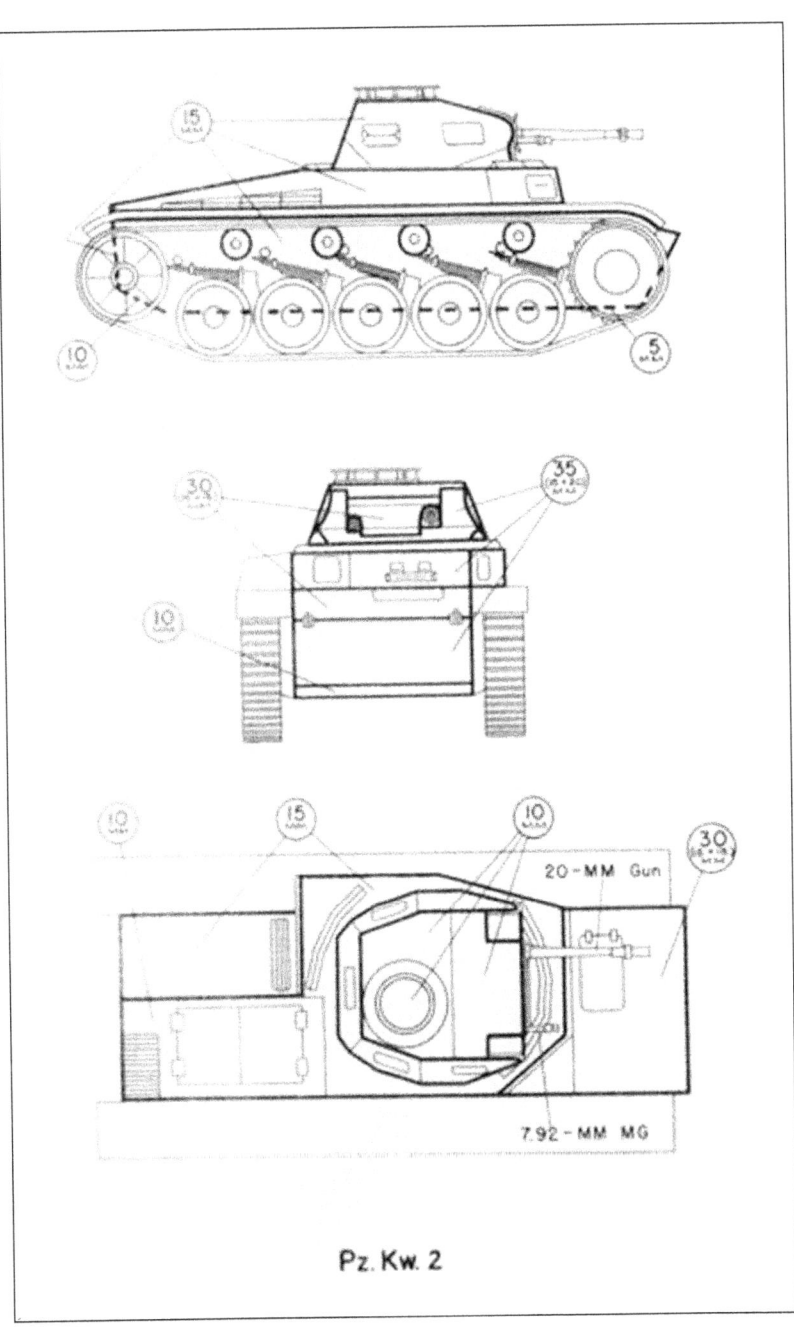

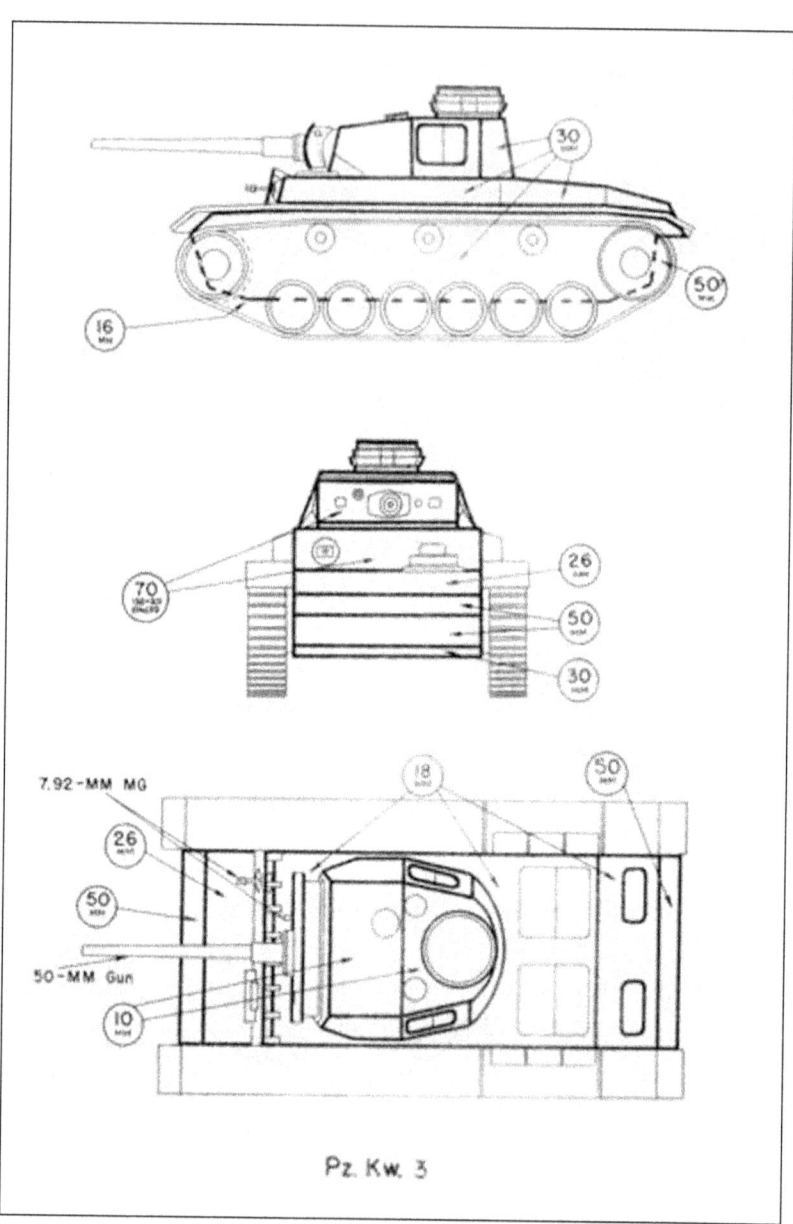

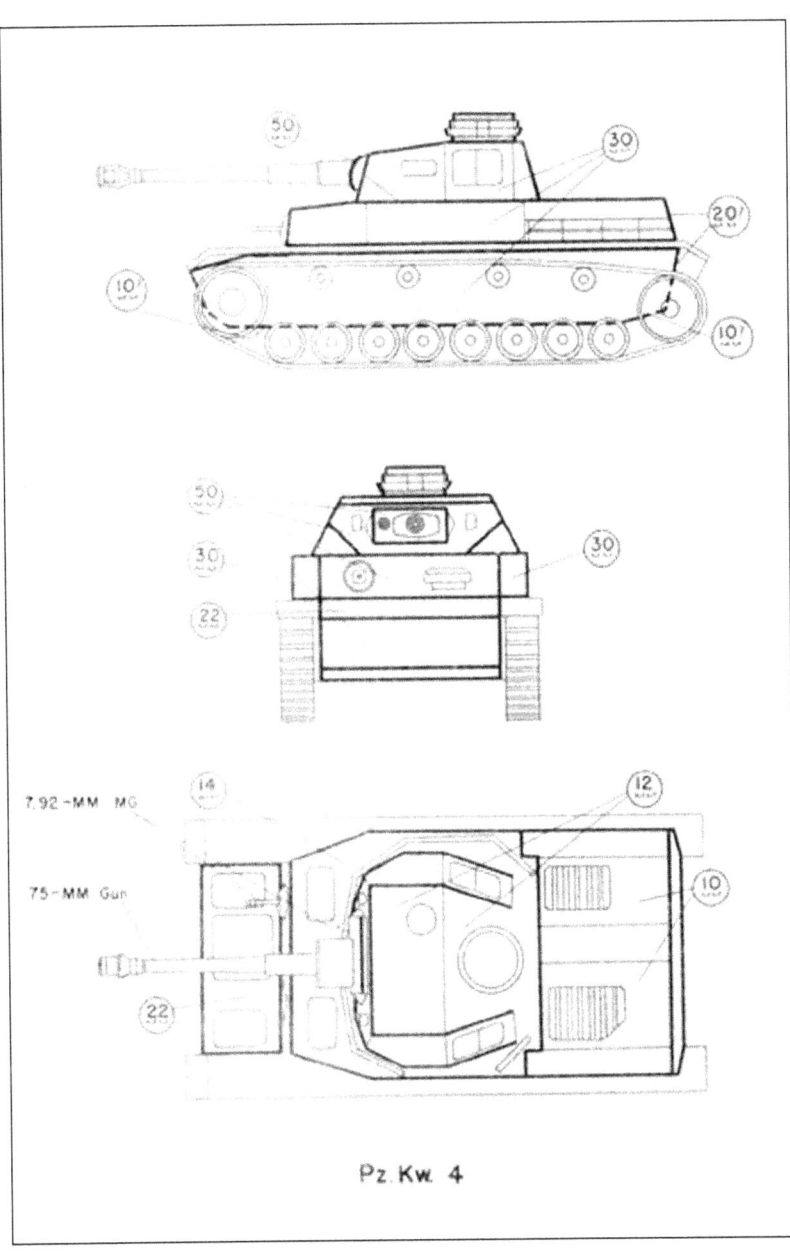

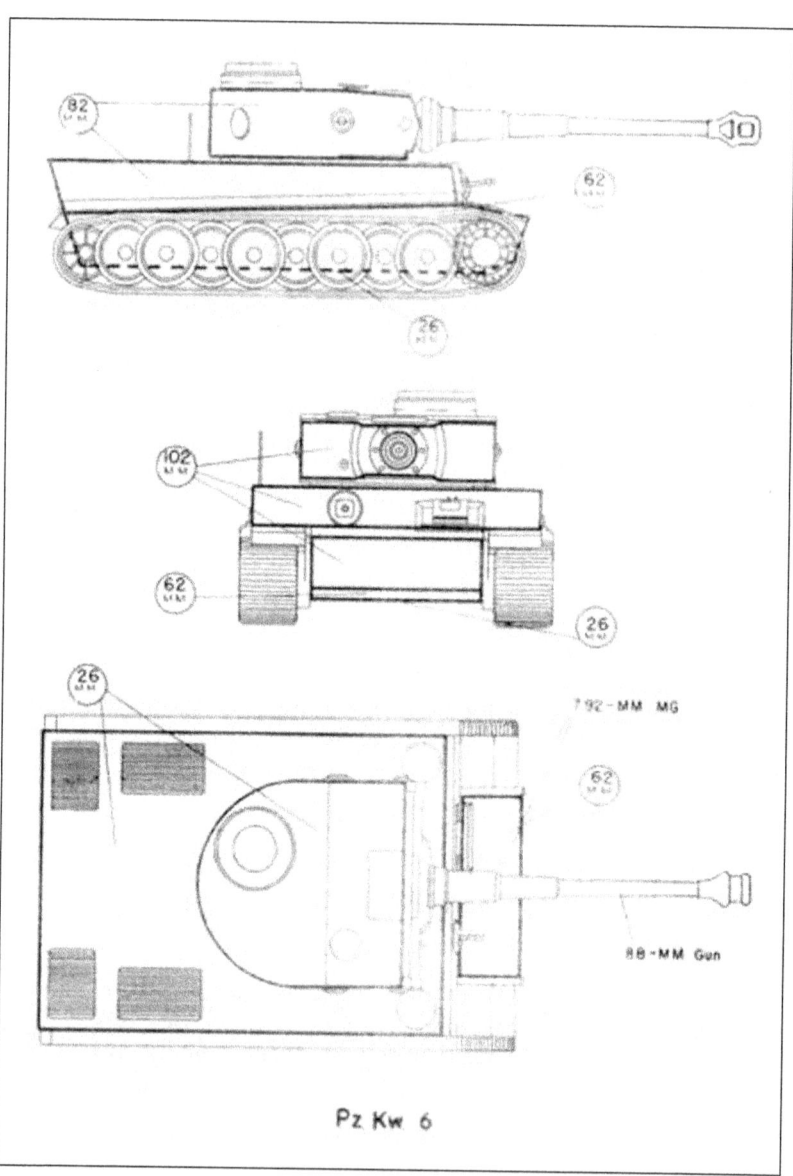

well. In April 1943, the KwK 40 L/43 was replaced by the longer 75-millimetre (2.95 in) KwK 40 L/48 gun, with a redesigned multi-baffle muzzle brake with improved recoil efficiency.

A U.S. report on the German practice of mounting armor skirts (Schürzen) on panzers in WWII, from Tactical and Technical Trends, No. 40, December 16, 1943 is reprinted below:

ARMOR SKIRTING ON GERMAN TANKS
Tactical and Technical Trends, No. 40, December 16th 1943

From both Allied and German sources, reports have come in of additional armored skirting applied to the sides of German tanks and self-moving guns to protect the tracks, bogies and turret. Photographs show such plating on the PzKw 3 and 4, where the plates are hung from a bar resembling a hand-rail running above the upper track guard and from rather light brackets extending outward about 18 inches from the turret.

What appeared to be a 75-mm self-moving gun was partially protected by similar side plates over the bogies. This armor is reported to be light — 4 to 6 millimeters (.16 to .24 in) — and is said to give protection against hollow-charge shells, 7.92-mm tungsten carbide core AT ammunition, and 20-mm tungsten carbide core ammunition. This armor might cause a high-velocity AP shot or shell to deflect and strike the main armor sideways or at an angle, but covering the bogies or Christie wheels would make the identification of a tank more difficult, except at short ranges.

***

A further U.S. military report on the German use of armor-skirting on tanks was published in Tactical and Technical Trends, No. 42, January 13, 1944.

Panzer IV Ausf.H in the Army Group South sector August 1943.

ENEMY USE OF SKIRTING ON TANKS
Tactical and Technical Trends, No. 42, January 13th 1944

An examination of German Pz Kw 3 and 4 tanks in Sicily, and a number of SP guns has confirmed prior reports that the Germans are using skirting both around the turret and along the sides of the hull. A prior reference to enemy use of armor skirting on German tanks may be found in Tactical and Technical Trends No. 40, p. 11.

On one Pz Kw tank, 1/4-inch mild steel plates were placed around the sides and rear of the turret, and extended from the turret top to the bottom, almost flush with the top of the superstructure. The front edges on both sides had been turned in, so as to line up with the front of the turret, thus filling the space between the turret and the outer mild steel plate. Doors are provided in the outer plate immediately opposite the doors of the turret. The plate is bolted on to brackets by 3/8-inch bolts and studs. The plates stand out about 18 inches from the top and 12 inches from the bottom of the turret. The depth of the plate is approximately 20 inches.

The skirting of 3/16 inch mild steel plates is in sections of 3 feet 9 inches x 3 feet 3 inches. It extends from the top of the superstructure to about the tops of the bogies, and for the full length of the hull. The sections are held in place by slots in them which match the supporting clips on a 1/4-inch angle-iron rail, welded on to the top of the superstructure and extending the full length of the hull, and by 5 brackets bolted on to the track mudguards. The angle-iron is spaced about 15 inches outwards away from the hull, and the brackets about 8 inches away from the mudguards.

Three other Pz Kw 4 tanks, similarly equipped with skirting were also seen, and a Pz Kw 3 tank had both sides completely covered with sheets of 3/16 inch boiler plate extending the whole length of the tank, and reaching from turret-top level to the tops of the bogies.

The 7.5-cm Stu.K. 42 SP equipment on a Pz Kw 3 chassis has been seen with similar additional side plates. The plates, which

extend vertically from the top of the equipment to the tops of the bogies, and laterally from the fifth bogie to the rear of the front-drive sprocket, are in three sections, the front section being cut to conform roughly with the shape of the equipment. A 15-cm s.F.H. 18 on Pz Kw 4 tank chassis is also reported to have been similarly equipped.

It would appear from available information that the use of spaced skirting on German armored vehicles and self-propelled guns is being adopted as standard practice. The fact that the side plates are in sections and held in place by clips suggests that they are detachable. This would, of course, be a great convenience in loading for transportation by rail.

It is believed that the skirting is designed to cause premature explosion of hollow charge, HE and AP HE shell, and thus minimize their effect. Although the plates have been described as mild steel, other sources have erroneously described them as armor.

Particular attention is drawn to the difficulty of recognition of tanks and SP equipments with this extensive skirting. Almost all of the features which are of primary importance in identification are obscured (see last sentence, Tactical and Technical Trends, No. 40, p. 11).

THE AUSF. H

The next version, the Ausf. H, began production in April 1943 and received the designation Sd. Kfz. 161/2. This variant saw the integrity of the glacis armor improved by manufacturing it as a single 80-millimetre (3.15 in) plate. To prevent adhesion of magnetic anti-tank mines, which the Germans feared would be used in large numbers by the Allies, Zimmerit paste was added to all the vertical surfaces of the tank's armor.

The vehicle's side and turret were further protected by the addition of 5-millimetre (0.20 in) side-skirts and 8-millimetre (0.31 in) turret skirts. During the Ausf. H's production run its

Panzer IV Auf.J with missing sideskirts Russia 1944.

rubber-tired return rollers were replaced with cast steel; the hull was fitted with triangular supports for the easily-damaged sideskirts. A hole in the roof, designed for the Nahverteidigungswaffe, was plugged by a circular armored plate due to shortages of this weapon. These modifications meant that the tank's weight jumped to 25 tonnes (27.56 short tons), reducing its speed, a situation not improved by the decision to adopt the Panzer III's six-speed SSG 77 transmission, which was inferior to that of earlier-model Panzer IVs.

The Ausf. J was the final production model, and was greatly simplified compared to earlier variants to speed construction. This shows an exported Finnish model.

Despite addressing the mobility problems introduced by the previous model, the final production version of the Panzer IV — the Ausf. J — was considered a retrograde from the Ausf. H. Born of German necessity to replace heavy losses, it was greatly simplified to speed production.

The electric generator that powered the tank's turret traverse was removed, so the turret had to be rotated manually. The space was later used for the installation of an auxiliary 200-litre (44 imp gal) fuel tank; road range was thereby increased to 320 kilometres (198.84 mi), The pistol and vision ports in the turret were removed, and the engine's radiator housing was simplified by changing the slanted sides to straight sides. In addition, the cylindrical muffler was replaced by two flame-suppressing mufflers. By late 1944, Zimmerit was no longer being applied to German armored vehicles, and the Panzer IV's side-skirts had been replaced by wire mesh, while to further speed production the number of return rollers was reduced from four to three.

In a bid to augment the Panzer IV's firepower, an attempt was made to mate a Panther turret—carrying the longer 75 mm (2.95 in) L/70 tank gun—to a Panzer IV hull. This was unsuccessful, and confirmed that the chassis had, by this time, reached the limits of its adaptability in both weight and available volume.

GERMAN HOLLOW-CHARGE AMMUNITION FOR 75-MM TANK GUN

From Tactical and Technical Trends, No. 19, February 25th, 1943

A sketch showing the details of the hollow-charge round for the German 7.5-cm KwK (75-mm tank gun) accompanies this report. The German nomenclature for this ammunition is 7.5-cm Pz. Gr. Patr. 38 KwK.

The round is of the fixed type. The cartridge case and the weight and type of propellant are similar to those for the other types of 75-mm antitank gun ammunition. The shell is fitted with a threaded hemispherical cap into which is screwed a small nose percussion fuze. From the nose fuze, a central tube runs down to a booster which is situated in the base of the shell.

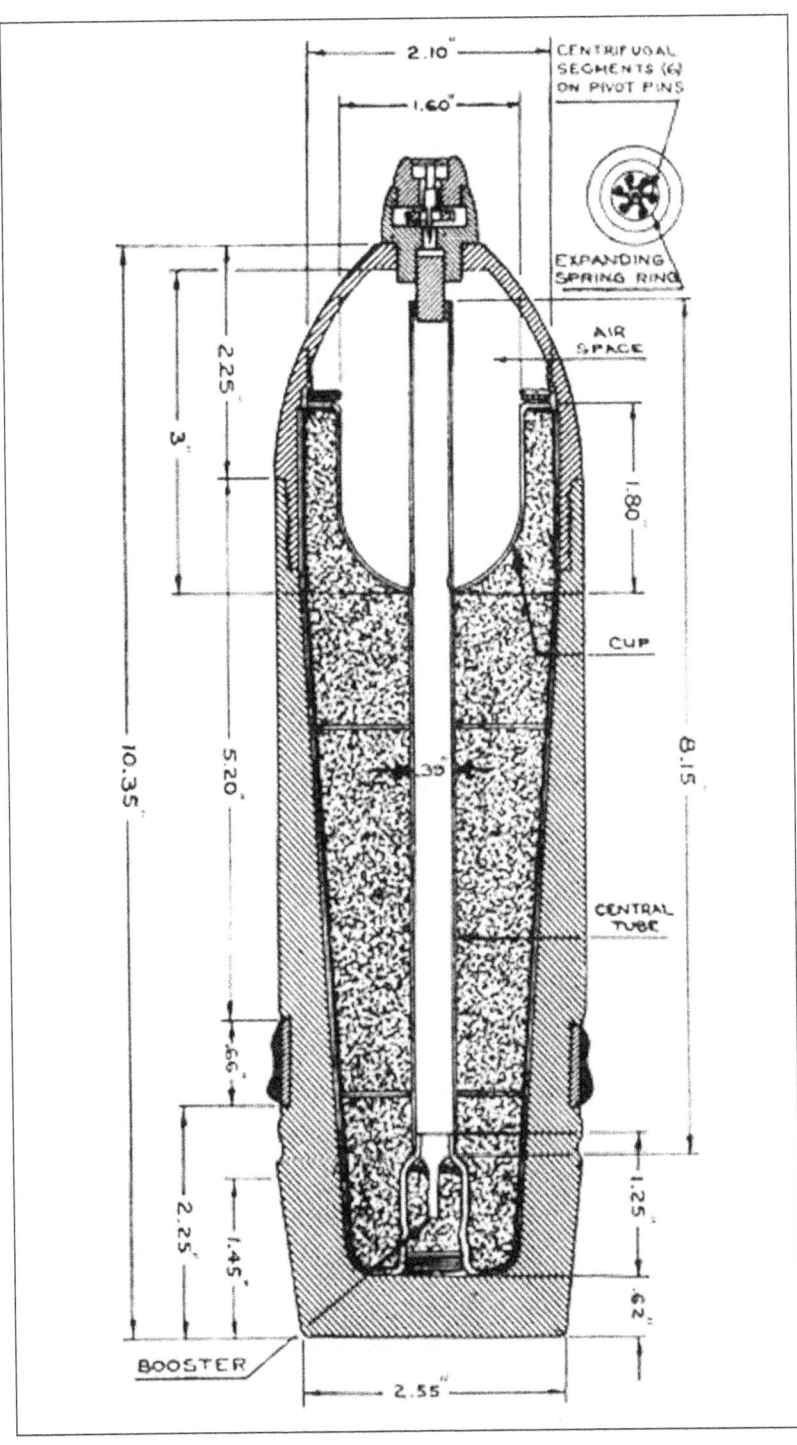

This booster consists of a detonator set in penthrite wax, the whole being contained in a perforated container. The bursting charge consists of three blocks of Hexagen (Trimethylene Trinitramine) the front one of which is concave, as shown in the sketch. The blocks are contained in waxed paper and are cemented into the shell.

The operation of the Aufschlag Zunder or percussion fuze (A.Z. 38-type fuze) is simple. The striker is held off the detonator assembly by six centrifugal segments which are surrounded by an expanding spring ring. After the shell has left the gun, centrifugal force causes the clock spring and the safety blocks to open, thus freeing the striker. Upon impact, the striker is driven onto the detonator. The detonation passes down the central tube to initiate the booster. This in turn initiates the bursting charge.

The shell is painted white and has black markings. The weight of the shell is 4.5 kilograms, and that of the bursting charge 450 grams.

Comments: This is another instance of the use of hollow-charge ammunition to increase the armor-shattering effect of a gun of comparatively low muzzle velocity. No data is available at this time concerning the performance of this type of projectile against armor at various ranges.

***

The Panzer IV was originally intended to be used only on a limited scale, so initially Krupp was its sole manufacturer. Prior to the Polish campaign, only 262 Panzer IVs were produced: 35 Ausf. A; 42 Ausf. B; 140 Ausf. C; and 45 Ausf. D. After the invasion of Poland, and with the decision to adopt the tank as the mainstay of Germany's armored divisions, production was extended to the Nibelungenwerke factory (managed by Steyr-Daimler-Puch) in the Austrian city of St. Valentin. Production increased as the Ausf. E was introduced, with 223 tanks delivered to the German army. By 1941, 462 Panzer IV

Panzer IV production by year		
Date	Number of Vehicles	Variant (*Ausführung* or *Ausf.*)
1937–1939	262	A – D
1940	278-386	E
1941	467-769	E, F1, F2, G
1942	est. 880	G
1943	3,013	G, H
1944	3,125	J
1945	est. 435	J
Total	**9,870**	**A - J**

Ausf. Fs had been assembled, and the up-gunned Ausf. F2 was entering production. The yearly production total had more than quadrupled since the start of the war.

As the later Panzer IV models emerged, a third factory, Vomag (located in the city of Plauen), began assembly. In 1941 an average of 39 tanks per month were built, and this rose to 83 in 1942, 252 in 1943, and 300 in 1944. However, in December 1943, Krupp's factory was diverted to manufacture the Sturmgeschütz IV, and in the spring of 1944 the Vomag factory began production of the Jagdpanzer IV, leaving the Nibelungenwerke as the only plant still assembling the Panzer IV. With the slow collapse of German industry under pressure from Allied air and ground offensives — in October 1944 the Nibelungenwerke factory was severely damaged during a bombing raid — by March and April 1945 production had fallen to pre-1942 levels, with only around 55 tanks per month coming off the assembly lines.

THE EXPORT OF THE PZ IV

The Panzer IV was the most exported German tank of the Second World War. In 1942 Germany delivered 11 tanks to Romania and 32 to Hungary, many of which were lost on the Eastern Front between the final months of 1942 and the beginning of 1943. Romania received approximately 120 Panzer IV tanks of different models throughout the entire war. To arm Bulgaria, Germany supplied 46 or 91 Panzer IVs, and offered Italy 12 tanks to form the nucleus of a new armored division. These were used to train Italian crews while Italian dictator Benito Mussolini was deposed, but were retaken by Germany during its occupation of Italy in mid-1943. The Spanish government petitioned for 100 Panzer IVs in March 1943, but only 20 were ever delivered, by December. Finland bought 30, but received only 15 Panzer IVs in 1944, and the same year a second batch of 62 or 72 were sent to Hungary (although 20 of these were diverted to replace German losses). In total some 297 Panzer IVs of all models were delivered to Germany's allies.

Combat history

The Panzer IV was the only German tank to remain in both production and combat throughout World War II, and measured over the entire war it comprised 30% of the Wehrmacht's total tank strength. Although in service by early 1939, in time for the occupation of Czechoslovakia, at the start of the war the majority of German armor was made up of obsolete Panzer Is and Panzer IIs. The Panzer I in particular had already proved inferior to Soviet tanks, such as the T-26, during the Spanish Civil War.

WESTERN FRONT AND NORTH AFRICA (1939–1942)

When Germany invaded Poland on 1 September 1939, its armored corps was composed of 1,445 Panzer Is, 1,223 Panzer IIs, 98 Panzer IIIs and 211 Panzer IVs; the more modern vehicles amounted to less than 10% of Germany's armored strength. The 1st Panzer Division had a roughly equal balance of types, with 17 Panzer Is, 18 Panzer IIs, 28 Panzer IIIs, and 14 Panzer

IVs per battalion. The remaining panzer divisions were heavy with obsolete models, equipped as they were with 34 Panzer Is, 33 Panzer IIs, 5 Panzer IIIs, and 6 Panzer IVs per battalion. Although the Polish army possessed less than 200 tanks capable of penetrating the German light tanks, Polish anti-tank guns proved more of a threat, reinforcing German faith in the value of the close-support Panzer IV.

Despite increasing production of the medium Panzer IIIs and IVs prior to the German invasion of France on 10 May 1940, the majority of German tanks were still light types. According to Heinz Guderian, the Wehrmacht invaded France with 523 Panzer Is, 955 Panzer IIs, 349 Panzer IIIs, 278 Panzer IVs, 106 Panzer 35(t)s and 228 Panzer 38(t)s. Through the use of tactical radios and superior tactics, the Germans were able to outmaneuver and defeat French and British armor. However, Panzer IVs armed with the KwK 37 L/24 75-millimetre (2.95 in) tank gun found it difficult to engage French tanks such as Somua S35 and Char B1. The Somua S35 had a maximum armor thickness of 55 mm (2.17 in), while the KwK 37 L/24 could only penetrate 43 mm (1.69 in) at a range of 700 m (2,296.59 ft). Likewise, the British Matilda Mk II was heavily armored, with at least 70 mm (2.76 in) of steel on the front and turret, and a minimum of 65 mm on the sides.

Although the Panzer IV was deployed to North Africa with the German Afrika Korps, until the longer gun variant began production, the tank was outperformed by the Panzer III with respect to armor penetration. Both the Panzer III and IV had difficulty in penetrating the British Matilda II's thick armor, while the Matilda's 40-mm QF 2 pounder gun could knock out either German tank; its major disadvantage was its low speed. By August 1942, Rommel had only received 27 Panzer IV Ausf. F2s, armed with the L/43 gun, which he deployed to spearhead his armored offensives. The longer gun could penetrate all

A PzKpfw IV Ausf. H of the 12th Panzer Division operating on the Eastern Front in the USSR, 1944.

American and British tanks in theater at ranges of up to 1,500 m (4,900 ft). Although more of these tanks arrived in North Africa between August and October 1942, their numbers were insignificant compared to the amount of matériel shipped to British forces.

The Panzer IV also took part in the invasion of Yugoslavia and the invasion of Greece in early 1941.

EASTERN FRONT (1941–1945)

With the launching of Operation Barbarossa on 22 June 1941, the unanticipated appearance of the KV-1 and T-34 tanks prompted an upgrade of the Panzer IV's 75 mm (2.95 in) gun to a longer, high-velocity 75 mm (2.95 in) gun suitable for antitank use. This meant that it could now penetrate the T-34 at ranges of up to 1,200 m (3,900 ft) at any angle. The 75 mm (2.95 in) KwK 40 L/43 gun on the Panzer IV could penetrate a T-34 at a variety of impact angles beyond 1,000 m (3,300 ft) range and up to 1,600 m (5,200 ft). Shipment of the first model to mount the new gun, the Ausf. F2, began in spring 1942, and by the summer offensive there were around 135 Panzer IVs with the L/43 tank gun available. At the time, these were the only German tanks that could defeat the Soviet T-34 or KV-1. They played a crucial role in the events that unfolded between June 1942 and March 1943, and the Panzer IV became the mainstay of the German panzer divisions. Although in service by late September 1942, the Tiger I was not yet numerous enough to make an impact and suffered from serious teething problems, while the Panther was not delivered to German units in the Soviet Union until May 1943. The extent of German reliance on the Panzer IV during this period is reflected by their losses; 502 were destroyed on the Eastern Front in 1942.

The Panzer IV continued to play an important role during operations in 1943, including at the Battle of Kursk. Newer types such as the Panther were still experiencing crippling reliability problems that restricted their combat efficiency, so much of the effort fell to the 841 Panzer IVs that took part in the battle. Throughout 1943, the German army lost 2,352 Panzer IVs on the Eastern Front; some divisions were reduced to 12–18 tanks by the end of the year. In 1944, a further 2,643 Panzer IVs were destroyed, and such losses were becoming increasingly difficult to replace. By the last year of the war, the Panzer IV was outclassed by the upgraded T-34-85, which had an 85 mm (3.35 in) gun, and other late-model Soviet tanks such as the 122 mm (4.80 in)-armed IS-2 heavy tank. Nevertheless, due to a shortage of replacement Panther tanks, the Panzer IV continued to form the core of Germany's armored divisions, including elite units such as the II SS Panzer Corps, through 1944.

In January 1945, 287 Panzer IVs were lost on the Eastern Front. It is estimated that combat against Soviet forces accounted for 6,153 Panzer IVs, or about 75% of all Panzer IV losses during the war.

British officers inspect a German Pzkw-IV knocked out in France in June 1944 by the Durham Light Infantry.

WESTERN FRONT (1944–1945)

Panzer IVs comprised around half of the available German tank strength on the Western Front prior to the Allied invasion of Normandy on June 6, 1944. Most of the 11 panzer divisions that saw action in Normandy initially contained an armored regiment of one battalion of Panzer IVs and another of Panthers, for a total of around 160 tanks, although Waffen-SS panzer divisions were generally larger and better-equipped than their Heer counterparts. Regular upgrades to the Panzer IV had helped to maintain its reputation as a formidable opponent. Despite overwhelming Allied air superiority, the Norman bocage countryside in the US sector heavily favored defense, and German tanks and anti-tank guns inflicted horrendous casualties on Allied armor during the Normandy campaign. On the offensive, however, the Panzer IVs, Panthers and other armored vehicles proved equally vulnerable in the bocage, and counter-attacks rapidly stalled in the face of infantry-held anti-tank weapons, tank destroyers and anti-tank guns, as well as the ubiquitous fighter bomber aircraft. That the terrain was highly unsuitable for tanks was illustrated by the constant damage suffered to the side-skirts of the Ausf. H's; essential for defence against shaped charge anti-tank weapons such as the British PIAT, all German armored units were "exasperated" by the way these were torn off during movement through the dense orchards and hedgerows.

The Allies had also been developing lethality improvement programs of their own; the widely-used American-designed M4 Sherman medium tank, while mechanically reliable, suffered from thin armor and an inadequate gun. Against earlier-model Panzer IVs, it could hold its own, but with its 75 mm M3 gun, struggled against the late-model Panzer IV (and was unable to penetrate the frontal armor of Panther and Tiger tanks at virtually any range). The late-model Panzer IV's 80 mm (3.15 in) frontal hull armor could easily withstand hits from the 75 mm (2.95 in) weapon on the Sherman at normal combat ranges, though the turret remained vulnerable.

The British up-gunned the Sherman with their highly effective QF 17 pounder anti-tank gun, resulting in the Firefly; although

Pzkw-IV in Belgrade Military Museum, Serbia.

A Syrian Panzer IV Ausf. G, captured during the Six-Day War, on display in the Yad La-Shiryon Museum, Israel.

this was the only Allied tank capable of dealing with all current German tanks at normal combat ranges, few (about 300) were available in time for the Normandy invasion. The other British tank with the 17 pdr gun could not participate in the landings and had to wait for port facilities. It was not until July 1944 that American Shermans, fitted with the 76-mm (3-inch) M1 tank gun, began to achieve a parity in firepower with the Panzer IV.

However, despite the general superiority of its armored vehicles, by August 29, 1944, as the last surviving German troops of Fifth Panzer Army and Seventh Army began retreating towards Germany, the twin cataclysms of the Falaise Pocket and the Seine crossing had cost the Wehrmacht dearly. Of the 2,300 tanks and assault guns it had committed to Normandy (including around 750 Panzer IVs), over 2,200 had been lost. Field Marshal Walter Model reported to Hitler that his panzer divisions had remaining, on average, five or six tanks each.

During the winter of 1944–45, the Panzer IV was one of the most widely used tanks in the Ardennes offensive, where further heavy losses—as often due to fuel shortages as to enemy action—impaired major German armored operations in the West thereafter. The Panzer IVs that took part were survivors of the battles in France between June and September 1944, with around 260 additional Panzer IV Ausf. Js issued as reinforcements.

OTHER USERS

In the 1960s Syria received a number of Panzer IVs from the French, replacing the turret's machine gun with a Soviet-made 12.7-millimetre (0.50 in) machine gun. These were used to shell Israeli settlements below the Golan Heights, and were fired upon during the 1965 "Water War" by Israeli Centurion tanks. Syria received 17 more Panzer IVs from Spain, which saw combat during the Six-Day War in 1967.

The Finns bought 15 new Panzer IV Ausf J in 1944, for 5,000,000 Finnish markkas each (about twice the production price). The tanks arrived too late to see action against the Soviets, but were instead used against the Germans in the Lapland War. After the war, they served as training tanks, and one portrayed a Soviet KV-1 tank in the movie The Unknown Soldier in 1955.

After 1945, Bulgaria incorporated its surviving Panzer IVs in defensive bunkers as gunpoints on the border with Turkey, along with T-34 turrets. This defensive line known as the "Krali Marko Line", remained in use until the fall of communism in 1989.

Most of the tanks Romania had received were lost in 1944 and 1945 in combat. These tanks, designated T4 in the army inventory, were used by the 2nd Armoured Regiment. On 9 May 1945 only two Panzer IV were left. Romania received another 50 Panzer IV tanks from the Red Army after the end of the war. These tanks were of different models and were in very poor shape. Many of them were missing parts and the side skirts. The T4 tanks remained in service until 1950, when the Army decided to use only Soviet equipment. By 1954, all German tanks were scrapped.

Variants

In keeping with the wartime German design philosophy of mounting an existing anti-tank gun on a convenient chassis to give mobility, several tank destroyers and infantry support guns were built around the Panzer IV hull. Both the Jagdpanzer IV, initially armed with the 75-millimetre (2.95 in) L/48 tank gun, and the Krupp-manufactured Sturmgeschütz IV, which was the casemate of the Sturmgeschütz III mounted on the body of the Panzer IV, proved highly effective in defense. Cheaper and faster to construct than tanks, but with the disadvantage of a very limited gun traverse, around 1,980 Jagdpanzer IV's and 1,140 Sturmgeschütz IVs were produced. The Jagdpanzer IV eventually received the same 75 millimeter L/70 gun that was mounted on the Panther.

Another variant of the Panzer IV was the Panzerbefehlswagen IV (Pz.Bef.Wg. IV) command tank. This conversion entailed the installation of additional radio sets, mounting racks,

A Jagdpanzer IV/48 tank destroyer, based on the Panzer IV chassis, mounting the 75 mm PaK L/48 anti-tank gun.

A Sturmpanzer IV Brummbär infantry-support gun (Casemate MG variant (flexible mount)).

transformers, junction boxes, wiring, antennas and an auxiliary electrical generator. To make room for the new equipment, ammunition stowage was reduced from 87 to 72 rounds. The vehicle could coordinate with nearby armor, infantry or even aircraft. Seventeen Panzerbefehlswagen were converted from Ausf. J chassis, while another 88 were based on refurbished chassis.

The Panzerbeobachtungswagen IV (Pz.Beob.Wg. IV) was an artillery observation vehicle built on the Panzer IV chassis. This, too, received new radio equipment and an electrical generator, installed in the left rear corner of the fighting compartment. Panzerbeobachtungswagens worked in cooperation with Wespe and Hummel self-propelled artillery batteries.

Also based on the Panzer IV chassis was the Sturmpanzer IV Brummbär 150-millimetre (5.91 in) infantry-support self-propelled gun. These vehicles were primarily issued to four Sturmpanzer units (Numbers 216, 217, 218 and 219) and used during the battle of Kursk and in Italy in 1943. Two separate versions of the Sturmpanzer IV existed, one without a machine gun in the mantlet and one with a machine gun mounted on

The Wirbelwind armored anti-aircraft vehicle.

the mantlet of the casemate. Furthermore, a 105-millimetre (4.13 in) artillery gun was mounted in an experimental turret on a Panzer IV chassis. This variant was called the Heuschrecke, or Grasshopper. Another 105 mm artillery/anti-tank prototype was the 10.5 cm K (gp.Sfl.) nicknamed Dicker Max.

Four different self-propelled anti-aircraft vehicles were built on the Panzer IV hull. The Flakpanzer IV Möbelwagen was armed with a 37-millimetre (1.46 in) anti-aircraft cannon; 240 were built between 1944 and 1945. In late 1944 a new Flakpanzer, the Wirbelwind, was designed, with enough armor to protect the gun's crew and a rotating turret, armed with the 20mm quadmount Flakvierling anti-aircraft cannon system; at least 100 were manufactured. Sixty-five similar vehicles were built, named the Ostwind, but with a single 37-millimetre (1.46 in) anti-aircraft cannon instead. This vehicle was designed to replace the Wirbelwind. The final model was the Flakpanzer IV

Kugelblitz, of which only five were built. This vehicle featured a covered turret armed with twin 30-millimetre (1.18 in) anti-aircraft cannons.

Although not a direct modification of the Panzer IV, some of its components, in conjunction with parts from the Panzer III, were utilized to make one of the most widely-used self-propelled artillery chassis of the war—the Geschützwagen III/IV. This chassis was the basis of the Hummel artillery piece, of which 666 were built, and also the 88 millimetres (3.46 in) gun armed Nashorn tank destroyer, with 473 manufactured. To resupply self-propelled howitzers in the field, 150 ammunition carriers were manufactured on the Geschützwagen III/IV chassis.

Heinz Wilhelm Guderian was a German general during World War II. He was a pioneer in the development of armored warfare, and was the leading proponent of tanks and mechanization in the Wehrmacht. Germany's panzer forces were raised and organized under his direction as Chief of Mobile Forces. During the war, he was a highly successful commander of panzer forces in several campaigns, became Inspector-General of Armored Troops, rose to the rank of Generaloberst, and was Chief of the General Staff of the Heer in the last year of the war.

THE PANTHER

Guderian's Problem Child

From late 1942 onwards the German engineers employed in the hard pressed armaments industry produced a remarkable range of armoured fighting vehicles. They were driven by the desperate demands of an insatiable front line which was showing the first warning signs that it might ultimately roll back and consume their homeland in a red tide. The race against time was remorseless, and this ominous situation was compounded by Adolf Hitler who harboured unrealistic expectations that new and improved tank designs were somehow capable of turning back the surge of the Red Army. The weight of Hitler's expectancy and his unreasonable deadlines placed the engineers and manufacturers under extreme pressure to design, develop and supply new and unproven battlefield technology as quickly as possible. The war in the East was a demanding and remorseless taskmaster which consumed every new offering as soon as it was ready for action, the price of failure was unthinkable and, not surprisingly, this unsettling combination of concerns actually drove the German armaments industry on to some remarkable achievements. Chief among these was the development and deployment of the Panzer Mark V - The Panther.

Among the many excesses which the Nazi regime condoned was its willingness to embrace the concept of slave labour. The German armaments industry workforce, both willing and enslaved, worked ceaselessly in gloomy war ravaged factories to design, develop and produce an astonishing variety of highly effective armoured fighting vehicles which appeared on the battlefield in an incredibly short period of time. It has often been said that the German armaments industry placed the best possible weapons in the worst possible hands; that is certainly true of the Panther.

Under peacetime conditions a new fighting vehicle would generally be designed, built and tested over a period of three to five years. Between 1941 and 1945 however some very successful designs for armoured fighting vehicles were produced in just 12 months. As war progressed the Red Army received huge volumes of increasingly sophisticated vehicles and weapons and as a result it became imperative that ne w German vehicles should be brought into action as quickly as possible. Many of the most successful German machines were adaptions of existing vehicles which were modified to produce specialist tank destroyers such as the Jagdpanzer IV and the Nashorn. Other armoured fighting vehicles such as the Tiger and the Panther, were completely designed and built from scratch, these designs were more innovative and, in most respects, more effective, but the hasty development process meant that significant teething problems often remained unsolved. In the case of the Panther the evidence of this hurriedness was evident for all to see. On his way up to the front lines prior to the battle of Kursk SS Panzer Grenadier Hofstetter recalled seeing the new Panther for the first time.

> "As we passed the unfamiliar column of Panzers, it was soon obvious that there had been a serious problem with one machine in particular that was reduced to a burnt out wreck with no sign of any enemy activity. We later learnt that this was the Panther – Guderian's problem child!"

The omens pointed towards dismal failure, but against heavy odds, the Panther gradually gained a fearsome reputation and eventually produced a legacy which shaped the face of tank

Minister of Armaments and War Production for the Third Reich, Albert Speer, inspects a Panther tank. The vehicle has already received a factory coating of Zimmerit anti-magnetic paste.

The original T-34 Model 1940 - recognizable by the low-slung barrel of the L-11 gun below a bulge in the mantlet housing its recoil mechanism. This pre-production A-34 prototype has a complex single-piece hull front.

design in the post war era. The Panther's excellent combination of firepower and mobility produced a fighting machine which has frequently been hailed as one of the best tank designs of World War II. It has been estimated that every Panther deployed accounted for, on average, five allied tanks and as many as nine Russian tanks.

The statistics are unproven and in reality it may well be the case that the Panther was actually a very expensive failure which drew much needed resources away from the real requirements of the *Panzertruppen*. At the time it was strongly argued, by Guderian and others, that what the hard pressed front line troops really needed was to a high volume of reliable main battle tanks in the shape of the Mark IV F2, a machine which could at least attain parity with the T-34. There remains the strong argument that the decision to develop the Panther was a wrong option, especially as the problems caused by the poor quality components used in the final drive were never overcome. This serious flaw made the Panther highly susceptible to breakdowns which were so frequent as to be almost a certainty. These catastrophic mechanical failures were particularly common during the long road marches which became increasingly numerous as the war progressed and the Panthers had to be rushed from place to place. Many of the repairs required, particularly those on the final drive, were very difficult and frequently could not be managed at divisional workshops and required the vehicle being returned to army depots far behind the lines. On the retreat it was not always possible to recover the broken down vehicles and this led to many, otherwise salvageable, Panthers having to be destroyed.

The other principal disadvantage of the Panther lay in its comparatively weak side armour which made it highly vulnerable to attack from any direction other than head on. As a result of the poor ammunition stowage design, the tank was also highly susceptible to "brewing up" when hit. Taken together these negative aspects of the Panther are the main reasons why the Panther has not attained the legendary status of the Tiger I which was much loved by its crews.

Like the Tiger, the development of the Panther resulted from the Wehrmacht's unpleasant surprise encounter with the Soviet T-34 during Operation Barbarossa, the German invasion of Russia, in June 1941. During the first weeks of Barbarossa, the men of the *Panzertruppen* repeatedly encountered the T-34/76 medium tank. Although in short supply, the T-34 made a quick and lasting impression on the German armoured forces who were shocked to be confronted with this formidable vehicle with its near perfect combination of speed and mobility, rugged reliability, sloped armour protection and firepower. As a result of numerous adverse encounters with the T-34, especially the battering sustained by the 4th Panzer division at Mtsensk on 4th October 1941, Colonel General Heinz Guderian, leading *Panzergruppe* 2 in Army Group Centre, requested the establishment of a Commission of Enquiry into the relative strengths of the tank armies on the Eastern Front.

Although Guderian suggested simply copying the T-34, this proposal was rejected and the report of the enquiry instead recommended that the main attributes of the T-34 be incorporated into a new German built machine. The main points which were desirable in the new design the T-34 were its excellent main armament which was capable of firing both high velocity anti-tank rounds and a reasonably effective high explosive shell , well sloped armour and a highly effective suspension design with wide tracks which gave good cross country mobility.

The outcome of Hitler's itervention in the debate was the decision to produce a brand new medium tank – the Panther. Hitler however demanded a crash building programme and as soon as the new machine was off the drawing board and into production, the Panther underwent a complex and difficult development cycle which included overcoming problems with the vehicle's transmission, steering, main gun, turret and fuel pump. Despite having to contend with these and a host of other issues the first 200 Panthers were nonetheless readied for participation in the Wehrmacht's 1943 summer offensive in the East. The Panther then saw action from mid-1943 to the end of the European war in 1945. It was intended as a counter to the T-34, and to replace the Panzer III and Panzer IV. However a remorseless allied bombing campaign meant that production did not reach the necessary levels and Panther formations served alongside those equipped with the Mark IV and the heavier Tiger tanks until the end of the war.

The Panther Manual: The Pantherfibel

The crew of the Panther comprised five members: a driver, a radio operator (who also operated the bow machine gun), a gunner who aimed and fired the main gun and co-axial machine gun , a gun loader, and a commander.

The crews selected for duty on the Panther were selected among the very best that could be found. Due to the high number of teething issues the Panther required extremely sympathetic handling by knowledgeable crews, but by 1943 the process of identifying and training crews was becoming increasingly difficult. Maintaining and fighting the Panther demanded a great deal of specialist knowledge, both theoretical and practical, which required long hours of class room study as well as, ideally, months familiarisation and training on the Panther itself. However, the declining war situation and a shortage of training machines dictated that the time and resources which

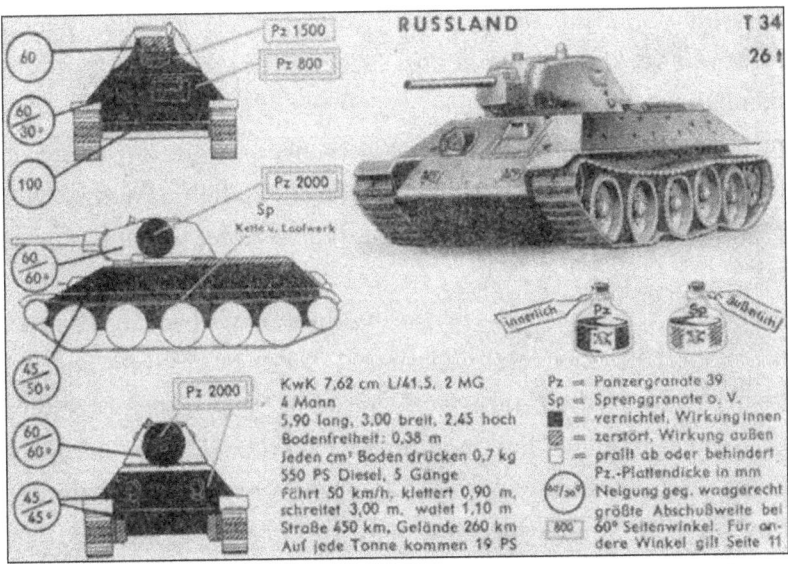

A page from the Pantherfibel the crew manual published in 1944 demonstrating graphically how to combat the T-34 visually illustrating the weak spots (in black) as aiming points.

The introductory page from the Pantherfibel which offered the crew the opportunity to learn with ease.

would normally be allocated to crew training were seriously curtailed.

One successful element of the training programme was the introduction *Pantherfibel* an illustrated crew manual which followed the style of the highly successful Tiger I crew training manual, the *Tigerfibel*. Surviving copies of the The *Pantherfibel* provide a fascinating primary source insight into the world of the men of the Panzertruppen who crewed the Panther and extensive use has been made of the *Pantherfibel* throughout this book.

The man responsible for the evolution of the *Pantherfibel* was Oberstleutnant Hans Christern, head of training for the Inspectorate of the *Panzerwaffe* based at Paderborn. Christern was an experienced tank commander who could provide proof to his own practical experience by dint of his the possession of the Knight's Cross awarded to him for bravery in the field.

With the introduction of the Tiger I (Ausf H) in late 1942 Christern found himself faced with the need to rapidly instruct crews in the operation of a very different type of vehicle. Like the Panther this tank had to be handled very differently on the battlefield like the Panther it needed far more care and attention than any other machine so far delivered to the *Panzerwaffe*. The *Tigerfibel* therefore dealt with the same set of issues which were encountered with the later introduction of the Panther.

Faced with a rapidly declining war situation everything needed to be done in a hurry. Christern therefore decided it would help to move matters along if he were to replace the usual dusty tank instruction manual with a special training booklet for Tiger I students which was simple yet memorable. The end result was certainly a success on both counts. The simplistic but effective style recalled a children's school book. It was therefore given the name *Tigerfibel*, which means Tiger primer. This booklet was assigned the official publication number of D656/27.

The task of actually writing the *Tigerfibel* was assigned to Leutnant Josef von Glatter-Goetz. Glatter-Goetz took the assignment to heart and gave serious consideration to the need

The five man crew of the Panther tank photographed in Italy in August 1944.

to impart such a large amount of information quickly and make it stick in the minds of bored young tank men. He therefore developed the idea of writing a humorous and highly risqué manual that would hold fast in the memories of the young men training on the Tiger I. To do this he used humorous and risque cartoon illustrations along with slang and the everyday situations which it was hoped the target audience would identify with.

The illustrations in the *Tigerfibel* were completed by two serving soldiers named Obergrenadier Gessinger and Unteroffizier Wagner. This wide range of images included the usual technical drawings and photographs supplemeted by a range of cartoons. Wherever possible the cartoons featured an attractive and curvaceous blonde named Elvira. She was depicted naked as often as possible and somewhat predictably was the romantic target for the affections of a Tiger crewman who gets the girl in the end.

The *Tigerfibel* also contains some short verses and rhyming

The Red Army menace is characterised as a ravenous bird of prey in this page from the Pantherfibel which cautions the men of the Panzertruppen to be constantly vigilant.

A Panther tank commander surveys the surrounding area on the eastern front in the summer of 1944.

couplets which do not lend themselves readily to an exact translation from German and English.

Both The *Tigerfibel* and the later *Pantherfibel* (published on 1st July 1944) included vital information concerning basic maintenance requirements and peculiarities, and in addition covered a wide range of additional subjects. There was important advice on gunnery and ammunition drill as well as a comprehensive run down the type of enemy targets likely to be encountered. In addition came advice on driving techniques, winter conditions, fuel conservation, how to deal with enemy infantry at close quarters, anti-tank mines, target spotting and a host of additional information.

Although it was quite unconventional when compared to any other manual hitherto produced and was somewhat racy by straight laced Third Reich standards, the *Tigerfibel* was actually authorized by Guderian himself and it proved to be very effective training aid. The *Pantherfibel*, which followed a year later was again personally authorised by Guderian, however it is the product of a far more sober environment and presents a much

The radio duty of the Commander from the Pantherfibel.

less saucy publication which reined in the gratuitous cartoon nudity in preference for some rather twee rhyming couplets which obviously don't have the same instant appeal to the common soldier. The *Pantherfibel* nonetheless featured good black and white photos and diagrammatic representations of the various Allied tanks which the Panther crew could be expected to encounter in the field. Another particularly interesting feature is the graphic cloverleaf demonstration of the range the Panther could be penetrated by or itself penetrate enemy tanks such as the Sherman M4 or T-34 or KV1.

In addition to the advice on fighting and maintaining the machine the *Pantherfibel* also affords a fascinating insight into the deteriorating supply situation in the form of exhortations to conserve ammunition and to overrun targets rather than use precious shells. Both the *Tigerfibel* and the *Pantherfibel* are also noteworthy for the fact that, despite Guderian's strong Nazi sympathies, no Nazi iconography appears anywhere in either the *Tigerfibel* or the *Pantherfibel*.

The Re-building Programme

The Panther was to all intents a prototype, but Hitler was intent on seeing the new tank in action by the middle of 1943. However by late 1942, with production now in progress it was all too obvious that the machines emerging from the production lines were far from perfect. A rebuilding and final proofing programme was therefore introduced in order to try and deal with the remaining teething troubles. Under very difficult circumstances the DEMAG factory entrusted with the rebuild programme managed to deliver 200, ostensibly combat ready, Panthers to the Eastern Front in time to make an operational debut in Operation Zitadelle, otherwise known as the Battle of Kursk. The last great German offensive in the East began on 5th July 1943 and the two battalions of Panthers involved were split across the 51st and 52nd Panzer Battalions, which were attached to the Grossdeutschland Panzergrenadier Division

The Pantherfibel emphasised the role of the hard pressed home front in producing the essential parts of the Panther.

on the southern flank of the Kursk salient. Inevitably, the continuing mechanical and design flaws and the limited time available for training had a disastrous effect. There was simply no available time to properly train the crews and this, when combined with the mechanical problems, severely hampered the Panthers' contribution to Zitadelle. Despite the fact that the Panthers on their first combat foray were credited with 267 enemy tanks destroyed, it was at Kursk, and for good reason, that the reputation of the Panther as Guderian's problem child took root. Germany simply did not have the resources to be able to loose tanks at this ratio and this sobering fact was obvious to all.

The rushed emergence of the Panther into action at Kursk not only compromised frontline performance, it also left a large number of Panther wrecks on the battlefield. The ability of the Russians to study captured machines meant that the cat was out of the bag and a series of counter measures designed to defeat the Panther in action were soon being implemented. The following report on the new German Panther tank, based on Russian intelligence sources, appeared in the US intelligence manual *Tactical and Technical Trends*, on November 4, 1943. As the Panther tank was first deployed on the Russian front initial US intelligence on the Panther tank was based entirely on Russian sources.

THE PZ-KW 5 (PANTHER) TANK
Tactical and Technical Trends, November 4, 1943.

The German tank series 1 to 6 has now been filled in with the long-missing PzKw 5 (Panther) a fast, heavy, well-armored vehicle mounting a long 75-mm gun. It appears to be an intermediate type between the 22-ton PzKw 4 and the PzKw 6 (Tiger) tank. The Panther has a speed of about thirty-one miles per hour. It approximates (corresponds roughly to) our General Sherman, a tank which evoked complimentary comment in the Nazi press.

The following is a description of the tank: (It should be noted that practically all data contained in this report come from Russian sources)

Weight	45 tons
Crew	5
Armament	75-mm (2.95 in) gun, long barrel, (1943) 1 machine gun, MG-42, 7.92-mm
Ammunition	75 rounds (AP & HE)
Motor	Maybach, gasoline, 640 hp in rear of tank The gas tanks are located on either side of motor
Cooling System	Water
Ignition	Magneto
Armor	Front of turret and cannon shield 100 mm (3.94 in) Upper front plate 85 mm (3.45 in) 57° inclination Lower front plate 75 mm (2.95 in) 53° inclination Side and rear plate 45 mm (1.78 in) Top of turret & tank and bottom of tank 17 mm (.67 in)
Dimensions:	
Width	11 ft 8 in (same as the PzKw 6)
Length	22 ft 8 in (1 1/2 ft longer than the PzKw 6)
Clearance	1 ft 8 in (10 cm)(3.9 in) more than the PzKw 6)
Caterpillar Section	Drive sprockets at front; rear idlers; 8 double rubber-tired bogie wheels 850 mm (33.46 in) in diameter on either side; torsion suspension system; hydraulic shock absorbers located inside tank; metal caterpillar tread, 660 mm (25.62 in) wide
Maximum Speed	50 km hr. (approx. 31 mph)
Range	170 km (approx. 105 miles)

The 75-mm gun is probably the new Pak. 41 AT gun with a muzzle velocity of 4,000 foot-seconds. The estimated armour penetration at 547 yards is 4.72 inches, and the life of the barrel from 500 to 600 rounds. The gun has direct sights to 1,500 meters or 1,640 yards. The 75-mm has an overall length of 18 feet 2 inches.

The Panther can also be easily converted for fording deep streams by attaching a flexible tube with float to the air intake. There is a special fitting in the top rear of the tank for attaching this tube.

Although provided with smaller armour and armament than the 6, the Panther has the same motor, thus giving it higher speed and manoeuvrability. This tank is also provided with light armour plate (not shown in the sketch) 4 to 6 millimetres thick along the side just above the suspension wheels and the inclined side armour plate.

Panther tanks are organized into separate tank battalions similar to the Tiger tanks. Many of these tanks have been used by the Germans during the July and August battles. The Russians state that this tank, although more manoeuvrable, is much easier to knock out than the PzKw 6. Fire from all types of rifles and machine guns directed against the peep holes, periscopes and the base of the turret and gun shield will blind or jam the parts. High-explosives and armour-piercing shells of 54-mm (2.12 in) calibre or higher, at 800 meters (875 yds) or less, are effective against the turret. Large calibre artillery and self-propelled cannon can put the Panther out of action at ordinary distances for effective fire. The inclined and vertical plates can be pierced by armour-piercing shells of 45 mm calibre or higher. Incendiary armour-piercing shells are especially effective against the gasoline tanks and the ammunition located just in the rear of the driver.

The additional 4 to 6 mm armour plate above the suspension wheels is provided to reduce the penetration of hollow-charge shells but the Russians state that it is not effective. Antitank grenades, antitank mines and "Molotov cocktails" are effective against the weak bottom and top plates and the cooling and ventilating openings on the top of the tank just above the motor.

This tank is standard but the quantity and rate of production is not known.

A Panther left destroyed in the aftermath of the Battle of Kursk.

The negative lessons of Kursk were many, but those improvements which could be made were quickly absorbed and modifications were adapted into the production lines. Improvements included stronger, lower-profile commander cupolas, rain guards on the gun mantlet, Zimmerit anti-magnetic mine paste and, on the later Ausf G, a simplified and strengthened hull. Given the production difficulties and the complex internal politics of German weapons manufacture, the Panther tank was inevitably a compromise of various requirements. It shared essentially the same engine as the Tiger I tank, it had better frontal armour, better gun penetration, was lighter overall, faster, and could handle rough terrain better than the Tigers.

The Achilles heel of the Panther was resultant trade off in the provision of weaker side armour which made the tank highly vulnerable to attack from any direction other than head on. Setting aside this glaring weakness the Panther still proved to be a fearsome adversary in open country especially in long range gunnery duels, but the Panther was extremely vulnerable in close-quarter combat. It should also be noted that the 75 mm

A close view of Close view of Zimmerit on the turret of a Panther in Italy in 1944. The coating was created by the German company Chemische Werke Zimmer AG.

gun fired a smaller shell than the Tiger's 88 mm gun, providing significantly less high explosive firepower against infantry and soft skinned targets.

The Panther was however far cheaper to produce than the Tiger tanks, and only slightly more expensive than the Panzer IV. The reason for this was unexpected outcome was that its production run coincided with the Reich Ministry of Armament and War Production's improved efforts to increase the efficient production of war materials. Nonetheless it cannot be stressed enough that key elements of the Panther design, such as its armour, transmission and final drive, were compromised and reductions in quality were made specifically to improve production rates and address Germany's requirement for numbers on the battlefield. Particularly with regard to the final drive, this was to prove a false economy.

Ironically other expensive and over engineered elements such as the Panther's complex suspension system remained. The net result of the various compromises was that some progress towards the achievement of the ambitious production goals was made and with 6000 machines being produced between 1943 and 1945 Panther tank production ran at a far higher rate than was possible for the Tiger tanks which saw only 1800 machines of both types produced between 1942 and 1945. It would appear on best estimates available however that the production run of 6000 Panthers was achieved at a very high opportunity cost. In all probability the Panther was created at the expense of some 20,000 Mark IV tanks which could otherwise have been built.

The main gun on the Panther was the 7.5 cm Rheinmetall-Borsig KwK 42 (L/70) with semi-automatic shell ejection and a supply of 79 rounds (82 on the Ausf. G). The main gun used three different types of ammunition: APCBC-HE (Pzgr. 39/42), HE (Sprgr. 42) and APCR (Pzgr. 40/42), the last of which was usually in short supply. While it was of only average calibre for its time, the Panther's gun was in fact one of the most powerful tank guns of World War II, this was due to the large propellant charge and the long barrel, which gave it a very high muzzle velocity and excellent armour-piercing qualities. The flat trajectory also made hitting targets much easier, since accuracy was less sensitive to range. The Panther's 75 mm gun had more penetrating power than the main gun of the Tiger I heavy tank, the 8.8 cm KwK 36 L/56, although the larger 88 mm projectile might inflict more damage if it did penetrate.

The tank typically had two MG 34 machine guns of a specific version designed for use in armoured combat vehicles featuring an armoured barrel sleeve. An MG 34 machine gun was located co-axially with the main gun on the gun mantlet; an identical MG 34 was located on the glacis plate and fired by the radio operator. Initial Ausf. D and early Ausf. A models used a "letterbox" flap opening, through which the machine gun was fired. In later Ausf A and all Ausf G models (starting in late November-early December 1943), a ball mount in the glacis plate with a K.Z.F.2 machine gun sight was installed for the hull machine gun.

The front of the turret was a curved 100 mm thick cast armour mantlet. Its transverse-cylindrical shape meant that it was more likely to deflect shells, but the lower section created a shot trap. If a non-penetrating hit bounced downwards off its lower section, it could penetrate the thin forward hull roof armour, and plunge down into the front hull compartment. Penetrations of this nature could have catastrophic results, since the compartment housed the driver and radio operator sitting along both sides of the massive gearbox and steering unit; more importantly, four magazines containing main gun ammunition were located between the driver/radio operator seats and the turret, directly underneath the gun mantlet when the turret was facing forward.

From September 1944, a slightly redesigned mantlet with a

The main armament of the Panther - a 75 mm KwK 42 (L/70), 1944.

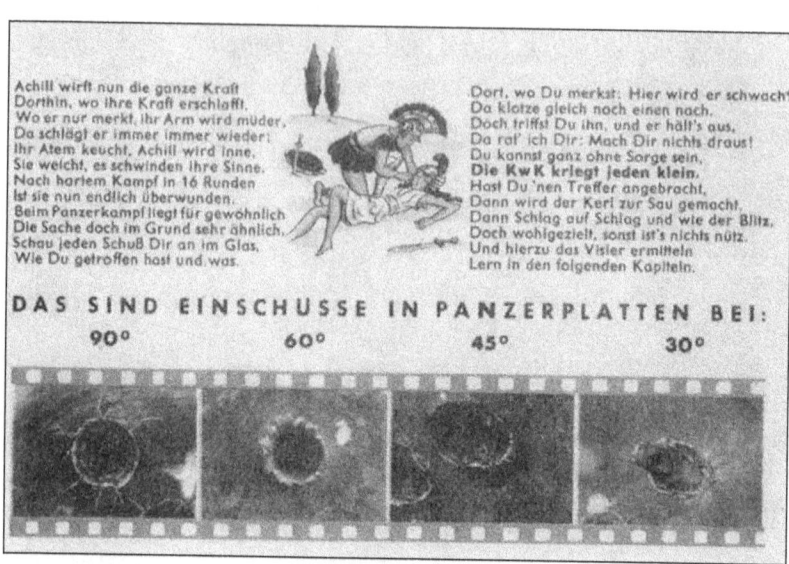

An important lesson from the Pantherfibel was the effect of the angle at which a shot struck the defensive plate.

flattened and much thicker lower "chin" design started to be fitted to Panther Ausf G models, the chin being intended to prevent such deflections. Conversion to the "chin" design was gradual, and Panthers continued to be produced to the end of the war with the rounded gun mantlet.

In most cases the Panther's gun mantlet could not be penetrated by the M4 Sherman's 75 mm gun, the T-34s 76.2 mm gun, or the T-34-85s 85 mm gun. But it could be penetrated by well-aimed shots at 100 m by the 76mm M1A1 gun used on certain models of the M4, at 500 m by the Soviet A-19 122 mm gun on the IS-2 and at over 2500 yards (2286 m) by the British Ordnance QF 17 pounder using APDS ammunition. The side turret armour of 45 mm (1.8 in) was vulnerable to penetration at long range by almost all Allied tank guns, including the M4's 75 mm gun which could penetrate it at 1,500 m (0.93 mi). These were the main reasons for continued work on a redesigned Panther turret, the Schmalturm.

The Ausf A model introduced a new cast armour commander's cupola, replacing the more difficult to manufacture forged cupola. It featured a steel hoop to which a third MG 34 or either the coaxial or the bow machine gun could be mounted for use in the anti-aircraft role, though it was rare for this to be used in actual combat situations.

The first Panthers (Ausf D) had a hydraulic motor that could traverse the turret at a maximum rate of one complete revolution in one minute, independent of engine speed. This slow speed was improved in the Ausf A model with a hydraulic traverse that varied with engine speed; one full turn taking 46 seconds at an engine speed of 1,000 rpm but only 15 seconds if the engine was running at 3,000 rpm. This arrangement was a slight weakness, as traversing the Panther's turret rapidly onto a target required close coordination between the gunner and driver who had to run the engine to maximum speed. By comparison, the turret of the M4 Sherman turret traversed at up to 360 degrees in 15 seconds and was independent of engine speed, which gave it an advantage over the Panther in close-quarters combat. As usual

Panther with regular mantlet.

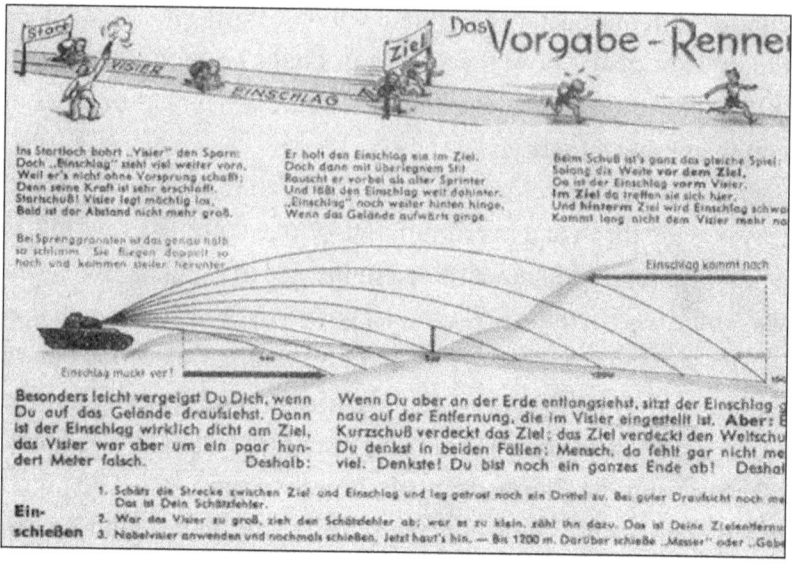

Advice on gunnery from the Pantherfibel.

for tanks of the period, a hand traverse wheel was provided for the Panther gunner to make fine adjustment of his aim.

Ammunition storage for the main gun was a weak point. All the ammunition for the main armament was stored in the hull, with a significant amount stored in the sponsons. In the Ausf D and A models, 18 rounds were stored next to the turret on each side, for a total of 36 rounds. In the Ausf G, which had deeper sponsons, 24 rounds were stored on each side of the turret, for a total of 48 rounds. In all models, 4 rounds were also stored in the left sponson between the driver and the turret. An additional 36 rounds were stored inside the hull of the Ausf D and A models - 27 in the forward hull compartment directly underneath the mantlet. In the Ausf G, the hull ammunition storage was reduced to 27 rounds total, with 18 rounds in the forward hull compartment. For all models, 3 rounds were kept under the turntable of the turret. The thin side armour could be penetrated at combat ranges by many Allied tank guns, and this meant that the Panther was vulnerable to catastrophic ammunition fires ("brewing up") if hit from the sides.

The loader was stationed in the right side of the turret. With the turret facing forward, he had access only to the right sponson and hull ammunition, and so these served as the main ready-ammunition bins.

Thanks to the Kwk 42 L/70 main gun The Panther offered a superb performance at longer ranges with excellent accuracy and a very high muzzle velocity which posed an extreme danger for every enemy tank. The tried and tested Panzer IV Ausf. G came on stream in April 1943 and although it was equipped with the less powerful KwK 40 L/48 main gun it nonetheless offered a similar battlefield performance to the Panther at shorter ranges and most importantly did not suffer from the appalling final drive issues which became the single major cause of breakdowns of the Panther tank, and which remained a problem throughout its service life.

The Panther was one of many German weapon systems with which Hitler became fixated. He placed a great deal of faith in his own assumption that the Panther could deliver a major

A Panther with a destroyed engine bay at the roadside in Normandy.

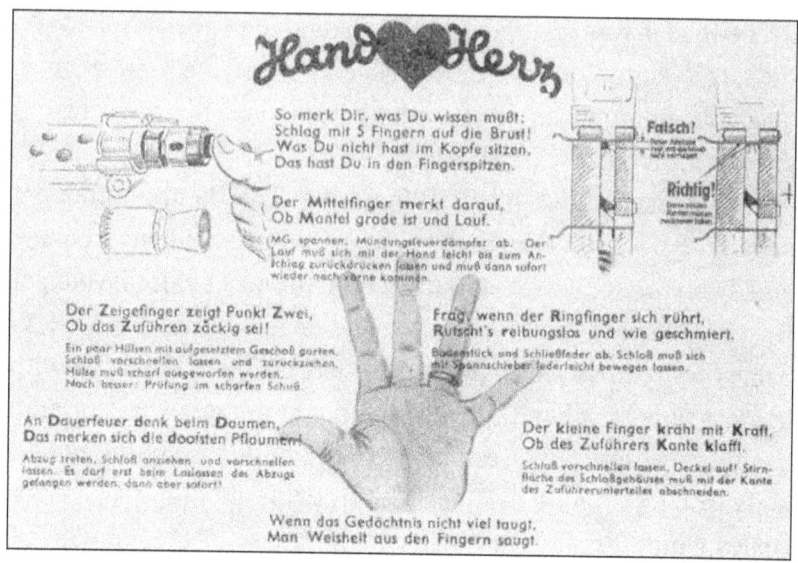

Advice on operating the machine gun in the Panther from the Pantherfibel.

contribution towards turning the course of the war in Russia. This high level of personal expectation, and the resulting pressure from the Fürher, led to the vehicles being rushed through the design process and into combat long before they were ready. The Panthers duly arrived on the battlefield in 1943 at a crucial phase in World War II for Germany and were rushed into combat at Kursk with a glaringly inefficient final drive system and before its obvious teething problems, including a porous fuel delivery system were corrected.

In the months that followed, to a limited extent, the most glaring difficulties were overcome. The Panther tank thereafter fought on outnumbered on the most important fronts as the German army steadily retreated before the Allies for the remainder of World War II. The faint possibility of the Panther proving a success as a battlefield weapon was drastically hampered by Germany's generally declining position in the war. The long logistical tail which supplied spare parts gradually dried up and major repairs became all but impossible to effect. With the loss of air cover more and more Panthers became victims of allied interdiction. The large poorly protected engine deck was particularly vulnerable to attack from above, and it has been estimated that 70% of Panthers were destroyed by aerial attack. As the war wore on towards a conclusion the desperate fuel situation led to many broken down Panthers, even those awaiting only minor repairs being destroyed. The pressure on training personnel and facilities allied to the declining quality of tank crews meant that the Panther, a tank which required the very best crews was often handled by novices and therefore faced a massive range of obstacles which could not be overcome.

It is a mark of the fighting qualities of the Panther that, despite all the factors ranged against it, this late introduction to the war, with its favourable combination of fire power and heavy frontal armour still drew accolades from the allies who fought against it. As a result of its high kill ratio in combat the Panther soon became feared and respected by the Allies, and regardless of its many short comings has become known to posterity one of the best all-round tanks of the war.

Panther wreckage Nortmandy at Kursk.

The Development Process

The Panther was a direct response to the lurking presence of the Soviet T-34 and KV-1 tanks which were first encountered on 23 June 1941. The T-34 was relatively easy to produce and was soon available in large numbers. The KV-1, although rarer, easily outclassed the existing Panzer III and IV of the Panzertruppen. At the insistence of General Heinz Guderian, a special Panzerkommision was dispatched to the Eastern Front to assess the T-34. Among the features of the Soviet tank which the Panzerkommision considered most significant were the sloping frontal armour, which gave much improved shot deflection and also increased the effective armour thickness against penetration, the wide tracks of the T-34 also provided excellent mobility over soft ground.

The 76.2 mm main gun of the T-34 in contrast to the short barrelled howitzer type of the Mark IV had a reasonably high muzzle velocity making for good armour penetration, furthermore it also fired an effective high explosive round. This type of main gun was therefore considered by the *Panzerkommision* to be the new minimum standard for the next generation of German tanks. However, it should be noted that the Germans already boasted a comparable main gun which was fitted to Mark IV F2 tanks from 1942 onwards. Other than the massive frontal armour of the Panther the Mark IV F2, although approaching the limits of the design, actually incorporated many of the features which the Panther was intended to deliver.

In November 1941, the decision to up-gun the Panzer IV to the 50 mm gun had been dropped, and instead Krupp was contracted in a joint development to modify Rheinmetall's pending 75 mm anti-tank gun design, later known as the PaK 40 L/46. As the recoil length was considered too long for PaK 40 to be mounted in the Mark IV turret, the recoil

This photograph showing shows the production of the wide tracks for the Panther, which as with the T-34, enabled the Panther to have improved mobility over soft ground.

mechanism and chamber had to be shortened in order that the weapon could serve as an effective *Kampfwagenkanone*. The conversion work was undertaken with the usual war time speed resulted in the new 75 mm KwK 40 L/43. This new tank gun, when firing an armour-piercing shot, achieved a dramatic rise in muzzle velocity was increased from 430 metres per second to 990 metres per second. Initially, the gun was mounted with a single-chamber, ball-shaped muzzle brake, which provided just under 50% of the recoil system's breaking ability. Firing the *Panzergranate* 39, the KwK 40 L/43 could penetrate 77 mm of steel armour at a range of 1,830 metres. This new *Kampfwagenkanone* was first introduced into the 1942 Panzer IV Ausf. F2 which was the equal of the T-34 in combat. A simple process of evolution and more efficient manufacturing programme could therefore have provided the hard pressed *Panzerwaffe* in 1942 with a large volume of tried and tested machines. In reality much needed resources were diverted to

Some graphic advice on how essential maintenance could avoid breakdowns from the Pantherfibel.

the Panther programme which did not bear fruit until 1944.

On 1st March 1943 Guderian, who had spent the previous year in the wilderness, was rehabilitated and appointed Inspector-General of the armoured Troops. His responsibilities were to determine armoured strategy and to oversee tank design and production and the training of Germany's panzer forces. According to Guderian, Hitler was far too easily persuaded to field a surfeit of new tank and tank destroyer designs, this resulted in unnecessary supply, logistical, and repair problems for the German forces in Russia. Guderian preferred the simple expedient of fielding large numbers of Panzer IIIs and Panzer IVs over smaller numbers of heavier tanks like the Panther which had limited range and required its own logistical channel of Panther spares. Guderian famously summed up these frustrations with the remark that *"logistics are the ball and chain of the tank forces"*.

The importance of an adequate supply of spare parts is often over looked when armoured affairs are considered, but without replacement parts tank formations soon grind to a halt. As Guderian was all too aware, the decision to deploy the Panther alongside the Mark III, IV and Tiger I added a real logistical headache. The introduction of the Panther meant that a system for the supply of an entire new set of spare parts had to be set up and drawn along a 2000 mile supply line as opposed to simply utilising the existing chain which provided Mark IV spares.

Despite the fact that, in Guderian's view, by utilising the existing Mark III and IV an acceptable battlefield solution lay within the grasp of the *Panzertruppen*, it was to prove fortunate that the Panther with the new longer barrelled L/70 was already under development. Had the tank not been a pet project enjoying Hitler's blessing, Guderian may well have prevailed in his desire to limit the number of German tank models. However, as a result of the inevitable evolution which was taking place on the battlefield, the presence of the Panther with its heavy hitting punch would soon be required and welcomed. The Russian T-34 equipped with an 85mm gun first appeared in late1942. This up-gunned version of the T-34 was known to the Germans as the T-43 and it began to appear in large numbers during 1943.

The race towards producing tanks with a larger main gun was all about achieving increased muzzle velocity; the speed a projectile achieves at the moment it leaves the muzzle of the gun. Longer barrels give the propellant force more time to develop the speed of the shell before it leaves the barrel. For this reason longer barrels generally provided higher velocities and hence more penetrating power. During World War II the constant introduction of faster burning propellant, improved shells and longer barrel length led to constantly enhanced armour piercing capabilities on both sides.

Providing the antidote to the T-43 and T-43 required the introduction of a tank equipped with ideally the 8.8 cm KwK 36 L/56 of the Tiger I or alternatively the long barrelled 7.5 cm L/70.

There was no prospect of fitting either *Kampfwagenkanone* into the turret of the Mark IV. It was fortunate therefore that, driven on by Hitler's mania for radical new solutions, in late November 1941 Daimler-Benz (DB) and Maschinenfabrik Augsburg-Nürnberg AG (MAN) were each given the task of designing a completely new 30- to 35-ton tank. This development machine was designated VK30.02 and was required to was to be ready by April 1942 in time to be shown to Hitler for his birthday.

The Daimler Benz design imitated the T-34 almost completely. It closely resembled the T-34 in both hull and turret form and therefore posed obvious problems concerning battlefield recognition. Unusually for a German design it also incorporated a rear sprocket drive. The initial road wheel arrangement was also visually similar to that of the T-34 although Daimler's design initially used a leaf spring suspension whereas the T-34 incorporated coil springs. The Daimler Benz turret was smaller than that of the MAN design and had a smaller turret ring which was the result of the narrower hull required by the leaf spring suspension which lay outside of hull. The main advantages of the leaf springs over a torsion bar suspension were a lower hull silhouette and a simpler shock damping design. Unlike the T-34, the Daimler Benz design had the advantage of a three-man turret crew comprising commander, gunner, and loader whereas the T-34 turret initially allowed for only the commander and gunner. The planned L/70 75 mm gun was much longer and heavier than the L/43 and mounting it in the Daimler-Benz turret was difficult. Active consideration was given to reducing the turret crew to two men to address this problem but this retrograde step was eventually dropped.

The MAN design for the Panther embodied more conventional German thinking with the transmission and drive sprocket in the front and a turret placed centrally on the hull. One of the main design flaws of the Tiger lay in the low positioning of the

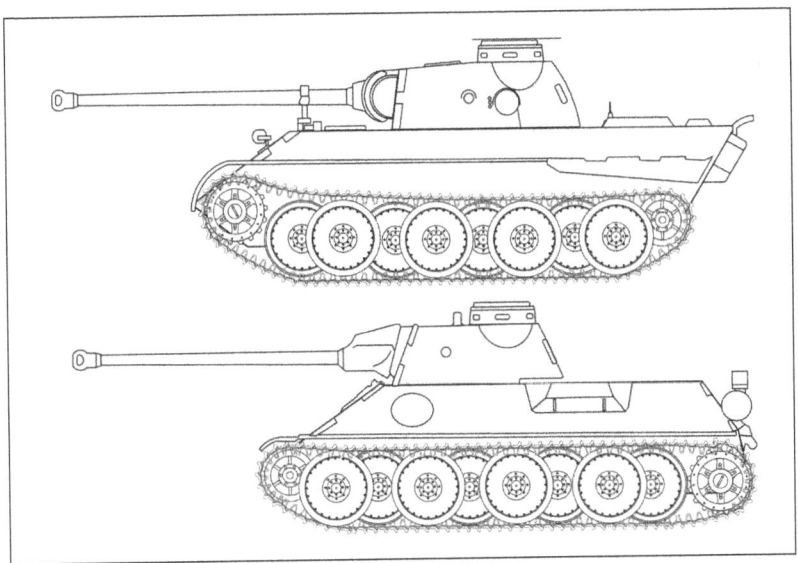

The VK30.02 prototype proposed by MAN (upper) seen alongside the alternative design proposed by Daimler-Benz (lower).

front sprocket which made obstacle crossing less efficient. The design for the Panther eliminated this draw back by situating the front drive sprockets much higher than the road wheels making obstacle crossing more efficient and improving cross country performance in muddy conditions.

The MAN design for the Panther incorporated a Maybach petrol engine and eight torsion-bar suspension axles per side. Because of the torsion bar suspension and the drive shaft running under the turret basket, the MAN Panther needed to be higher and had a wider hull than the Daimler Benz design. The MAN Panther incorporated the "slack-track" Christie-style pattern of large road wheels with no return rollers for the upper run of track. Like the Tiger the main road wheels were interleaved but were arranged in just two rows eliminating the worst aspects of the Tiger I design.

The two designs were reviewed over a period from January through March 1942. Following a significant programme of development in which the running gear of the Daimler

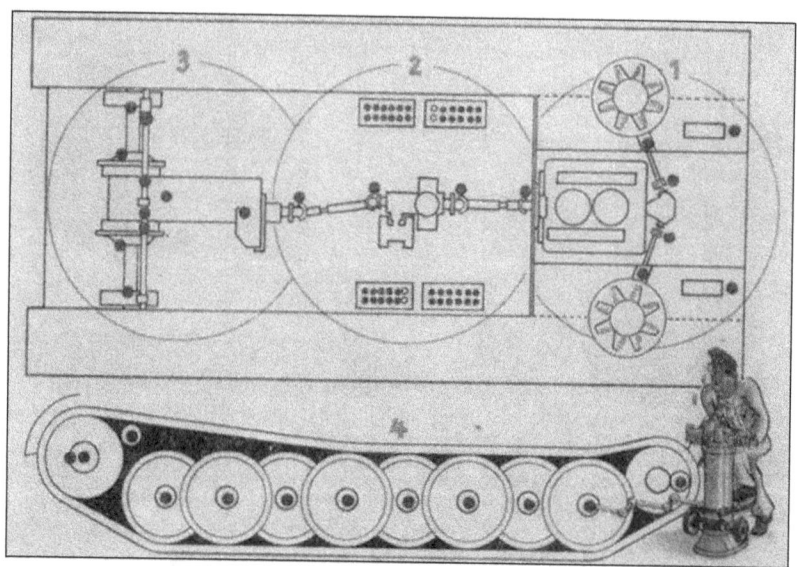

The complex drive arrangement of the Panther as shown in the Pantherfibel.

Benz design was altered to match that of the MAN design Reichminister Todt, and later, his replacement Albert Speer, both recommended the Daimler Benz design to Hitler because of its several advantages over the initial MAN design.

However, by the final submission, MAN had substantially improved their design, having incorporated the best elements of Daimler Benz proposal. A final review by a special commission appointed by Hitler in May 1942 belatedly settled on the MAN design. Hitler approved this decision after reviewing it overnight. One of the principal reasons given for this decision was that the MAN design used an existing turret designed by Rheinmetall-Borsig, while the Daimler Benz design would have required the tooling a brand new turret to be designed and produced which would have significantly delayed the commencement of production.

Albert Speer recalled the trials and tribulations concerning the development of the Panther in his autobiography *Inside the Third Reich*. It produces a primary insight into Hitler's hands on involvement in the Panther design process.

"Since the Tiger had originally been designed to weigh fifty tons but as a result of Hitler's demands had gone up to seventy five tons, we decided to develop a new thirty ton tank whose very name, Panther, was to signify greater agility. Though light in weight, its motor was to be the same as the Tiger's, which meant it could develop superior speed. But in the course of a year Hitler once again insisted on clapping so much armour on it, as well as larger guns, that it ultimately reached forty eight tons, the original weight of the Tiger."

The Panther In Production

The MAN design had better fording ability, easier gun servicing and higher mobility due to better suspension, wider tracks, and a bigger fuel tank. A mild steel prototype of the Panther was produced by September 1942 and, after testing at Kummersdorf, was officially accepted. It was ordered to be placed into immediate production. The start of production was delayed, however, mainly because there were too few specialized machine tools needed for the machining of the hull. Finished tanks were produced in December and suffered from reliability problems as a result of this haste. The demand for this tank was so high that the manufacturing was soon expanded beyond MAN to include Daimler-Benz, Maschinenfabrik Niedersachsen-Hannover (MNH) and Henschel & Sohn in Kassel.

The initial production target was 250 tanks per month at MAN. This ambitious output target was increased to 600 per month in January 1943. Despite the maximum effort by the German war industry, including the use of slave labour, this figure was never

A Panther tank production line.

reached. This was primarily as a result of disruption by Allied bombing, manufacturing bottlenecks, and other difficulties although it is possible that the target was simply too ambitious to be achieved even under favourable circumstances.

The use of slave labour in the complex production and logistical system which produced the Panther should not be overlooked. During the course of World War II the Germans abducted approximately 12 million people from almost twenty European countries; about two thirds of whom came from the Eastern Europe. These forced labourers provided the bulk of the labour in many of the German firms who supplied components and munitions for the Panther programme. Many of these workers died as a result of their inhuman living conditions, mistreatment, malnutrition, or exhaustion and so became civilian casualties of war. At its peak the forced labourers comprised 20% of the German work force. Counting deaths and turnover, about 15 million men and women were forced labourers at one point or another during the war.

It was by resorting to such measures that Panther production was maintained at any level but the projected figure of 600 per month remained a pipe dream. In 1943 production averaged 148 per month. In 1944, it averaged out at 315 a month with 3,777 machines being built in that year. Panther production peaked at 380 in July 1944 and ended around the end of March 1945, by which time at least 6,000 built in total. Front-line combat strength peaked on 1st September 1944 at 2,304 tanks, but that same month a record number of 692 Panther tanks were reported lost.

Both the Tiger and the Panther used Maybach engines so it was no surprise that Allied air forces were soon targeting the Maybach engine plant. This plant was first bombed the night of 27/28th April 1944 and the attack was so severe and accurate that production was completely shut down for five months.

Unlike the risqué illustrations in the Tigerfibel the young ladies in the Pantherfibel were all depicted with clothes on.

Fortunately for the *Panzerwaffe* this exigency had already been anticipated and a second plant had already been planned, the Auto-Union plant at Siegmar, and this came online in May 1944 ensuring continuity of supply.

Targeting of the factories which produced the Panther itself began with a bombing raid on the Daimler Benz plant on 6th August 1944, a follow up raid took place on the night of 23/24th August 1944. MAN was first struck on 10th September then again in rapid succession on 3rd October and 19th October 1944. Despite these attacks however, production was soon resumed at MAN and the allied air forces returned to the fray on 3rd January 1945 and finally on 20/21st February 1945. The MNH was not attacked until very late in the war and was not targeted until 14th March. There was one final raid on 28th March 1945.

In addition to interfering with tank production goals, the bombing forced a steep drop in the production of spare parts. Spare parts as a percentage of tank production dropped from 25–30 per cent in 1943, to 8 per cent in the fall of 1944. This only compounded the problems with reliability and numbers of operational Panthers, as tanks in the field had to be cannibalized for parts.

PRODUCTION FIGURES

The Panther was the third most numerous German armoured fighting vehicle.

Production by type			
Model	Number	Date	Notes
Prototype	2	11/42	Designated V1 and V2
Ausf. D	842	1/43 to 9/43	
Ausf. A	2,192	8/43 to 6/44	Sometimes called Ausf. A2
Ausf. G	2,953	3/44 to 4/45	
Befehlspanzer Panther	329	5/43 to 2/45	Converted
Beobachtungspanzer Panther	41	44 to 45	Converted
Bergepanther	347	43 to 45	

Panther production in 1944 by manufacturer	
Manufacturer	% of total
Maschinenfabrik Augsburg-Nürnberg (M.A.N.)	35%
Daimler-Benz	31%
Maschinenfabrik Niedersachsen-Hannover	31%
Other	3%

The Panther In Combat

Panthers were first supplied to form Panzer Abteilung 51 (tank Battalion 51) on 9 January, and then Pz.Abt. 52 on 6 February 1943.

The first production Panther tanks were plagued with mechanical problems. The engine was dangerously prone to overheating and suffered from connecting rod or bearing failures. Gasoline leaks from the fuel pump or carburettor, as well as motor oil leaks from gaskets easily produced fires in the engine compartment; several Panthers were destroyed in such fires. Transmission and final drive breakdowns were the most common and difficult to repair. A large list of other problems were detected in these early Panthers, and so from April through May 1943 all Panthers were shipped to Falkensee and Nuremburg for a major rebuilding program. This did not correct all of the problems, so a second program was started at Grafenwoehr and Erlangen in June 1943.

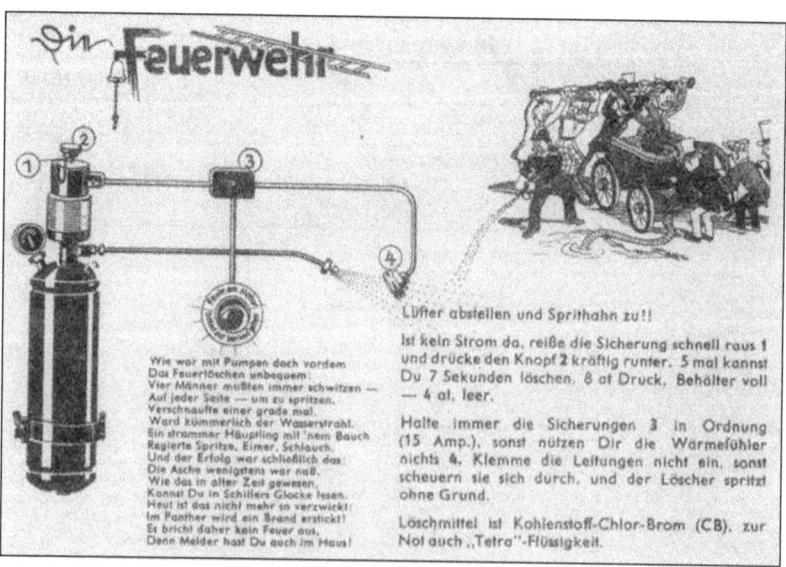

Fire was a constant threat to the Panther and in the Pantherfibel a strong emphasis was placed on fire fighting measures.

Panther tanks move into formation during Operation Citadel. These machines were part of the initial run of 200 tanks deployed in July 1943.

PANTHER ON THE EASTERN FRONT

The Panther tank was viewed by Hitler as an essential component of the forthcoming Operation Zitadelle, and on his orders the attack was delayed several times because of the mechanical problems which were still being encountered. The eventual start date of the battle was delayed as long as possible and commenced only six days after the last of the 200 Panthers had been delivered to the front. This hurriedness resulted in major problems in Panther units during the Battle of Kursk, as in addition to all of the other problems, tactical training at the unit level, co-ordination by radio, and driver training were all seriously deficient.

It was not until 29th June, 1943, that the last of a total of 200 rebuilt Panthers were finally issued to Panther Regiment von Lauchert, of the XLVIII Panzer Corps (4 Panzer Army). Two were immediately lost due to motor fires upon disembarking from the trains. By 5th July, when the Battle of Kursk started, there were only 184 operational Panthers. Within two days, this total had dropped to just 40. On 17th July 1943 after Hitler had

A Panther is left destroyed after the Battle of Kursk.

ordered a stop to the German offensive, Gen. Heinz Guderian sent in the following preliminary assessment of the Panthers:

"Due to enemy action and mechanical breakdowns, the combat strength sank rapidly during the first few days. By the evening of 10 July there were only 10 operational Panthers in the front line. 25 Panthers had been lost as total write offs (23 were hit and burnt and two had caught fire during the approach march). 100 Panthers were in need of repair (56 were damaged by hits and mines and 44 by mechanical breakdown). 60 percent of the mechanical breakdowns could be easily repaired. Approximately 40 Panthers had already been repaired and were on the way to the front. About 25 still had not been recovered by the repair service. On the evening of 1th July, 38 Panthers were operational, 31 were total write offs and 131 were in need of repair. A slow increase in the combat strength is observable. The large number of losses by hits (81 Panthers up to 10th July) attests to the heavy fighting."

During Zitadelle the Panthers claimed a total 267 destroyed Soviet tanks. Given the circumstances this was a remarkable achievement and pointed towards the fact that under the right circumstances this was could have been a very impressive design indeed.

A later report on 20th July 20, 1943 showed 41 Panthers as operational, 85 as repairable, 16 severely damaged and needing repair in Germany, 56 burnt out (due to enemy action), and 2 that had been completely destroyed by motor fires at the railhead.

Even before the Germans ended their offensive at Kursk, the Soviets began their counteroffensive and succeeded in pushing the Germans back into a steady retreat. As a result of the headlong withdrawal many Panthers could not be recovered and had to be left on the battlefield This was to lead to a drastic decline in operational numbers and a report 11th August 1943 showed that the numbers of total write offs in the Panther force swelled to 156, with only 9 operational. The German Army was forced into a fighting retreat and increasingly lost Panthers in combat as well as from abandoning and destroying damaged vehicles.

The Panther demonstrated its capacity to destroy any Soviet tank from long distance during the Battle of Kursk, and had a very

A Panther photographed on the Eastern Front in 1944.

Panther tanks of the Großdeutschland Division advance in the area of Iaşi, Romania in 1944.

high overall kill ratio. However, it comprised less than seven per cent of the estimated 2,400–2,700 total tanks deployed by the Germans in this battle, and its effectiveness was limited by its mechanical problems and the in-depth layered defence system of the Soviets at Kursk. Ironically the greatest contribution to this titanic battle may have been a highly negative one. Hitler's decisions to delay the original start of Operation Zitadelle for a total of two months was at least partially due to his desire to see the panther in action. The precious extra time was used by the Soviets to build up an enormous concentration of minefields, anti-tank guns, trenches and artillery defences which ultimately thwarted the German ambitions.

After the losses of the Battle of Kursk, the German Army was forced into a constant state of retreat before the advancing Red Army. The numbers of Panthers were slowly re-built on the Eastern Front, and the operational percentage increased as its reliability was improved. In March 1944, Guderian reported: *"Almost all the bugs have been worked out"*. Despite his bold words many units continued to report significant mechanical problems, especially with the final drive. There undoubtedly were some real advances in reliability and the greatly outnumbered Panthers for the remainder of the war were used as mobile reserves to fight off major attacks.

NEW HEAVY TANK: THE Pz. Kw. 5 (PANTHER)
INTELLIGENCE BULLETIN, JANUARY 1944

When the Pz. Kw. 6 (Tiger) became standard, the Pz. Kw. 5 (Panther) was still in an experimental stage. Now that the Panther has joined the German tank series as a standard model, a general description of this newest "land battleship" can be made available to U.S. military personnel. Much of the data presented here comes from Russian sources, inasmuch as the Pz. Kw. 5 has thus far been used only on the Eastern Front.

The Panther is a fast, heavy, well-armoured vehicle. It mounts a long 75-mm gun. Weighing 45 tons, the new tank appears to be of a type intermediate between the 22-ton Pz. Kw. 4 and the 56-ton Pz. Kw. 6. The Panther has a speed of about 31 miles per hour. It corresponds roughly to our General Sherman, which the Germans have always greatly admired. It is believed that the 75-mm gun is the Kw.K.. This tank gun is a straight-bore weapon with a muzzle brake, and has an over-all length of 18 feet 2 inches.

Although equipped with the same motor as the Tiger, the Panther has lighter armour and armament. For this reason it is capable of higher speed and greater maneuverability. The Panther is also provided with additional armour plate, 4- to 6-mm thick, (not shown in fig. 1) along the side, just above the suspension wheels and the sloping side armour plate.

When a flexible tube with a float is attached to the air intake, the Panther has no difficulty in fording fairly deep streams. There is a special fitting in the top of the tank for attaching this tube.

Like the Pz. Kw. 6's, the Pz. Kw. 5's are organized into separate tank battalions. During the summer of 1943, the Germans used many of these new tanks on the Russian front.

Although the Russians have found the Pz. Kw. 5 more manoeuvrable than the Pz. Kw. 6, they are convinced that the new tank is more easily knocked out. Fire from all types of rifles and machine guns directed against the peep holes, periscopes, and the base of the turret and gun shield will blind or jam the parts, the Russians say. High explosives and armour-piercing shells of 54-mm (2.12 inches) calibre, or higher are effective against the turret at ranges of 875 yards or less. Large-calibre artillery and self-propelled cannon can put the Panther out of action at ordinary distances for effective fire. The vertical and sloping plates can be penetrated by armour-piercing shells of 45-mm (1.78 inches) calibre, or higher. Incendiary armour-piercing shells are said to be especially effective, not only against the gasoline tanks, but against the ammunition, which is located just to the rear of the driver.

The additional armour plate above the suspension wheels is provided to reduce the penetration of hollow-charge shells. According to the Russians, it is ineffective; antitank grenades, antitank mines, and Molotov cocktails are reported to be effective against the weak top and bottom plates and the cooling and ventilating openings on top of the tank, just above the motor.

However, it should definitely be stated that the Pz. Kw. 5 is a formidable weapon—a distinct asset of the German Army.

1. With certain alterations the Pz. Kw. 6 may weigh as much as 62 tons. For an illustrated discussion of the Pz. Kw. 6, see Intelligence Bulletin, Vol. I, No. 10, pp. 19-23.

2. Kampfwagenkanone-tank gun.

***

The highest total number of operational Panthers on the

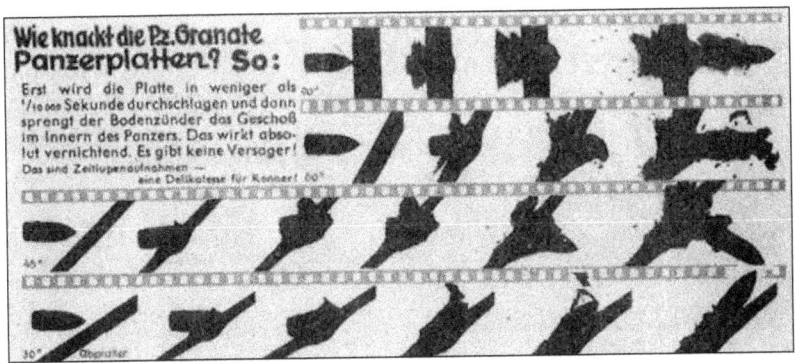

The missile defeating qualities of sloped armour is graphically demonstrated in this page from the Pantherfibel.

Eastern Front was achieved in September 1944, when some 522 were listed as operational out of a total of 728 machines. Throughout the rest of the war, Germany continued to deploy the majority of available Panther forces on the Eastern Front. The last recorded status, on 15th March 1945, listed 740 Panthers on the Eastern Front with 361 operational. By this time the end was in sight as the Red Army had already entered East Prussia and was advancing through Poland.

In August 1944 Panthers were deployed in Warsaw during the uprising as a mobile artillery and troops support. At least two of them were captured in the early days of the conflict and used in actions against Germans, including the liberation of Gęsiówka concentration camp on 5th August, when the soldiers of "Wacek" platoon used the captured Panther (named "Magda") to destroy the bunkers and watchtowers of the camp. Most of the Germans in the camp were killed; insurgents had lost two people and liberated almost 350 people. After several days they were immobilized due to the lack of fuel and batteries and were set ablaze to prevent them from being re-captured by the German forces.

The organisation of Panther battalions varied but an optimal organisation is set out below. In practice the number of operational machines was never achieved.

- Battalion Command
  (Composed of Communication and Reconnaissance platoons)
- Communication Platoon -
  3 × *Befehlswagen* Panther SdKfz.267/268
- Reconnaissance Platoon - 5 × Panther
- 1st Company - 22 × Panther
   Company Command - 2 × Panther
      1st Platoon - 5 × Panther
      2nd Platoon - 5 × Panther
      3rd Platoon - 5 × Panther
      4th Platoon - 5 × Panther
- 2nd Company - 22 × Panther (composed as 1st Company)
- 3rd Company - 22 × Panther (composed as 1st Company)
- 4th Company - 22 × Panther (composed as 1st Company)
- Service Platoon - 2 × *Bergepanther* SdKfz.179

From 3rd August 1944, the new Panzer-Division 44 organisation called for a Panzer division to consist of one Panzer regiment with two Panzer battalions – one of 96 Panzer IVs and one of 96 Panthers. Actual strengths tended to differ, and in reality were far lower after combat losses were taken into account.

The Panzer Mark V seen here in combat accompanied by infantry support.

Panthers in a French village, Summer 1944.

PANTHERS IN COMBAT ON THE WESTERN FRONT - FRANCE

At the time of the invasion of Normandy, there were initially only two Panther-equipped Panzer regiments on the entire Western Front, they fielded a total of 156 Panthers. From June through August 1944, an additional seven Panther regiments were sent into France, reaching a maximum strength of 432 in a status report dated 30th July, 1944.

The majority of German panzer forces in Normandy – six and a half divisions, were stationed around the vital town of Caen facing the Anglo-Canadian forces of the 21st Army Group; and the numerous battles to secure the town became collectively known as the Battle of Caen. While there were sectors of heavy bocage around Caen, there were also many open fields over which the Allied armour had to attack. This allowed the Panther to play to its strengths and engage the attacking enemy armour at long range. By the time of the Normandy Campaign however, British Divisional Anti-tank Regiments were well equipped with the excellent 17 pounder gun (the 17pdr also replaced the US gun on some M10 tank Destroyers in British

Panther in bocage, Summer 1944.

service), making it equally as perilous for the Panthers to launch attacks across these same killing fields. The British had begun converting regular M4 Shermans to carry the 17 pounder gun (nicknamed Firefly) prior to the D-day landings, and while limited numbers meant that during Normandy not more than one Sherman in four was of the Firefly variant, the lethality of its gun against German armour made them priority targets for German gunners.

US forces in the meantime, facing one and a half German panzer divisions, mainly the Panzer Lehr Division, struggled in the heavy, low-lying bocage terrain west of Caen. Against the M4 Shermans of the Allied tank forces during this time, the Panther tank again proved to be most effective when fighting in open country and firing at long range - its combination of superior armour and firepower allowed it to engage at distances from which the Shermans could not respond. However, the Panther struggled in the enclosed bocage country of Normandy, and was vulnerable to side and close-in attacks in the built-up areas of cities and small towns. The commander of the Panzer Lehr Division, Gen. Fritz Bayerlein, reported the weaknesses of the Panther tank in the fighting in Normandy in a very damning report:

"While the PzKpfw IV could still be used to advantage, the PzKpfw V [Panther] proved ill adapted to the terrain. The Sherman because of its manoeuvrability and height was good... [the Panther was] poorly suited for hedgerow terrain because of its width. Long gun barrel and width of tank reduce manoeuvrability in village and forest fighting. It is very front-heavy and therefore quickly wears out the front final drives, made of low-grade steel. High silhouette. Very sensitive power-train requiring well-trained drivers. Weak side armour; tank top vulnerable to fighter-bombers. Fuel lines of porous material that allow gasoline fumes to escape into the tank interior causing a grave fire hazard. Absence of vision slits makes defence against close attack impossible."

Through September and October, a series of new Panzerbrigades equipped with Panther tanks were sent into France to try to stop the Allied advance with counterattacks.

A pair of Panthers rendered useless after they have been knocked-out and left at the roadside, Normandy, Summer 1944.

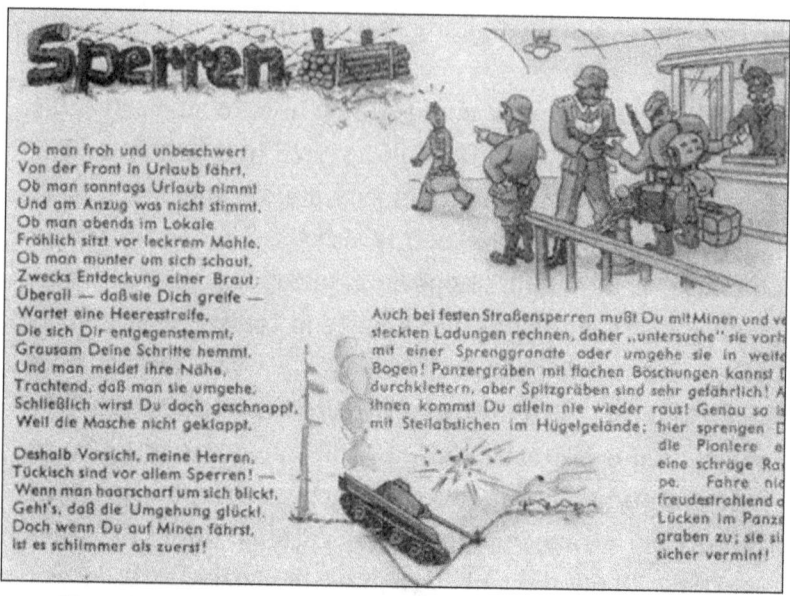

The subject of how to avoid anti-tank defences was an important consideration and was represented graphically in the Pantherfibel.

This culminated in the Battle of Arracourt (September 18–29, 1944), in which the mostly Panther equipped German forces suffered heavy losses fighting against the 4th armoured Division of Patton's 3rd Army, which were still primarily equipped with 75 mm M4 Sherman tanks and yet came away from the battle with only a few losses. The Panther units were newly formed, poorly trained, and tactically disorganized; most units ended up stumbling into ambush situations against seasoned U.S. tank crews.

WESTERN FRONT - ARDENNES OFFENSIVE

A status report on 15th December, 1944 listed a record high of 471 Panthers deployed the Western Front, with 336 operational accounting for a healthy 71 per cent of the available force. This was one day before the start of the Battle of the Bulge; 400 of the tanks assigned to the Western Front were in units detailed for the offensive.

During the Battle Of The Bulge The Panther once again

demonstrated its prowess in open country, where it could destroy its victims at long range with near-impunity. The reverse side of the coin was once again in evidence as the vulnerability of the Panther in the close-in fighting of the small towns of the Ardennes, was cruelly exposed and there were consequently very heavy losses. A status report on January 15, 1945 showed only 97 operational Panthers left in the units involved in the operation, out of 282 still in their possession. Total write-offs were listed as 198.

The Operation Greif commando mission included five Panthers assigned to Panzerbrigade 150, disguised to look like M10 tank Destroyers by welding on additional plates, applying US-style camouflage paint and markings. This was carried out as part of a larger operation that involved soldiers disguised as Americans and other activities. The disguised Panthers were detected and destroyed and their story was reported in the US intelligence magazine *Tactical and Technical Trends* No. 57, April 1945.

A burnt out Panther Ausf. G at the Battle of the Bulge, which has been penetrated in the sponson.

Panther disguised as an M10 Tank Destroyer.

GERMANS DISGUISE PANTHERS CLEVERLY IMITATE M10 GUN CARRIAGE
Tactical and Technical Trends No. 57, April 1945.

Investigation of four German Panther tanks knocked out in the Malmedy area in the December breakthrough in Belgium revealed that the tanks were carefully and cleverly disguised as U.S. M10 gun motor carriages.

After inspecting the tanks and realizing the amount of time, work, and materials involved in order to imitate the appearance of the M10, Ordnance intelligence investigators expressed the opinion that these disguised tanks, used in the proper tactical situation and at the proper time, would have caused considerable damage.

Because the false vehicle numbers of the tanks knocked out were B-4, B-5, B-7, and B-10, investigators concluded that at least ten similarly disguised tanks might have been in action.

Inside the one tank which was not blown up too badly to be inspected were found items of U.S. clothing such as a helmet, overcoat, and leggings. To heighten the deception, U.S. stars were painted on both sides and also on the top of the turret, the entire tank was painted O.D., and U.S. unit markings were painted on the false bow and rear.

In disguising the Panther the distinctive cupola was removed from the turret and two semicircular hatch covers were hinged in its place to the turret top in order to cover the opening. In addition, it was necessary to remove extra water cans, gas cans, the rammer staff container, and other external accessories.

The tank then was camouflaged or disguised with sheet metal, that used on the turret and upper bow being three twenty-seconds of an inch thick and that on time sides of the hull being nine sixty-fourths of an inch thick. The lower part of the false

Top view of Panther tank disguised as U.S. M10 gun carriage, showing hatch covers used in place of cupola.

Left front view with turret reversed. Note false final-drive housing at bottom of bow and false side apron.

Front view showing plate over machine-gun opening, false lifting rings and brackets, and markings.

bow was thicker, possibly made of double plates. To accomplish the deceptive modifications, which pointed to at least fourth or fifth echelon alterations, the work probably was done by maintenance units rather than at a factory. The work probably was divided into four sections: turret, bow, rear, and sides.

TURRET CHANGES

The turret was disguised by using five pieces of sheet metal, two of which were cut to resemble the distinctive sides of the M10 turret and then were flanged on the edges, bent to shape, and stiffened with small angle iron. The gun shield was carefully formed from another sheet to the exact shape of the M10 shield, and a hole was made to the right of the gun hole in the shield for the co-axial M.G. 34, a hole which does not exist in the M10 shield. Two pieces of sheet metal made up the rear of the turret, one representing the bottom slant surface of the rear and one representing the counterweight. The pieces representing the sides and rear were joined together and braced with angle iron, and the whole was attached to the turret. The false gun shield was attached to the Panther gun shield, and all the lifting rings, brackets, extra-armour studs, etc., found on the M10 turret were carefully duplicated and welded to the false turret.

FALSE BOW

Approximately four pieces of sheet metal, shaped to imitate as closely as possible the contours of the M10 bow, made up the false bow, necessary because the Panther bow is bulkier than the M10. The false bottom was shaped to give the characteristic appearance of the front drive sprocket housing of the M10, and the top was shaped carefully and various component pieces attached to the front of the tank. All the brackets, lifting rings, towing devises, etc., of the M10 bow were also imitated. A square opening was cut in the false bow to permit the use of the bow M.G. 34, but a removable cover attached with a small chain was made for this opening.

Rear view showing false tail plate. Note exhausts and dummy fittings.

FALSE REAR AND SIDES

The false rear was made of sheet metal. It was a faithful duplicate of the M10 rear except for two holes to permit the twin exhaust elbows of the Panther to protrude.

An attempt was made to imitate the skirting armour of the M10 which appears to hang lower than the side armour of the Panther and is bevelled in at the bottom. A long flat strip of sheet metal was attached to the sides parallel to the ground, and a vertical sheet strip was attached at right angles to this strip to give the appearance of low skirting armour.

Features which aid in recognizing disguised Panthers and which cannot be camouflaged easily are:

- The distinctive Panther bogie suspension. (The M18 motor gun carriage now has a somewhat similar suspension.)
- The muzzle brake on the 7.5 cm Kw.K. 42.
- The wide and distinctive track of the Panther tank.

***

In February 1945, eight Panzer divisions with a total of 271 Panthers were transferred from the West to the Eastern Front. Only five Panther battalions remained in the west.

One of the top German Panther commanders was SS-*Oberscharführer* Ernst Barkmann of the 2nd SS-Panzer Regiment "*Das Reich*". By the end of the war, he had some 80 tank kills claimed.

Building The Panther

The cost of a Panther tank was 117,100 Reichmarks (RM). This compared favourably with 82,500 RM for the StuG III, 96,163 RM for the Panzer III, 103,462 RM for the Panzer IV, and 250,800 RM for the Tiger I. These figures did not include the cost of the armament and radio. Expressed in terms of Reichmarks per ton the Panther tank was arguably one of the most cost-effective German tanks of World War II. However, these cost figures should be understood in the context of the time period in which the various tanks were first designed, as the Germans armaments industry increasingly strove for designs and production methods that would allow for higher production rates, and thereby steadily reduced the cost of their tanks.

The process of streamlining the production of German tanks first began after Speer became Reichminister in early 1942, and steadily accelerated through 1943 reaching a peak in 1944; production of the Panther tank therefore coincided with this period of increased manufacturing efficiency.

In the pre-war era German tank manufacturers relied heavily on a large pool of skilled and willing workers. Even after the outbreak of World War II the armaments industry continued to utilize heavily labour-intensive and costly manufacturing methods unsuited to mass production. Under the influence of

Albert Speer the increasing use of forced labour and increased production efficiencies led to a jump in output; although it should be noted that, even with streamlined production methods and slave labour, Germany could not hope to approach the efficiency of Allied manufacturing during World War II.

Initial production Panthers had a face-hardened frontal armour which formed the glacis plate the benefits of face-hardening was that it caused uncapped rounds to shatter, but as capped armour-piercing capped rounds became the standard in all armies this expensive and difficult process was no longer relevant and the requirement was deleted on 30th March1943. By August 1943, Panthers were being built only with a homogeneous steel glacis plate which helped to bring down costs and speed up production.

Although the front hull of the panther boasted only 80 mm of armour as opposed to the 100m of the Tiger I, the fact that the armour sloped back at 55 degrees from the vertical, gave it additional advantages and effectively produced the same benefits as the thicker Tiger armour. In addition the front glacis plates were welded and interlocked for additional strength. The combination of a steep slope and thick armour meant that few Allied or Soviet weapons could hope to penetrate the Panther frontally other than at very close ranges.

It was an altogether different matter with regard to the side armour. In order to acheive the weight savings which allowed the Panther to function at all the armour for the side hull and superstructure however was much thinner at just 40–50 mm. The thinner side armour was essential to keep the overall weight within reasonable bounds, but it made the Panther extremely vulnerable to attacks from the side at relatively long ranges by most Allied and Soviet tank and anti-tank guns. German tactical doctrine for the use of the Panther thus emphasized the importance of flank protection. Five millimetre thick skirt armour, known as Schürzen, was fitted to the sides of

Panther with track segments hung on the turret sides to augment the armour, 1944.

the Panthers. This flimsy addition was intended to provide protection for the lower side hull from Soviet anti-tank rifle fire and was fixed on the hull side by means of a series of brackets. In the rough conditions encountered in the field these plates were constantly being torn off and many surviving pictures show Panthers missing these side panels.

Zimmerit coating against Soviet magnetic mines was applied at the factory on late Ausf D models commening in September 1943; an order for field units to apply Zimmerit to older versions of the Panther was issued in November 1943. However in September 1944, these orders were countermanded and a new to stop all application of Zimmerit were issued. This new order was based on combat reports that hits on the Zimmerit had caused vehicle fires.

Panther crews were aware of the weak side armour and made unauthorized augmentations by hanging track links or spare road wheels onto the turret and the hull sides. The rear hull top armour was soon recognised as the extreme weak point of the Panther it was only 16 mm thick, and housed two radiator

Pantherturm fortification under inspection in Italy in June 1944.

fans and four air intake louvres over the engine compartment. This made the Panther highly vulnerable to strafing attacks by aircraft. With such thin armour even those aircraft armed with just machine guns were potentially dangerous opponents. The Panther was also highly vulnerable to shrapnel damage from airbursts.

As the war progressed, Germany was forced to curtail the use of certain critical alloy materials in the production of armour plate, such as nickel, tungsten, molybdenum, and manganese. The loss of these alloys resulted in substantially reduced impact resistance levels compared to earlier armour. Manganese from mines in the Ukraine ceased when the German Army lost control of this territory in February 1944. Allied bombers struck the Knabe mine in Norway and stopped a key source of molybdenum; other supplies from Finland and Japan were also cut off. The loss of molybdenum, and its replacement with other substitutes to maintain hardness, as well as a general loss of quality control resulted in an increased brittleness in German armour plate, which developed a tendency to fracture when struck with a shell. Testing by U.S. Army officers in August 1944 in Isigny, France showed catastrophic cracking of the armour plate on two out of three Panthers examined.

PANTHER TURRETS AS FORTIFICATIONS

From 1943, Panther turrets were mounted in fixed fortifications, some were normal production models, but most were made specifically for the task, with additional roof armour to withstand artillery. Two types of turret emplacements were used; (Pantherturm III - Betonsockel - concrete base) and (Pantherturm I - Stahluntersatz - steel sub-base). They housed ammunition storage and fighting compartment along with crew quarters. A total of 182 of these were installed in the fortifications of the Atlantic Wall and West Wall, 48 in the Gothic Line and Hitler Line, 36 on the Eastern Front, and 2 for training and experimentation, for a total of 268 installations by March 1945. They proved to be costly to attack, and difficult to destroy.

PANTHER BATALLION ORGANIZATION

From September 1943, one Panzer battalion with 96 Panthers comprised the Panzer regiment of a Panzer-Division 43.
- Battalion Command
(Composed of Communication and Reconnaissance platoons)
- Communication Platoon -
3 × *Befehlswagen* Panther SdKfz.267/268
- Reconnaissance Platoon - 5 × Panther
- 1st Company - 22 × Panther
    Company Command - 2 × Panther
        1st Platoon - 5 × Panther
        2nd Platoon - 5 × Panther
        3rd Platoon - 5 × Panther
        4th Platoon - 5 × Panther
- 2nd Company - 22 × Panther (composed as 1st Company)
- 3rd Company - 22 × Panther (composed as 1st Company)

- 4th Company - 22 × Panther (composed as 1st Company)
- Service Platoon - 2 × *Bergepanther* SdKfz.179

From 3rd August 1944, the new Panzer-Division 44 organisation called for a Panzer division to consist of one Panzer regiment with two Panzer battalions – one of 96 Panzer IVs and one of 96 Panthers. Actual strengths tended to differ, and in reality were far lower after combat losses were taken into account.

THE SOVIET RESPONSE

The importance of the tank on the Eastern Front led to an arms race between the Germans and Soviets to produce tanks with ever greater armour and firepower. The Tiger I and Panther tanks were German responses to encountering the T-34 in 1941. Soviet firing tests against a captured Tiger in April 1943 showed that the T-34's 76 mm gun could not penetrate the front of the Tiger I at all, and the side only at very close range. An existing Soviet 85 mm antiaircraft gun, the 52-K, was found to be very effective against the frontal armour of the Tiger I, and so a derivative of the 52-K 85 mm gun (F-34 tank gun) was developed for the T-34. The Soviets thus had already embarked on the 85 mm gun upgrade path before encountering the Panther tank at the Battle of Kursk.

After much development work, the first T-34-85 tanks entered combat in March 1944. When tested by Wehrmacht, the production version of the T-34's new 85 mm F-34 gun proved to be ineffective against the Panther's frontal armour at the standard Panzerwaffe engagement range of 2,000m, meaning the Soviet tanks were out-ranged in open country, while the Panther's main gun could penetrate the T-34 frontal armour at this range from any angle. Although the T-34-85 tank was not quite the equal of the Panther, it was much better than the 76.2 mm-armed versions and made up for its quality shortcomings by being produced in greater quantities than the Panther. New

Panzerbefehlswagen Panther Ausf. A (Sd.Kfz. 267) of the Panzergrenadier-Division Großdeutschland photographed in southern Ukraine in 1944.

self-propelled anti-tank vehicles based on the T-34 hull, such as the SU-85 and SU-100, were also developed. A German Army study dated October 5, 1944 showed that from a 30 degree side angle the Panther's gun could easily penetrate the turret of the T-34-85 from the front at ranges up to 2000 m, and the frontal hull armour at 300 m, whereas from the front, the T-34-85 could only penetrate the non-mantlet part of the Panther turret by closing to a range of 500 m. From the side, the two were nearly equivalent as both tanks could penetrate the other from long range. T-34-85 production was soon varied to allow for the introduction of two replacement guns, the D-5T and ZiS-S-53, the later becoming a production standard for the rest of the war.

The Battle of Kursk convinced the Soviets of the need for even greater firepower. A Soviet analysis of the battle in August 1943 showed that a Corps artillery piece, the A-19 122 mm gun, had performed well against the German tanks in that battle, and so development work on the 122 mm equipped IS-2 began in late 1943. Soviet tests of the IS-2 versus the Panther included a claim of one shot that could penetrate the Panther from the front

A Panther tank is passing anti-tank obstacles of the Westwall near Weissenburg / Bergzabern, January 1945.

armour through the back armour. However, German testing showed that the 122 mm gun could not penetrate the glacis plate of the Panther at all, but it could penetrate the front turret/mantlet of the Panther at ranges up to 1500 m. At a 30 degree side angle the Panther's 75 mm gun could penetrate the front of the IS-2s turret at 800 m and the hull nose at 1000 m. From the side, the Panther was more vulnerable than the IS-2. Thus the two tanks, while nearly identical in weight, had quite different combat strengths and weaknesses. The Panther carried much more ammunition and had a faster firing cycle than the IS-2, which was a lower and more compact design; the IS-2s A-19 122 mm gun used a two piece ammunition which slowed its firing cycle.

THE AMERICAN AND BRITISH RESPONSE

The Western Allies' response was inconsistent between the Americans and the British. Although the western Allies were aware of the Panther and had access to technical details through the Soviets, the Panther was not employed against the western

Allies until early 1944 at Anzio in Italy, where Panthers were employed in small numbers. Until shortly before D-Day, the Panther was thought to be another heavy tank that would not be built in large numbers. However, just before D-Day, Allied intelligence investigated Panther production, and using a statistical analysis of the road wheels on two captured tanks, estimated that Panther production for February 1944 was 270, thus indicating that it would be found in much larger numbers than had previously been anticipated. In the planning for the Battle of Normandy, the US Army expected to face a handful of German heavy tanks alongside large numbers of Panzer IVs, and thus had little time to prepare to face the Panther. Instead, 38% of the German tanks in Normandy were Panthers, whose frontal armour could not be penetrated by the 75 mm guns of the US M4 Sherman.

The British were more astute in their recognition of the increasing armour strength of German tanks, and by the time of the Normandy invasion their program that mounted the excellent 17-pounder anti-tank gun on some of their M4 Shermans had provided more than 300 of these Sherman Fireflies. The British lobbied during the war to use American production lines for

M4 Shermans in combat.

British Firefly in Namur, 1944.

building many Fireflies but these demands were ignored due to suspicion of British tank designs after they had done poorly in North Africa. There were also 200 interim Challenger tanks with the 17 pounder and improved tank designs under development. British and Commonwealth tank units in Normandy were initially equipped at the rate of one Firefly in a troop with three Shermans or Cromwells. This ratio increased until, by the end of the war, half of the British Shermans were Fireflies. The Comet with a similar gun to the 17 pdr had also replaced the 75 mm gun Sherman in some British units. The 17-pounder with APCBC shot was more or less equivalent in performance to the Panther's 75 mm gun, but superior with APDS shot.

The US armour doctrine at the time was dominated by the head of Army Ground Forces, Gen. Lesley McNair, an artilleryman by trade, who believed that tanks should concentrate on infantry support and exploitation roles, and avoid enemy tanks, leaving them to be dealt with by the tank destroyer force, which were a mix of towed anti-tank guns and lightly armoured tanks with open top turrets with 3-inch (M-10 tank destroyer), 76 mm (M18 Hellcat) or later, 90 mm (M36 tank destroyer) guns. This doctrine led to a lack of urgency in the US Army to upgrade the armour and firepower of the M4 Sherman tank, which had previously performed well against the most common German tanks, the Panzer III and Panzer IV, encountered in Africa and Italy. As with the Soviets, the German adoption of thicker armour and the 7.5 cm KwK 40 in their standard tanks prompted the U.S. Army to develop the more powerful 76 mm version of the M4 Sherman tank in April 1944. Development of a heavier tank, the M26 Pershing, was delayed mainly by McNair's insistence on "battle need" and emphasis on producing only reliable, well-tested weapons, a reflection of America's 3,000 mile supply line to Europe.

An AGF (Armored Ground Forces) policy statement of November 1943 concluded the following:

"The recommendation of a limited proportion of tanks carrying a 90mm gun is not concurred in for the following reasons: The M4 tank has been hailed widely as the best tank of the battlefield today... There appears to be no fear on the part of our forces of the German Mark VI (Tiger) tank. There can be no basis for the T26 tank other than the conception of a tank-vs-tank duel-which is believed to be unsound and unnecessary. Both British and American battle experience has demonstrated that the antitank gun in suitable numbers is the master of the tank... There has been no indication that the 76mm antitank gun is inadequate against German Mark VI tank."

U.S. awareness of the inadequacies of their M4 tanks grew only slowly. All U.S. M4 Shermans that landed in Normandy in June 1944 had the 75 mm gun. The 75 mm M4 gun could not penetrate the Panther from the front at all, although it could penetrate various parts of the Panther from the side at ranges from 400 to 2,600 m (440 to 2,800 yd). The 76 mm gun could also not penetrate the front hull armour of the Panther, but could penetrate the Panther turret mantlet at very close range. In August 1944, the HVAP (high velocity armour-piercing) 76 mm round was introduced to improve the performance of the 76 mm M4 Shermans. With a tungsten core, this round could still not penetrate the Panther glacis plate, but could punch through the Panther mantlet at 730 to 910 m, instead of the usual 90 meteres for the normal 76 mm round. However, tungsten production shortages meant that this round was always in short supply, with only a few rounds available per tank, and some M4 Sherman units were not issued with any ammunition of this type.

Sherman tank shells used a high flash powder, making it easier for German crews to spot their opponents. German tanks conversely used a low flash powder making it harder for Allied crews to spot them. Due to the narrowness of their tracks which did little to spread the weight the Sherman also possessed an inferior cross country mobility in relation to the Panthers. This proved to be the case on all adverse surfaces from mud through to sheet ice. Meanwhile it is important to note that the Panther is around 15 tons heavier than the M4. Brig. Gen. J.H. Collier noted:

> "I saw where some Mark V tanks crossed a muddy field without sinking the tracks over five inches, where we in the M4 started across the same field the same day and bogged down."

The 90 mm M36 tank destroyer was finally introduced in September 1944; the 90 mm round also proved to have difficulty penetrating the Panther's glacis plate, and it was not until an HVAP version of the round was developed that it could effectively penetrate it from combat range. It was very effective against the Panther's front turret and from the side, however.

The high U.S. tank losses in the Battle of the Bulge against a force composed largely of Panther tanks brought about a clamour for better armour and firepower. At General Eisenhower's request, only 76 mm gun-armed M4 Shermans were shipped to Europe for the remainder of the war. Small numbers of the M26 Pershing were also rushed into combat in late February 1945. A dramatic newsreel film was recorded by a U.S. Signal Corps cameraman of an M26 successfully stalking and then knocking out a Panther in the city of Cologne, however only after the Panther had already knocked out two M4 Shermans.

Production of Panther tanks and other German tanks dropped off sharply after January 1945, and eight of the Panther regiments still on the Western Front were transferred to the Eastern Front in February 1945. The result was that for the rest of the war during 1945, the greatest threats to the tanks of the Western Allies were no longer German tanks, but infantry anti-tank weapons such as the 88 mm calibre Panzerschreck (the German bazooka) and Panzerfaust anti-tank grenade launcher, and infantry anti-tank guns such as the ubiquitous 7.5 cm Pak 40, and mobile anti-tank guns such as the Marder, StuG III, StuG IV, and Jagdpanzer. A German Army status report dated March 15, 1945 showed 117 Panthers left in the entire Western Front, of which only 49 were operational.

According to US Army Ground Forces statistics, destruction of a single Panther was achieved after destruction of 5 M4 Shermans or some 9 T-34s.

DESIGN CHARACTERISTICS

Hitler personally reviewed the final designs for the Panther and it was he who insisted on an increase in the thickness of the frontal armour. Under his orders the front glacis plate was increased from 60 mm to 80 mm and the turret front plate was increased from 80mm to 100 mm.

As a result of Hitler's intervention the weight of the production model was increased to 45 metric tons an increased by 10 tons from the original plans for a 35 ton tank. To exacerbate matters the Panther was rushed into combat before all of its teething problems were corrected. Reliability was considerably improved over time, and the Panther did prove to be a very effective fighting vehicle; however, some design flaws, such as its weak final drive units were never corrected due to various shortages in German war production.

THE MAYBACH ENGINE

The first 250 Panthers were powered by a Maybach HL 210 P30 engine, a V-12 petrol engine which delivered 650 hp at 3,000 rpm and was protected by three simple air filters. Starting in May 1943, the next run of Panthers were built using the 700 PS (690 hp, 515 kW)/3000 rpm, 23.1 litre Maybach HL 230 P30 V-12 petrol engine. The designs of both engines were excellent and gave a remarkably high output for such a compact device. Two multistage "cyclone" air filters were used to automate some of the dust removal process. Once more however the increasingly difficult supply system encroached and the British control of aluminium supplies from Turkey dictated that the light alloy block used in the HL 210 was soon replaced by a less effective cast iron block. This was done to preserve the limited aluminium supply which was desperately needed elsewhere particularly in the production of jet engines. In practice the engine power output of the engines employed in the Panther was reduced due to the use of low grade petrol. With a full tank of fuel, a Panther could in theory cover 130 km on surfaced roads and 80 km cross country.

The HL 230 P30 engine was a very compact design, which kept the space between the cylinder walls to a minimum. The crankshaft comprised of seven discs, each with an outer race of roller bearings, and a connecting crankshaft pin between each disc. To reduce the length of the engine further, by one half a cylinder diameter, the usual practice was abandoned and

The importance of engine coolants was strongly emphasised in the Pantherfibel.

the two banks of 6 cylinders of the V-12 were not offset. The centre points of the connecting rods of each cylinder pair in the "V" where they joined the crankshaft pin were thus at the same spot rather than offset; to accommodate this arrangement, one connecting rod in the pair of cylinders was forked and fitted around the other "solid" connecting rod at the crankshaft pin. (A more typical "V" engine would have had offset cylinder banks and each pair of connecting rods would have fit simply side by side on the crankshaft pin). This unusual arrangement with the connecting rods was the source of considerable teething problems.

The cylinder head gaskets were another major problem and the combination of poor fuel and lubricants led to a large instance of blown head gaskets. This was one problem which could be corrected with the introduction of improved seals from September 1943. Another advance lay in the improved bearings which were introduced in November 1943. In common with the Tiger I it was soon discovered that allowing the engine speed

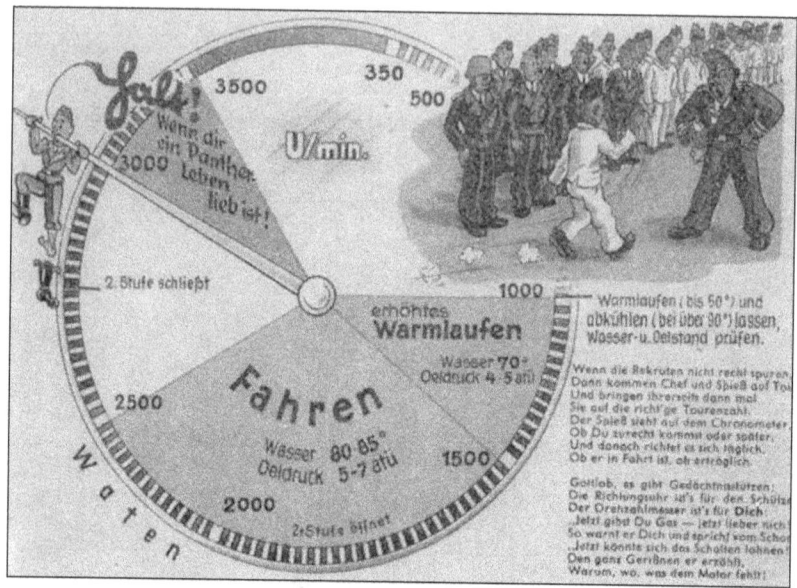

The importance of keeping the engine revs in a band between 1500 and 2500 is graphically demonstrated in the Pantherfibel.

to rise to 3000 rpm led to catastrophic failures. The obvious solution was to incorporate an engine governor which was added in November 1943. This essential device reduced the maximum engine speed to 2500 rpm. The situation was further improved by the addition of an eighth crankshaft bearing which was added to the production process beginning in January 1944. This too helped to reduce the previously high rate of motor engine failures.

The weight of the Panther posed major problems for bridge crossings. Like the Tiger I the engine compartment space of the Panther was therefore designed to be watertight so that the Panther could be submerged and cross waterways. The consequence of this was that the engine compartment was poorly ventilated and prone to overheating. In addition the fuel connectors in the early models were non-insulated, leading to leakage of fuel fumes into the engine compartment. This unfortunate combination was the source of many engine fires which blighted the deployment of the early Panthers. The solution was to add additional ventilation venting through the engine deck which was designed to draw off these gasses. To an extent this reduced the instance of engine fires but it did not completely solve the problem and engine fires continued to claim precious Panther tanks. Other measures taken to reduce this problem included improving the coolant circulation inside the motor and adding a reinforced membrane spring to the fuel pump. As far as the crews were concerned it was fortunate that the Panther had a solid firewall separating the engine compartment and the fighting compartment in order to keep engine fires from spreading.

The engines fitted into the Panther undoubtedly became more reliable over time, but as events demonstrated there was simply not enough time. In the aftermath of World War II a French assessment of their stock of captured Panthers conducted in 1947 concluded that the engine had an average life of 1,000 km and maximum life of 1,500 km.

The simple gearing for the final drive system of the Panther was easy to manufacture but was far less robust than the relatively complex gearing system on the Tiger.

SUSPENSION

The suspension system of the Panther closely resembled that of the Tiger I and consisted of two front drive sprockets, two rear idlers and eight double-interleaved rubber-rimmed steel road wheels on each side. The road wheels were suspended on a dual torsion bar suspension. The dual torsion bar system was designed by Professor Ernst Lehr and was purpose designed to allow for a wide travel stroke and rapid oscillations with high reliability. The result of the innovative dual torsion bar system was meant that it was possible for the Panther to attain a relatively high cross country speed and the impressive ability to travel at high speed cross country was a defining feature of this remarkable heavy tank. The high speed of the Panther could be maintained over undulating terrain. However, the speed of the Panther came at a very high price. The extra space required for the bars running across the length of the bottom of the hull, below the turret basket significantly increased the overall height of the tank and also prevented the incorporation of an escape hatch in the hull bottom. When damaged by mines, the finely engineered torsion bars were easily bent out of shape required a welding torch for removal.

The Panther's suspension was complicated to manufacture and in common with the Tiger I incorporated the interleaved system which required the outer wheels to be removed in order to access the rear wheels and made replacing inner road wheels time consuming. The crews of the Panther would no doubt have been relieved to discover that the road wheels on their vehicle were arranged in just two rows as opposed to the three of the Tiger I.

One tiresome feature of the interleaved wheels was that they exhibited a tendency to become clogged with mud, snow and ice, and could easily freeze solid overnight in the harsh winter weather of the Eastern Front. Shell damage could also cause

Taken in Northen France in October 1943, this photograph clearly shows the interleaved wheels of the Panther.

the road wheels to jam together and become extremely difficult to separate. Interleaved wheels had long been standard on all German half-tracks. The extra wheels did provide better flotation and stability, and also provided more armour protection for the thin hull sides than smaller wheels or non-interleaved wheel systems, but the complexity and the tedious processes involved in maintenance meant that no other country ever adopted this cumbersome design for their tanks.

The road wheels of the Panther were rubber rimmed but in September 1944, and again in March/April 1945, M.A.N. the shortages of this vital substance led to the building of a limited number of Panther tanks with steel road wheels which were originally designed for the Tiger II and late series Tiger I tanks. Steel road wheels were introduced from chassis number 121052.

Once the Allied air forces began targeting Schweinfurt the resultant shortage of ball bearings was another major issue and in consequence, from November 1944 through February 1945, an emergency conversion process began which revolved around

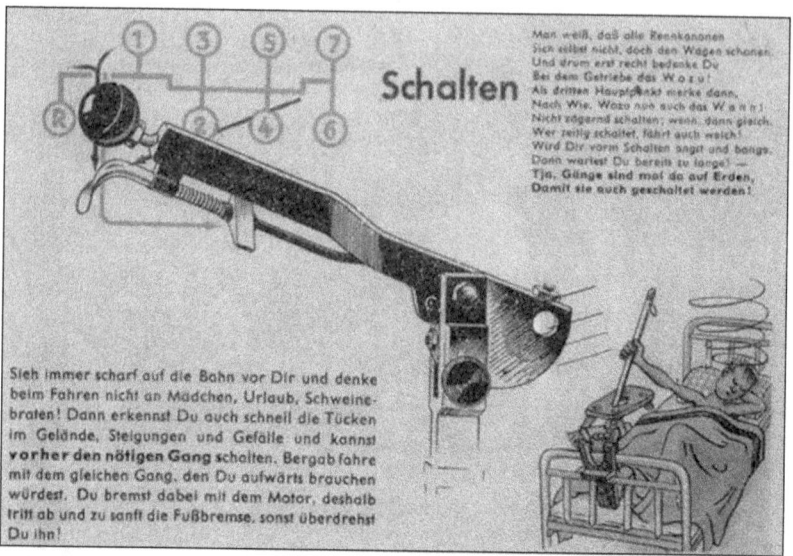

The seven forward and one reverse gear of the Panther from the Pantherfibel.

the use of sleeve bearings as an alternative to ball bearings. The sleeve bearings were primarily used in the running gear although contingency plans were made should the need arise to convert the transmission to sleeve bearings, but these were not carried out as production of Panther tanks came to an end.

STEERING AND TRANSMISSION

In the Panther, steering was accomplished through a seven-speed AK 7-200 synchromesh gearbox. It was designed by Zahnradfabrik Friedrichshafen, and incorporated a MAN single radius steering system which, unlike the Tiger I with its steering wheel operation, the Panther utilised the traditional arrangement of steering levers.

On the Panther each gear had a fixed radius of turning, ranging from five meters for 1st gear up to 80 meters for 7th gear. The driver was expected to anticipate the sharpness of a turn and shift into the appropriate gear to turn the tank. The driver also had the option of engaging the brakes on one side to force a sharper turn. This manual steering was a much simplified design, compared to the more sophisticated dual-radius hydraulically controlled steering system of the Tiger I and ease of manufacturing compared to the Tiger I was therefore much enhanced. The AK 7-200 transmission was also capable of pivot turns, but this method of turning placed a great deal of additional strain which could accelerate failures of the final drive.

Throughout its career, the weakest part of the Panther was its final drive unit. The problems arose from a combination of factors. The original MAN proposal had called for the Panther to have an epicyclic gearing (hollow spur) system in the final drive, similar to that used in the Tiger I. However, Germany at the time suffered from a shortage of gear-cutting machine tools and, unlike the Tiger tanks, the Panther was intended to be produced in large numbers. To achieve the goal of higher production rates, numerous simplifications were made to the design and its manufacture. This process was aggressively pushed forward, sometimes against the wishes of designers

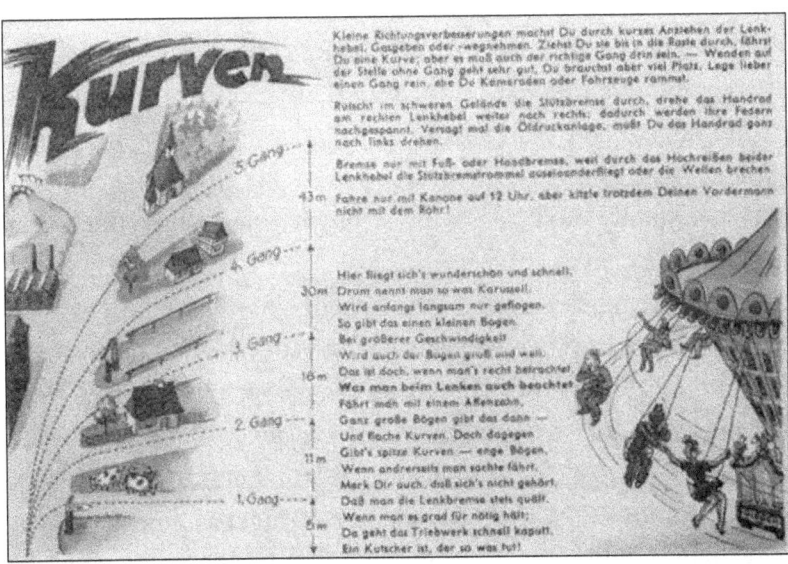

The turning radius of each of the Panther's forward gears from the Pantherfibel.

and army officers, by the Chief Director of Armament and War Production, Karl-Otto Saur (who worked under, and later succeeded, Reichminister Speer). Consequently, the final drive was changed to a more simple double spur system. Although much simpler to produce, the double spur gears had inherently higher internal impact and stress loads, making them prone to failure under the high torque requirements of the heavy Panther tank. Furthermore, high quality steel intended for double spur system was not available for mass production, and was replaced by 37MnSi5 tempered steel, which was unsuitable for such a high stress gearing arrangement. In contrast, both the Tiger II and the US M4 Sherman tank had double helical (herringbone gears) in their final drives, a system that reduced internal stress loads and was less complex than epicyclic gears.

Compounding these problems was the fact that the final drive's housing and gear mountings were too weak because of the poor type of steel available and the tight space allotted for the final drive. The final gear mountings deformed easily under the high torque and stress loads, pushing the gears out of alignment and resulting in failure. Due to the weakness of the final drives their average fatigue life was only 150 km. In Normandy, about half of the abandoned Panthers were found by the French to have broken final drives. However, at least the final gear housing was eventually replaced with stronger one, while final gear problem was never solved.

Plans were made to replace the final drive, either with a version of the original epicyclic gears planned by MAN, or with the final drive of the Tiger II. These plans were intertwined with the planning for the Panther II, which never came to fruition because Panzer Commission deemed that temporary drop in production of Panther due to merger of Tiger II and Panther II was unacceptable. It was estimated that building the epicyclic gear final drive would have required 2.2 times more machining

Repair of the transmission of a Panther, Russia, May 1944.

A knocked out Panther tank lies redundant in the river at Houffalize, 1945.

work than double spur gears, and this would have affected manufacturing output.

Most of the shortcomings were considered acceptable once design flaws were rectified. Due to the mechanical unreliability of final gear the Panther had to be driven by experienced drivers with extreme care, a characteristic shared with the Tiger tanks as well as Jagdtigers. Long road marches would inevitably result in a significant number of losses due to breakdowns, and so the German Army had to ship the tanks by rail as close to the battlefield as possible. This theoreticaly convenient and sensible arrangement was not always achievable in practice and the Panthers continued to face unfeasibly long road marches which led to numerous breakdowns.

THE PANTHER II

The early impetus for upgrading the Panther came from the concern of Hitler and others that it lacked sufficient armour. Hitler had already insisted on an increase in its armour once so far and further discussions involving Hitler, in January 1943, resulted in a call for further increased armour; initially referred to by an Arabic numeral as the Panther 2, it was redesignated with the Roman numeral becoming the Panther II after April 1943. This upgrade increased the glacis plate to 100 mm, the side armour to 60 mm, and the top armour to 30 mm. Production of the Panther 2 was slated to begin in September 1943.

In a meeting on February 10, 1943, further design changes were proposed - including changes to the steering gears and final drives. Another meeting on February 17, 1943 focused on sharing and standardizing parts between the Tiger II tank and the Panther 2, such as the transmission, all-steel roadwheels, and running gear. Additional meetings in February began to outline the various components, including use of the 88 mm L/71 KwK 43 gun. In March 1943, MAN indicated that the first prototype would be completed by August 1943. A number of engines were under consideration, among them the new Maybach HL 234 fuel-injected engine (900 hp operated by an 8-speed hydraulic transmission).

It was a sign of the rapid pace of events that the up-grade path to replace the original Panther design with the Panther II were already underway even before the first Panther had even seen combat. However from May to June 1943, work on the Panther II ceased as the focus shifted to expanding production of the original Panther tank. It is not clear if there was ever an official cancellation - this may have been because the Panther II upgrade pathway was originally started at Hitler's insistence. The direction that the design was headed would not have been consistent with Germany's need for a mass-produced tank, which was the goal of the Reich Ministry of Armament and War Production.

One Panther II chassis was completed and eventually captured by the U.S.; it is now on display at the Patton Museum in Fort Knox. An Ausf G turret is mounted on this chassis.

PANTHER AUSF. F

After the Panther II project was abandoned, a more limited upgrade of the Panther was planned, centered around a re-designed turret. The Ausf F variant was slated for production in April 1945, but the war ended these plans.

The earliest known redesign of the turret was dated November 7, 1943 and featured a narrow gun mantlet behind a 120 mm (4.7 in) thick turret front plate. Another design drawing by Rheinmettall dated March 1, 1944 reduced the width of the turret front even further; this was the Turm-Panther (Schmale Blende) (Panther with narrow gun mantlet). Several experimental Schmalturm (literally: "narrow turret") were built in 1944 with modified versions of the 75 mm KwK 42 L/70, which were given the designation of KwK 44/1. A few were captured and shipped back to the U.S. and Britain. One is on display at the Bovington tank Museum.

The Schmalturm had a much narrower front face of 120 mm (4.7 in) armour sloped at 20 degrees; side turret armour was increased to 60 mm (2.4 in) from 45 mm (1.8 in); roof turret armour increased to 40 mm (1.6 in) from 16 mm (0.63 in); and a bell shaped gun mantlet similar to that of the Tiger II was used. This increased armour protection also had a slight weight saving due to the overall smaller size of the turret.

The Panther Ausf F would have had the Schmalturm, with its better ballistic protection, and an extended front hull roof which was slightly thicker. The Ausf F's Schmalturm was to have a built-in stereoscopic rangefinder and lower weight than the original turrets. A number of Ausf F hulls were built at Daimler-Benz and Ruhrstahl-Hattingen steelworks; however there is no evidence that any completed Ausf F saw service before the end of the war.

Proposals to equip the Schmalturm with the 88mm KwK 43 L/71 were made from January through March 1945. These would have likely equipped future German tanks but none were built, as the war ended.

One of the most famous studies of the Tiger I. This early production model appears to be in almost factory fresh condition.

THE TIGER I

The Tiger I was the most famous heavy tank used in World War II. It was developed in great haste during 1942 by the Henschel & Sohn company as the answer to the unexpectedly formidable Soviet armour encountered during 1941 in the closing stages of Operation Barbarossa. During that titanic campaign an unpleasant surprise for the German armies appeared in the ominous form of the T-34 and the KV-1 to which the German tank designs of the time could provide no answer. The 50mm calibre high velocity gun of the German Mark III lacked projectile mass and penetrating power while the low velocity gun mounted on the German Mark IV was incapable of penetrating the well sloped armour of the T-34 at anything but the shortest range. The high velocity 88mm anti-aircraft gun, which had been forced into action in an anti-tank role in Russia and the western desert, was the only gun which had demonstrated its effectiveness against even the most heavily armoured ground targets such as The KV1.

Rushed into service in August 1942 the Tiger I design at least gave the Panzerwaffe its first tank capable of mounting the fearsome 88mm gun as its main armament. For the hard pressed men of the Panzewaffe however there was a very high price to pay for the Tiger in both literal and metaphorical terms. The highest price of all, or course, was paid by the slave labourers who were forced to build the Tiger.

The Roman numeral I was only officially added in 1944 when the later Tiger II entered production. The initial official German designation was Panzerkampfwagen VI Ausführung H ('Panzer VI version H'), abbreviated to PzKpfw VI Ausf. H. Somewhat

A Tiger I with the turret number 133 of 1. SS-Pz.-Korps Leibstandarte Adolf Hitler in transit by road march; in the foreground is Schwimmkübel; PK 698.

confusingly the tank was redesignated as PzKpfw VI Tiger Ausf. E in March 1943. It also enjoyed the ordnance inventory Sonderkraftzug designation SdKfz 181.

The Tiger I first saw action on 22nd September 1942 near Leningrad. It was not an instant success. Under pressure from Hitler, the tank was driven into action in unfavourable terrain, months earlier than planned. Many early models proved to be mechanically unreliable; in this first action most broke down. More worryingly two others were easily knocked out by dug-in Soviet anti-tank guns. Of even more concern was the fact that one disabled tank was almost captured intact by the Soviets. It was finally blown up in November 1942 to prevent it falling into Soviet hands. In any event the Soviets used the battlefield experience well and used the time to study the design and begin to prepare a response which, in due course, would emerge as the fearsome Josef Stalin heavy tank which was to prove equal to the Tiger in every respect.

A rare photograph shows the interior of the Tiger I factory Henschelwerk III at Kassel-Mittelfeld.

Production Of The Tiger

Production of the Tiger I began in August 1942, and 1,347 were built by August 1944 when production ceased. Production started at a rate of 25 per month and peaked in April 1944 at 104 per month. Battlefield strength peaked at 671 on 1st July 1944. Generally speaking, it took about twice as long to build a Tiger I as any other German tank of the period. However, none of the obvious lessons concerning the need to husband scarce resources were learned and astonishingly when the "improved" model began production in January 1944, the Tiger I was soon phased out in favour of an even more resource hungry monster in the form of the massive, less efficient and even more resource intense Tiger II.

The major problem with the Tiger I was that it simply used too many scarce resources in terms of both manpower and material, especially when compared with the spartan simplicity of the T-34. As a general rule of thumb each the Tiger I cost over twice as much as a Panzer IV and four times as much as a StuG III assault gun. Each Tiger I actually cost 250,000 Reichsmarks as compared to the 103,500 it cost to manufacture a Panzer IV. The Tiger I was also significantly over engineered which made it difficult to manufacture at a fast rate. The result was an increasing production gap which Speer's hard pressed German tank industry could never hope to close. During the Second World War, over 58,000 American Shermans and 36,000 Soviet T-34s were produced, compared to just 1,347 Tiger I and 492 Tiger II. The closest counterpart to the Tiger from the United States was the M26 Pershing around 200 of which deployed during the war and the Soviet IS-2 of which about 3,800 were built during the war.

THE DEVELOPMENT PROCESS

Henschel & Sohn began development of the vehicle that eventually became the Tiger I in January 1937 when the Waffenamt requested Henschel to develop a *Durchbruchwagen* (breakthrough vehicle) in the 30 metric ton range (see DW 1 hulk opposite). Only one prototype hull was ever built and it never was mounted with a turret. The general configuration and suspension of the Durchbruchwagen prototype in many

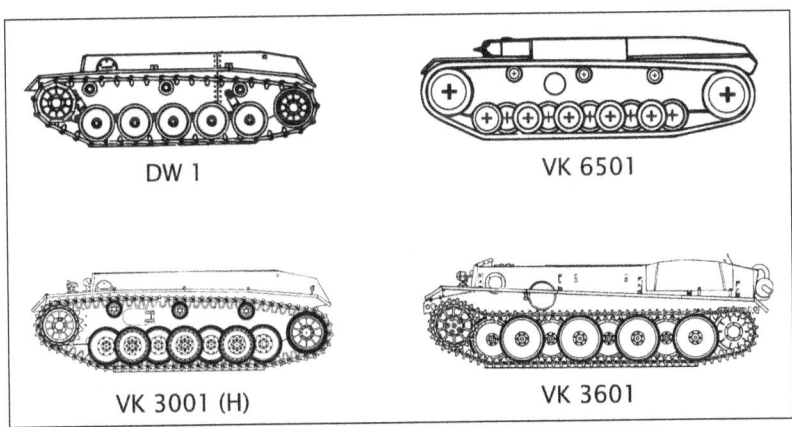

Early development prototype hulls for the Henschel heavy tank programme which ultimately produced the Tiger I.

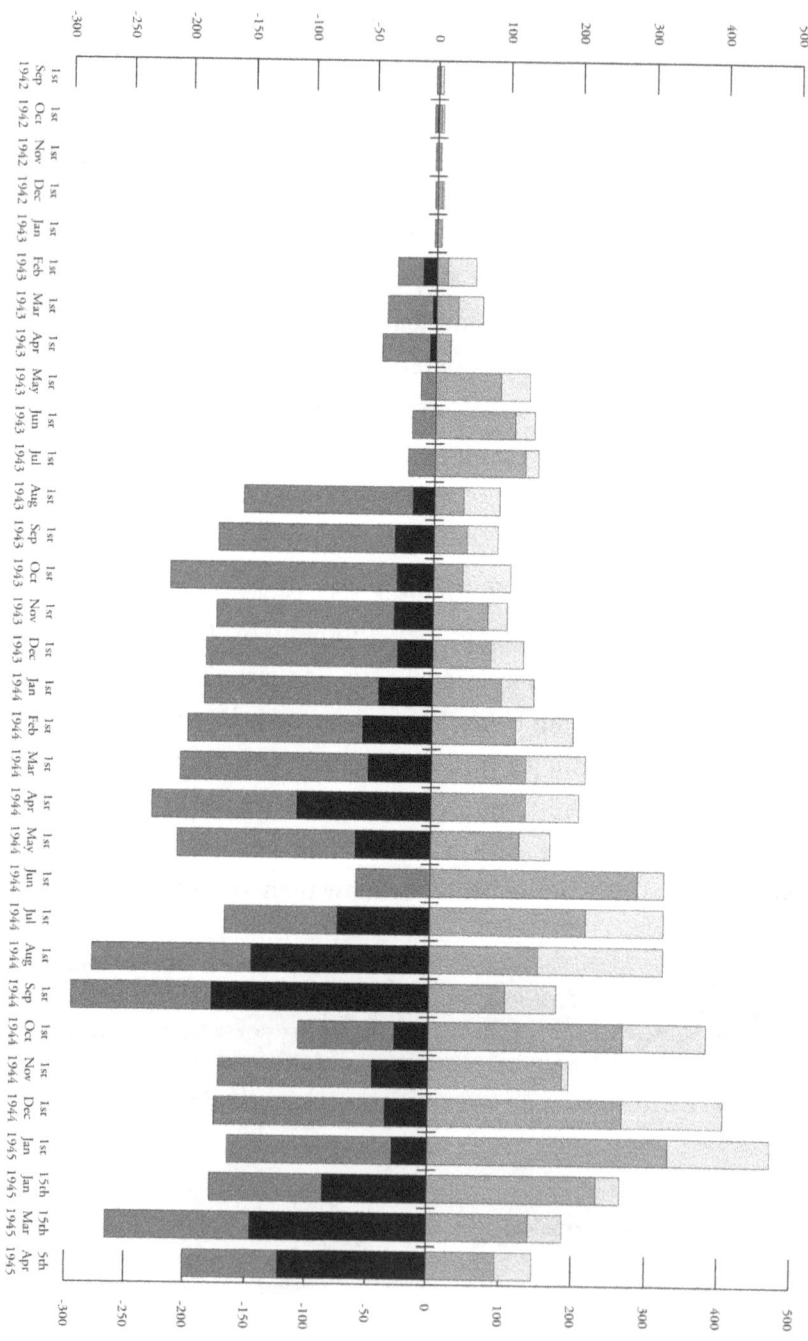

Operational status of Tigers on the eastern and western fronts 1st September 1942 to 5th April 1945

respects resembled the Panzer III. The proposed turret also bore similarities to existing machines and,had it been completed, it would have greatly resembled the early Panzer IV C turret which sported the short barrelled 7.5cm L/24 cannon.

Before Durchbruchwagen I was completed, however, a new request was issued for a heavier 30 tonne class vehicle with thicker armour; this was known as the Durchbruchwagen II (see VK 6501 opposite). This tank would have carried 50mm of frontal armour and have mounted a Panzer IV turret with the standard 7.5cm L/24 cannon. Overall weight would also have been approximately 36 metric tons. Again only one hull was ever built and a turret was never actually fitted. Development of this vehicle was cancelled in the autumn of 1938 in favour of the more advanced VK3001(H) and VK3601(H) designs. However, both the Durchbruchwagen I and II prototype hulls were used as test vehicles until 1941.

On 9th September 1939, with the invasion of Poland underway, Henschel & Sohn received permission to continue development of a VK3001(H)

The War Office commissioned this illustration on the basis of a photograph from the German newspaper above published in December 1942. Note the lack of muzzle brake on the gun.

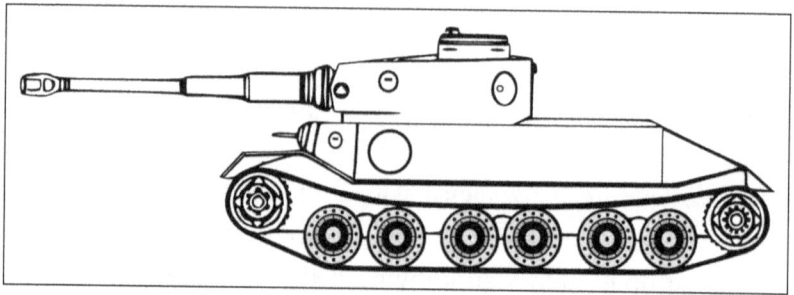

Prototype drawing for the Porsche version of the Tiger I. There were many problems with this design including forward location of the turret made manoeuvring difficult. There were also many mechanical breakdowns during testing.

medium tank and a VK3601(H) heavy tank, both of which apparently pioneered the overlapping and interleaved main road wheel concept as adapted for tank chassis use. Interleaved road wheels were already being used on German military half-tracked vehicles such as the SdKfz 7 although there was very little comparison with regard to the weight of a heavily armoured tank compared to a lightweight half track.

The VK3001(H) was intended be produced in three main variants the first of which was to mount a 7.5cm L/24 low velocity infantry support gun, the second was intended to carry a 7.5cm L/40 dual purpose anti-tank gun, and the third a 10.5cm L/28 artillery piece in a Krupp turret. Overall weight was to be 33 metric tons. The armour was designed to be 50mm on frontal surfaces and 30mm on the side surfaces. Four prototype hulls were completed for testing. Two of these were later used to create the 12.8cm Selbstfahrlafette L/61, also known as Sturer Emil.

The VK3601(H) was intended to weigh 40 metric tons, and carry 100mm of armour on its frontal surfaces, 80mm on turret sides and 60mm on hull sides. The VK3601(H) was also intended to appear in four variants adapted to house a 7.5cm L/24, or a 7.5cm L/43, or a 7.5cm L/70, or a 12.8cm L/28 cannon in a Krupp turret that looked very similar to an enlarged Panzer IVC turret. One prototype hull was built, followed later by five more prototype hulls. The six turrets intended for the prototype hulls were built but never actually fitted and ended their working lives as static defences mounted the Atlantic Wall. The development of the VK3601(H) project was discontinued in early 1942 in favour of the VK4501 project. German combat experience with the French Somua S35 cavalry tank and Char B1 heavy tank, and the British Matilda I and Matilda II infantry tanks in June 1940 showed that the German Army needed better armed and armoured tanks. In 1940 superior tactics had overcome superior enemy armour, but Rommel had endured a nasty shock on the form of a successful British counter attack at Arras. The German tank designers however, took notice of the lessons from the battlefield. Accordingly on 26th May 1941, at an armaments meeting, Henschel and Porsche were asked to submit designs for a 45 tonne heavy tank, to be ready by June 1942. Porsche worked hard and fast to submit an updated version of their VK3001(P) Leopard tank prototype while Henschel worked to develop an improved VK3601(H)tank. Henschel built two prototypes. A VK4501(H) H1 which used the 88mm L/56 cannon and a VK4501(H) H2 which used the 75mm L/70 cannon.

THE UNPLEASANT SURPRISE

On 22 June 1941, Germany launched Operation Barbarossa, the invasion of the Soviet Union. The Germans were shocked to encounter Soviet T-34 medium and KV-1 heavy tanks which completely outclassed anything the Germans were then able to put into the field. The T-34 was almost immune frontally to every gun in German service except the 88mm FlaK 18/36 gun. The Panzer Mark III with the 50mm KwK 38 L/42 main armament could penetrate the sides of a T-34, but had to be very close to do so. To have any chance of penetrating the frontal armour the Panzer III had to close to suicidally short range. The KV-1 was even more heavily armoured and in consequence almost

Dr. Erwin Aders (front row right) was head of Henschel's Tiger I development and construction project and the Tiger's chief designer, tours shop 5 in company with high ranking army officers on September 5th, 1942.

immune to anything but the 88mm FlaK 18/36. The emergence of the Soviet T-34 and KV-1 was a very unpleasant surprise and the shock of the discovery was later recalled by the lead Henschel designer Erwin Aders, "There was great consternation when it was discovered that the Soviet tanks were superior to anything available to the Heer." In the scramble to come up with an strong defensive alternative to the Russian armour an immediate weight increase to 45 tonnes and an increase in gun calibre to 88mm was ordered. The due date for new prototypes was brought forward to 20th April 1942, Adolf Hitler's birthday.

Porsche and Henschel submitted prototype designs, Tiger (P) and Tiger (H), and they were put through their paces at Rastenburg before Hitler. The Henschel design was accepted as the best overall design. The Porsche gasoline-electric hybrid power unit performed poorly on the day with frequent breakdowns. It also used large quantities of copper, a strategic war material which was in very short supply. The contract was duly awarded to Henschel & Sohn.

Unlike the later Panther tank however, the designs for the Tiger did not incorporate any of the design innovations incorporated into the T-34: the defensive benefits of sloping armour and the corresponding saving in terms of weight were absent from both the Henschel and the Porsche designs, with the thickness and weight of the Tiger's armour making up for this oversight.

With the contract in the bag there was no time to loose and Henschel began production of the Panzerkampfwagen VI Ausf. H in August 1942 at its tank factory Henschelwerk III in Kassel-Mittelfeld.

The official designation from March 1943 onwards was Panzerkampfwagen VI SdKfz 181 Tiger Ausf E until Hitler's order, dated February 27th, 1944, abolished the designation Panzerkampfwagen VI and ratified the use of the new designation Panzerkampfwagen Tiger Ausf. E. This was to remain the official designation until the end of the war. For common use the

A newly completed Tiger is lowered on to a railway carriage ready to commence its journey to the front.

A particularly fine study of a Tiger I in profile.

name was frequently shortened to Tiger - the name purportedly given to the machine by its frustrated rival designer Ferdinand Porsche.

The firm of Henschel & Sohn was established in the early 1800s as a builder of locomotives and it was only during World War I that the firm undertook the business of armament manufacturing for the first time. The company kept up the new operations during the inter-war years and by the time Hitler was ready to re-arm Germany Henschel was ready and waiting to oblige. By the time of the second World War, the company was producing locomotives, tanks, diesel engines, trucks, aeroplanes and artillery pieces. Henschel manufactured all of the main battle tank types with the exception of the Panzer IV. This meant that at various times the Panzer I, II and III as well as the Panther, Tiger I and Tiger II all rolled off the Henschel production lines.

The firm of Henschel & Sohn incorporated three huge engineering works in and around Kassel. Werk I in Kassel was devoted to locomotive assembly and gun production, Werk II in the Rothenditmold area consisted of a large foundry, boiler and other locomotive component shops and Werk III in Mittelfeld was primarily devoted to tank assembly and component manufacture.

The Mittelfeld Werkes were situated on both sides of a railway line running north to south. Looking south, those buildings on the right side of the railway line were used for manufacturing locomotive components and truck and engine repair. The main storage area for tank components was also on the right side of the track including sheds that held Tiger hulls and turrets. On the right side of the track were 4 main shops numbered 1, 2, 3 and 5. (Shop 4 was planned but never built.). Tiger manufacturing took place in shops 3 and 5.

At its peak the factory employed a total of over 8000 workers for tank production. Sadly, extensive use was made of slave labour and the victims were treated abominably being effectively worked to death. The Henschel works were in production round the clock seven days a week. The labour force, both slave labourers and willing workers performed two exhausting 12 hour shifts but the night shift for a variety of reasons produced only 50% of the output of the day shift.

A manufacturing process known as the *"takte"* system was used in the assembly shops. That system relied on a timed rhythm for each step in the manufacturing process. There were nine steps or *takte* used in manufacturing the Tiger I. In surviving factory photos the reader should note the takte signs on the shop wall denoting which step is being performed in that location.

Each *takte* took six hours. The total time to complete a Tiger, including the various machining processes, was estimated to be 14 days and incorporated 300,000 man hours. An average of 18 to 22 tanks were carried at any one time in the hull assembly line and approximately ten tanks were carried in the final assembly line.

The first 4 *takte* revolved around hull machining and preparation. Henschel itself did not have the capability to weld or bend the massive heavy armour plates used in the Tiger and actually received the raw hulls and turrets from sub contractors. The turrets were manufactured by Wegmann und Company, which was conveniently also located in Kassel. The raw hulls were manufactured by two firms, Krupp and Dortmund-Hoerder Huettenverein. The hull processing steps all took place in shop 3.

NEW GERMAN TANKS
Technical and Tactical Trends no. 18, 1943

Several new types of German tanks have been reported to be in existence:

a) Mark I (C) - No details are known but it is probable that this is a redesigned Mark I intended for airborne or landing operations. The original Mark I tank weighed about 6 tons.

b) Mark II Special - The original Mark II tank (weight about 9 tons) has for some time been considered obsolescent as a combat tank. The new tank probably has thicker armour and a more powerful engine. One of the most important features is that it is reportedly armed with the long-barrelled 50mm gun which is used in the new Mark III tanks. The result should be a comparatively light, fast tank with adequate striking power, probably suitable for use as a tank destroyer.

c) Mark VI - This is a heavy tank. No details other than the actual nomenclature are known, but it seems probable that this model is an entirely new departure in German tank design. It has been anticipated for some time that the Marks III and IV might be superseded by a new type incorporating the best features of each model and introducing features borrowed from British and possibly American designs. Having obtained a tank gun of first quality in the long-

The Tiger was deployed late in August 1942 but first saw action on 22nd September 1942. The machines were operating in the Army Group North sector near Lenningrad where the terrain was marshy and entirely unsuited to a colossus such as the Tiger I. This rare photograph gives a vivid impression of the type of terrain which the first Tigers were expected to traverse.

barrelled 75mm tank gun (40), the weapon mounted in the new Mark IV tanks, it is probable that this weapon or an 88mm weapon is the principal armament. The basic armour may be as thick as 80 or 100mm, and spaced armour, at least in front, is probably incorporated. There may also be skirting armour. Face-hardened armour is probably used, and the speed is not expected to be under 25mph.

Reports of a German heavy tank have been received over a considerable period of time. Apparently the most recent is the statement of a German captured in Tunisia. According to the prisoner, he belonged to an independent heavy tank battalion, which consisted of a headquarters company and two armoured companies. Each armoured company was equipped with nine 50 ton tanks. The tanks were armed with 88mm guns and were capable of a speed of 50 kilometers (about 30 miles) an hour. Whether or not this is the Mark VI tank is not known.

A Tiger I deployed to supplement the Afrika Korps operating in Tunisia, January 1943.

Deployment

Besides Russia, the Tiger was also deployed in Tunisia as it was this theatre which gave the western allies their first glimpse of the tank in the field. Prior to the arrival of the Tiger in Tunisia allied intelligence had been forced to rely on carefully placed German newspaper stories and limited intelligence provided by the Soviets. The first widely circulated intelligence report appeared in the US army intelligence publication entitled *Tactical and Technical Trends No. 18* which was published on 11th February 1943 some five months after the Tiger had first appeared in combat in Russia. It is interesting to note that the name Tiger had not yet come to be associated with the tank.

As the Tunisian campaign developed, Tiger tanks began appear more frequently on the battlefield albeit in limited numbers. However, their heavy armour and powerful armament allowed them dominate the initial tank battles fought in the open terrain of North Africa, but their mechanical unreliability and lack of numbers meant that they were never to be massed in great numbers and that they served in a primarily supporting role.

The following pages feature a further U.S. intelligence report describing the German Tiger tank originally appeared in *Tactical and Technical Trends*, No. 20 on 11th March 1943. By this time, accurate information on the Tiger tank was starting to be received from destroyed remnants of Tigers captured by the British forces in Tunisia. This is the second glimpse of how allied intelligence reported the arrival of the Tiger on the battlefield. At this stage the name Tiger was still not in use and the Americans did not use the Roman numerals with the new machine being simply refereed to as the PZ.KW. 6

GERMAN HEAVY TANK IN ACTION IN TUNISIA

As reported in the press and as previously indicated in Tactical and Technical Trends (No. 18, p.6) a German heavy tank has been in action in Tunisia. So far as can be definitely determined, this is the first time the Germans have used a heavy tank in combat. Whether or not it is the Pz.Kw. 6 cannot be definitely stated. At least one heavy tank has been captured, and while complete details are not yet available, there is sufficient reasonably confirmed data to warrant at least a partial tentative description at this time.

The chief features of this tank are the 88mm gun, 4-inch frontal armour, heavy weight, and lack of spaced armour. The accompanying sketch roughly indicates the appearance of the tank, but should not be accepted as wholly accurate.

The tank has a crew of 5. It is about 20 feet long, 12 feet wide, and 9 $1/2$ feet high. The gun overhangs the nose by almost 7 feet. It is reported that the weight is 56 tons or, with modifications, as much as 62 tons.

The power unit is a single 12-cylinder engine. A speed of at least 20 mph can be achieved. Two types of track are thought to exist: an operational track 2 feet 4.5 inches wide, and a loading track which is just under 2 feet. The suspension system consists of a front driving sprocket, a small rear idler, and 24 Christie-type wheels on each side giving it an appearance similar to the familiar German half-track suspension system. There are 8 axles.

There is no armour skirting for protection of the suspension. The armour plating is as follows:

Lower nose plate	62mm (2.4 in)	60° inwards
Upper nose plate	102mm (4 in)	20° inwards
Front plate	62mm (2.4 in)	80° outwards
Driver plate	102mm (4 in)	10° outwards
Turret sides and rear	82mm (3.2 in)	Vertical
Lower sides (behind bogies)	62mm (2.4 in)	Vertical
Upper sides	82mm (3.2 in)	Vertical
Rear	82mm (3.2 in)	20° inwards
Floor	26mm	(1 in)
Top	26mm	(1 in)

The turret front and mantlet range in thickness between a minimum of 97mm (3.8 in) to a (possible) maximum of 200mm (7.9 in). It appears that the armour is not face-hardened.

The armament of the tank consists of an 88mm gun and two 7.92mm (.315-in) machine guns. The 88mm has a double-baffle muzzle brake and fires the same fixed ammunition as the usual 88mm AA/AT gun. As already indicated, the gun overhangs the nose of the tank by almost 7 feet. The turret rotates through 360 degrees and is probably power-operated. Three smoke-generator dischargers are located on each side of the turret.

Comment

From the above characteristics, it is apparent that the Pz.Kw. 6 is designed to be larger and more powerful than the Pz.Kw. 4. As far as known, a Pz.Kw. 5 tank has not been used in combat. The noteworthy differences between the Pz.Kw. 4 and Pz.Kw. 6 are as follows:

Armour	Pz.Kw. 4	Pz.Kw. 6
Minimum	20mm	26mm
Maximum	50 to 80mm*	102mm**
Principal Armament	75mm (long-barrelled gun)	88mm (AA/AT gun)

A 360-degree rotating turret is used in both the Pz.Kw. 6 and Pz.Kw. 4.

The appearance of the Pz.Kw. 6 indicates that the Germans continue to see the need for a fully armoured vehicle equipped with a weapon capable of dealing with hostile tanks as well as with other targets that might hold up the advance of attacking elements.

This tank is undoubtedly an effective weapon, but not necessarily formidable. In the first place, a vehicle weighing from 56 to 62 tons presents many difficult logistical problems. Also, it is reported that one heavy tank was destroyed by a British six-pounder (57mm) antitank gun at a range of about 500 yards; out of 20 rounds fired, 5 penetrated the tank, 1 piercing the side of the turret and coming out the other side, and another penetrating an upper side plate at an angle of impact of about 15 degrees.

*Attained by attaching extra armour plate to protect critical points on the tank.

**Basic armour plate. The turret front and mantlet may possibly be 200mm thick.

***

The Mechanics Of The Tiger I

The Tiger was essentially at the prototype stage when it was first hurried into service, and therefore changes both small and large were made throughout the production run. A redesigned turret with a lower, less bulky commander's cupola was the most significant early change. To cut costs, the submersion capability

The cumbersome road wheel assembly of the Tiger I can be clearly seen in this photograph taken at the Henschel works. It is easy to understand why these wheels could become jammed solid with mud, ice or snow requiring huge efforts to repair.

was reduced and an external air-filtration system was dropped.

The rear of the tank held an engine compartment flanked by two floodable rear compartments each containing a fuel tank, radiator, and fans. German industry had not developed an adequate heavy diesel engine, so a fuel hungry petrol power plant had to be used. The initial engine was a 21 litre (1282 cu. in.) 12 cylinder Maybach HL 210 P45 with 650 PS (641hp, 478kW). Although a good and reliable engine, it was inadequate for the size and weight vehicle. From the 250th production Tiger Chassis 250251, this engine was replaced by the updated HL 230 P45 (23 litres/1410 cu. in.) with 700 PS (690hp, 515kW). The engine was in V-form, with two cylinder banks at 60 degrees. An inertial starter was mounted on its right side, driven via chain gears through a port in the rear wall. The engine could be lifted out through a hatch on the hull roof. The engine drove two front sprockets, which were mounted low to the ground.

The eleven-tonne turret had a hydraulic motor the drive for which was powered by mechanical drive from the engine. Rotation was slow and took about a minute to swing through 360°. The suspension used sixteen torsion bars, with eight suspension arms per side. To save space, the swing arms were leading on one side and trailing on the other. There were three road wheels on each arm, giving a good cross-country ride. However the smoothness of the ride was bought at a high price. The constant need to remove the front road wheels in order to gain access to the rear wheels was to become the bane of Tiger I crews from day one.

The problem from the crew's point of view was that the heavy wheels which had a diameter of 800mm (31 in) were overlapped and interleaved. Removing one inner wheel that had lost its tyre, which was a fairly common occurrence, could therefore require the removal of up to nine outer wheels. This was bad enough under calm conditions but it meant there was no way of making a fast change in the combat zone and many precious Tigers were blown up which could otherwise have been saved. The wheels could also become packed with mud or snow that could then freeze. Eventually, a new 'steel' wheel design, closely resembling those on the Tiger

An extract from the Tigerfibel, the commander's manual: "If you travel 7km, your wide tracks will throw up the dust from 1 hectare of land. You will be recognised from far away and will lose your most efective weapon - surprise."

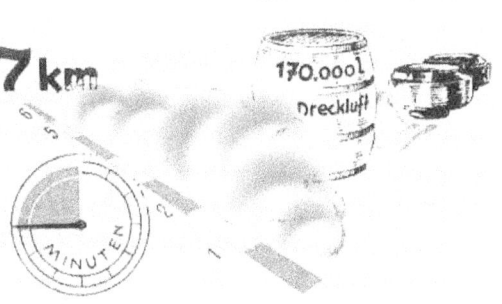

During action the laborious process of re-fuelling and re-arming the Tiger I was a never ending task for the hard pressed crew members.

II, with an internal tire was substituted, and which like the Tiger II, were only overlapped, and not interleaved.

Another new feature which was to cause problems was the untested Maybach-Olvar hydraulically-controlled pre-selector gearbox and semi-automatic transmission. The extreme weight of the tank also required a new steering system. Instead of the clutch-and-brake designs of lighter vehicles, a variation on the tested and proven British Merritt-Brown single radius system was used. The Tiger I, like all German tanks, used regenerative steering which was hydraulically operated - the separate tracks could therefore be turned in opposite directions at the same time, so the Tiger I could pivot in place, and completely turn around in a distance of only 3.44 meters (11.28 ft.). Since the vehicle had an eight-speed gearbox, it thus had sixteen different radii of turn. If an even smaller radius was needed, the tank could be turned by using brakes. There was an actual steering wheel and the steering system at least was robust, reliable, easy to use and ahead of its time. The British T. I. Summary No. 104 was issued on 16th May 1943 gave the British troops in the field a pretty accurate summary of the type of tank they were facing.

Pz. Kw. VI

The following additional information on the Pz. Kw. VI has been collated from captured documents and reports from Russian and North Africa:

(a) The tank can be submerged to a depth of up to 16ft for fording rivers and other water obstacles. Further information on this development is contained at Appendix C.

(b) An automatic fire extinguisher is provided. Heat-sensitive elements are arranged in suitable positions in the engine compartment. If fire breaks out, one of these elements will cause an electric circuit to operate the extinguisher which will there upon discharge a fire-extinguishing agent for a period of seven seconds. If the fire is severe, the circuit will remain closed and the process will be repeated one or more times until either the fire is put out or the reservoir of the fire extinguisher is exhausted. The reservoir holds 9lbs of extinguishing agent.

(c) The gearbox is preselective and is cooled by a fan which also cools the manifold.

(d) Standard German petrol with an octane number of 74 or 78 is used for the engine.

(e) Reference summary 102, appendix D, North Africa now reports that the total amount of 8.8cm ammunition carried is 92 rounds stowed in racks and bins, 46 rounds each side of the tank.

(f) It is confirmed that the 8.8cm tank gun is electrically fired.

(g) Oil capacities are as follows:

Engine	28 litres (6.2 galls)
Gearbox & steering units (common sump)	32 litres (7 galls)
Final drive units	8 litres (14 pints)
Turret traversing gear	5 litres (8.75 pints)
Fan drive	6 litres (10.5 pints)

***

Production History

While the Tiger I was justifiably feared by many of its opponents, it was also over-engineered, used expensive labour intensive materials and production methods, and was time-consuming to produce. Despite its lasting reputation the tank was actually produced in relatively small numbers. Only 1,347 were built between August 1942 and August 1944 when production ceased. Throughout its brief life the Tiger I was particularly prone to certain types of track failures and immobilisations, it

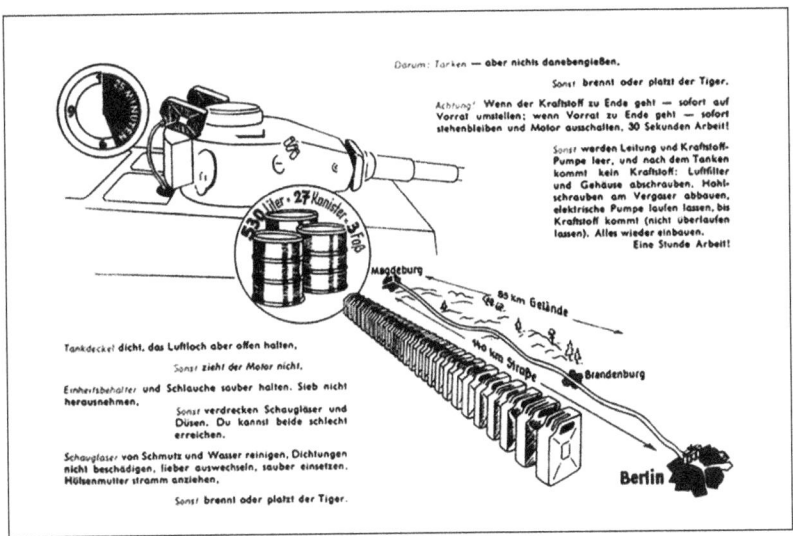

The humorous instruction manual for the tank, the Tigerfibel, was somewhat unorthodox by Third Reich standards. Full of risque sketches and irreverant statements, this is one of the more conventional pages which compares the tank's cross country capability against a road march.

was unreliable mechanically reliable and ferociously expensive to maintain and complicated to transport. Due to its wide tracks powered by interlocking and over lapping road wheels the Tiger I required that a total of eight road wheels consisting of the outer four road wheels on both of the vehicle were to be removed if it was to be transported by rail.

The other huge drawback of the Tiger was the enormous fuel consumption associated with such a heavy vehicle. The 1943 log book a captured Tiger circulated by the British M.I.10 intelligence unit which gives a fascinating insight into the fuel consumption characteristics of the Tiger I.

With the conclusion of the Tunisian campaign there was adequate time to study the battlefield results achieved by the Tiger. Captured vehicles provided a wealth of accurate technical information A far more detailed account of the Tiger in combat was reported by the US army intelligence service in their monthly update for June 1943 which refers to the vehicle, for the first time, as the "Tiger".

During the course of the war, the Tiger I saw combat on the three main German battlefronts. It was usually deployed in independent tank battalions, which on occasion proved to be extremely formidable. In the right hands the Tiger I could be relied upon to turn some spectacularly one sided tactical situations in favour of the hard pressed men of the Heer. At the operational level however, there were never enough Tigers to affect the outcome of a major battle. In the tactical arena the Tiger I demanded good handling by experienced crews who knew and respected the limitations of the machine. Even with the very best crews it was soon apparent that the Tiger I was by no means a miracle weapon. It was always vulnerable to regular battlefield weapons such as the British 6 pounder which could prove deadly if the Tiger I was within range as this account from the US intelligence briefing update *Tactical and Technical Trends* clearly demonstrates. American reports tended to favour the use of the Arabic numeral 6 as opposed to the German designated VI.

NOTE ON ENTRIES IN LOG BOOK OF PZ.KW.VI (H)
M I.10 Germany Rcd.at D.T.D Sept 43
Pz.Kw.VI(H) TIGER Mechanical behaviour under service conditions

Entries show that 4917 litres of petrol went into the fuel tanks of this vehicle during a period in which 489km were covered. In other words the apparent petrol consumption was over 10 litres per km. Even if it is assumed that the tanks (total capacity 530 litres) were empty at the start and full at the finish, the consumption would still work out at about 9 litres per km.

These figures are higher than the petrol consumption quoted in the official German specs, viz:

- **Roads:** 4.5 litres per km, 1.58 galls per mile
- **Cross country:** 7.8 litres per km, 2.76 galls per mile

The following additional points have been noted in the log book:

- 120 km - Log started
- 136 km - Wireless Tested
- 160 km - Test run by workshops company
- 200 km - Wireless Tested/Engine oil and air cleaner oil
- 343 km - New gearbox fitted
- 365 km - Tooth sprocket ring (offside sprocket) changed
- 482 km - New engine & new nearside fan drive clutch fitted
- 609 km - Log closes

NEW GERMAN HEAVY TANK

In Tunisia the German Army sent into combat, apparently for the first time, its new heavy tank, the Pz. Kw. 6, which it calls the "Tiger". The new tank's most notable features are its 88mm gun, 4-inch frontal armour, great weight, and lack of spaced armour. Although the Pz. Kw. 6 has probably been adopted as a

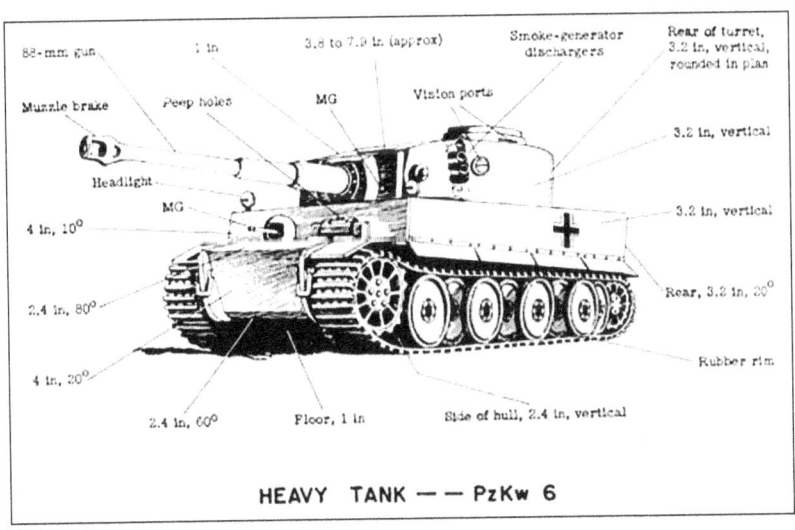

HEAVY TANK — — PzKw 6

standard German tank, future modifications may be expected.

The "Tiger" tank, which is larger and more powerful than the Pz. Kw. 4,1 is about 20 feet long, 12 feet wide, and 9 1/2 feet high. The barrel of the 88mm gun overhangs the nose by almost 7 feet. The tank weighs 56 tons in action (or, with certain alterations, as much as 62 tons), and is reported to have a maximum speed of about 20 miles per hour. It normally has a crew of five.

The armament of the Pz. Kw. 6 consists of the 88mm tank gun (Kw. K. 36), which fires fixed ammunition similar to, or identical with, ammunition for the usual 88mm antiaircraft-antitank gun; a 7.92mm machine gun (MG 34) which is mounted coaxially on the left side of the 88mm; and a second 7.92mm machine gun (MG 34) which is hull-mounted and fires forward.

In addition, a set of three smoke-generator dischargers is carried on each side of the turret.

The turret rotates through 360 degrees, and the mounting for the gun and coaxial machine gun appears to be of the customary German type.

The suspension system, which is unusually interesting, is illustrated in figure 4. The track is made of metal. To the far right in figure 4 is the front-drive sprocket and to the far left the rear idler. There are no return rollers, since the track rides on top of the Christie-type wheels, which are rubber rimmed. It will be noted that there are eight axles, each with three wheels to a side, or each with one single and one double wheel to a side. There are thus 24 wheels - 8 single wheels and 8 double wheels on each side of the tank. The system of overlapping is similar to the suspension system used on German half-tracks.

The tank is provided with two tracks, a wide one (2 feet, 4.5 inches) and a narrow one (just under 2 feet). The wide track is the one used in battle, the narrow being for administrative marches and where manoeuvrability and economy of operation take precedence over ground pressure. The dotted line in figure 4 indicates the outer edge of the narrow track. When the narrow track is used, the eight wheels outside the dotted line can be removed.

The armour plating of the Pz. Kw. 6 has the following thicknesses and angles:

Lower nose plate	62mm (2.4 in)	60° inwards
Upper nose plate	102mm (4 in)	20° inwards
Front plate	62mm (2.4 in)	80° outwards
Driver plate	102mm (4 in)	10° outwards
Turret front and mantlet	Up to 200mm (8 in)	Rounded
Turret sides and rear	82mm (3.2 in)	Vertical
Lower sides (behind bogies)	60mm (2.4 in)	Vertical
Upper sides	82mm (3.2 in)	Vertical
Rear	82mm (3.2 in)	20° inwards
Floor	26mm (1 in)	
Top	26mm (1 in)	

The angular (as opposed to rounded) arrangement of most of the armour is a bad design feature; reliance seems to be placed on the quality and thickness of the armour, with no effort having been made to present difficult angles of impact. In addition, none of the armour is face-hardened. The familiar German practice of increasing a tank's frontal armour at the expense of the side armour is also apparent in the case of the Pz. Kw. 6.

Undoubtedly the Germans developed the "Tiger" tank to meet the need for a fully armoured vehicle equipped with a heavy weapon capable of dealing with a variety of targets, including hostile tanks. Although the "Tiger" can perform these duties, its weight and size make it a logistical headache. It is entirely probable that the Germans, realizing this disadvantage, are continuing to develop tanks in the 30-ton class. Further, it is interesting to note that the Pz. Kw. 6 has proved vulnerable to the British 6-pounder (57mm) antitank gun when fired at a range of about 500 yards.

Design Features

The Tiger I differed from earlier German tanks principally in its design philosophy. Its predecessors all sought balance mobility, armour and firepower, and as a result were being outgunned by their opponents. The Tiger I represented a brand new approach which emphasised firepower and armour at the expense of mobility. Nonetheless the new heavy tank was surprisingly sprightly and was not that much slower than the best of its opponents. However, with over 50 metric tons dead weight, suspensions, gearboxes and other vital items had clearly reached their design limits and as a result Tiger I breakdowns were infuriatingly frequent.

Design studies for a new heavy tank had actually been started in 1937, but had stalled long before production planning stage was reached. Renewed impetus for the Tiger was provided by the discovery of outstanding battlefield qualities of the Soviet T-34 encountered in 1941. Although the general design and layout

A Tiger captured by Allied Forces near Tunis, 1943. It was vehicles such as this which allowed the Allies to unlock the secrets of the Tiger I.

The 88mm ammunition carried by the Tiger I was exceptionally bulky and an ingenious array of stowage solutions were incorporated which allowed the tank to accommodate up to 100, and sometimes more, of these space consuming rounds.

were broadly similar to the previous medium tank, the Panzer IV, the Tiger weighed more than twice as much. This was due to its substantially thicker armour, the larger main gun, greater volume of fuel and ammunition storage, larger engine, and more solidly-built transmission and suspension. Unfortunately for the Panzerwaffe not all of the lessons from the T-34 were absorbed. Sloping angular armour deflects most shots away from the vehicle and can therefore afford to be thinner and lighter. The Armour plates on the Tiger were mostly flat, with interlocking construction however the armour joints were of high quality, being stepped and welded rather than riveted which overcame one of the main disadvantages of riveted construction found in many allied tanks of the early war period.

The nominal armour of the Tiger at its thickest point on the gun mantlet was 200mm and an unprecedented 120mm thick on most of the mantlet. The Tiger I had frontal hull armour 100mm (3.9in) thick and frontal turret armour of 120mm (4.7in), as opposed to the 80mm (3.1in) frontal hull and 50mm (2 in) frontal turret armour of contemporary models of the Panzer IV. It also had 60mm (2.4in) thick hull side plates and 80mm armour on the side superstructure and rear, turret sides and rear was 80mm. The top and bottom armour was 25mm (1in) thick; from March 1944, the turret roof was thickened to 40mm (1.6in).

The gun's breech and firing mechanism were derived from the famous German "88" dual purpose flak gun, the Flugabwehrkanone. The 88mm Kampfwagonkanone 36 L/56 gun was the variant developed for the Tiger and was the most effective and feared tank guns of World War II. The Tiger's gun had a very flat trajectory and extremely accurate Leitz Turmzielfernrohr TZF 9b sights (later replaced by the monocular TZF 9c). In British wartime firing trials, five successive hits were scored on a 16 by 18 inch (410 by 460mm) target at a range of 1,200 yards (1,100m). Tigers were reported to have knocked out enemy tanks at ranges greater than 2.5 miles (4,000m), although most World War II engagements were fought at much shorter ranges.

Ammunition types :
    i) 8.8 cm KwK 36# Ammunition (General Issue)
    ii) PzGr.39 (Armour Piercing Capped Ballistic Cap)
    iii) PzGr.40 (Armour Piercing Composite Rigid)
    iv) Hl. Gr.39 (High Explosive Anti-Tank)
    v) Sch Sprgr. Patr. L/4.5 (Incendiary Shrapnel)

ATTACK AGAINST GERMAN HEAVY TANK Pz. Kw. 6

The following report by an observer on the Tunisian front furnishes some comments as a guide to training in antitank action against this tank.

It appears that the first of these tanks to be destroyed in this theatre were accounted for by British 6-pounders (57mm). An

A tank commander confers with supporting infantry from the Waffen-SS. This shot was taken in the summer of 1943.

account of this action, as reported by a British Army Officer, follows:

"The emplaced 6-pounders opened fire at an initial range of 680 yards. The first rounds hit the upper side of the tank at very acute angles and merely nicked the armour. As the tank moved nearer, it turned in such a manner that the third and fourth shots gouged out scallops of armour, the fifth shot went almost through and the next three rounds penetrated completely and stopped the tank. The first complete penetration was at a range of 800 yards, at an angle of impact of 30 degrees from normal, through homogeneous armour 82mm (approximately 3 1/3 inches) thick. Ammunition used was the 57mm semi-AP solid shot.

"One element of this action contains an important lesson that should be brought to the attention of all AT elements and particularly tank destroyer units."

    (a) "The British gunners did not open until the enemy tank was well within effective range."

    (b) "In addition to opening fire with the primary weapon - the 57mm - the AT unit also opened with intense light machine-gun fire which forced the tank to button up and in effect blinded him. His vision apparently became confused and he was actually traversing his gun away from the AT guns when he was knocked out for good.

(c) "Once they opened fire, the British gunners really poured it on and knocked out one more heavy tank and six Pz. Kw. 3s. Also, for good measure, one armoured car."

The conclusions to be drawn from this action, according to the British officer quoted, are:

(a) "The unobstructed vision of the gunner in a tank destroyer gives him a very real advantage over his opponent squinting through the periscope or narrow vision slits of a tank.

(b) "The tank destroyer unit must force the enemy tank to 'button up' by intense fire from every weapon he has, including machine-guns, tommy guns, and rifles."

The size and weight of a tank such as the Pz. Kw. 6 present many problems. It has been indicated from unofficial enemy sources that extensive reconnaissance of terrain, bridges, etc., was necessary before operations with this tank could be undertaken. Bridges have to be reinforced in many cases, and soil conditions must be good for its effective operation. It can therefore be assumed that its field of operation is limited.

Reports so far indicate that the use of this tank is chiefly to support other armoured units, including employment as mobile artillery. As a support tank it is always in rear of lighter units. In one reported skirmish in Tunisia, the lighter units formed the spear-head; as soon as enemy tanks were decoyed into range the lighter tanks fanned out, leaving the heavier tanks in the rear to engage the enemy units.

The Pz. Kw. 6 is now considered a standard German tank. Present production figures are believed to be at a maximum of 800 per month.

***

Getting To The Battlefield

The problems of moving the Tiger tank from place to place were significant and were especially marked in relation to rail movement by rail. The Tiger's width placed the vehicle at the very limits of the abilities of Europe's rail systems to cope with the vehicle and special transit tracks had to be developed if the tanks were to be moved at all. In order to support the considerable weight of the Tiger, the tracks were an unprecedented 725mm (28.5in) wide. Which was too wide to be carried by rail. To meet rail-freight size restrictions, the outer row of wheels had to be removed and special 520mm (20in) wide transport tracks installed. With a good crew, a track change took 20 minutes. British intelligence was bolstered by the 1944 interrogation of a POW who had experience of the enormous difficulties entailed in moving the Tiger by rail.

Another early U.S. report on the German heavy Tiger tank, Pz. Kw. 6 was featured in *Tactical and Technical Trends*, 6th May 1943 while the Tunisian campaign was coming to a close. By now the Tiger I was becoming increasingly familiar on the battlefields and as a result the intelligence reports were increasingly accurate.

As German prisoners began to be taken in Tunisia so the knowledge available to the allies increased. *Notes On Tank Tactics* was derived from interrogations of these prisoners and was published in April 1943 by the R.A.C. liaison unit. By this stage more and more detail was beginning to emerge on the exact statistical role in which the Tiger I was employed in Tunisia.

The first reports of the Tiger I in combat in Tunisia had actually begun to filter in from January 1943. From the speed at which the German battlefield tactics were altered it appears fairly clear that the German tank crews were quickly disabused of the notion that the new tank was invincible. The Tiger I

Routine maintenance of the Tiger I was incredibly difficult and required a mobile crane as it was necessary to remove the turret in order to change the gear box. This was a frustratingly frequent occurrence.

was without a doubt a strongly built tank with many superior attributes, but it could be easily destroyed by regular battlefield weaponry, especially if the crew were not constantly vigilant for attacks from the rear or the side. This further extract from a British intelligence report from M.I.10 dated September 1943 underlines the fact that the British were fast learning the weaknesses of the Tiger in action.

PRISONER OF WAR DESCRIBES RAIL EMBARKATION

A PW states that the narrow loading tracks for Tiger tanks belong permanently on the special platform truck and are put back on it when the truck returns to its home station.

Tiger tanks only just fit on the width of the truck and are secured by laying wooden beams against the inner sides of the trucks and securing them to the flooring by means of heavy bolts passing through prepared holes.

One PW described the loading of Tiger tanks at Maille-Le-Camp (France) early in Feb 44 and the unloading a few days later at Ficulie (Italy).

"Conditions at both ends were very bad. Deep mud, rain or snow, and biting winds hindered operations and made the job very trying.

The 80 ton platform truck was shunted up to an end loading ramp and secured in position.

By means of an 18 ton half tracked towing vehicle, the narrow loading tracks were towed off the platform truck and manoeuvred into position on the ground in echelon and at the correct width apart. One broad track was then undone and the tank driven forward on one track so that the bogie wheels on the opposite side ran off the broad track onto the narrow track.

The intended joining point of the narrow track was between the driving sprocket and the ground. To bring the upper run of the track round the rear idler and over the tops of the bogie wheels, the sprocket hub was used as a capstan by passing a wire rope round it. With the broad track locked and the sprocket on the opposite side rotating slowly, the crew pulled on the end of the wire rope and so brought the track up and over.

Having joined the first narrow track, the broad track on the opposite side was undone and the tank driven forward on the

The cumbersome process of preparing the Tiger I for rail transport included removing the outermost road wheels, changing the wide combat tracks to fit the narrow guage tracks shown here.

narrow track until the bogie wheels ran over the second narrow track.

Once the tank was fitted with the narrow tracks, the crew had to remove the four outside bogie wheels on both sides.

When this had been done, the half tracked towing vehicle had to tow the broad tracks side by side in front of the loading ramp.

The Tiger was then driven forward so that it straddled the tracks on the ground. Wire ropes were attached to the two lifting eyes at the front of the turret, passed over the front armour and secured at their other ends to the tracks.

The Tiger was finally driven up the ramp, towing its own broad tracks underneath it between the narrow tracks. Once it was in position on the platform truck the ultimate operation was to bring up the overhanging ends of the broad tracks over the rear armour of the tank, a feat accomplished by wire ropes and pulleys, with the attendant towing vehicle providing the motive power.

Before the tank was ready to travel, the turret had to be traversed to approx 5 o'clock to allow for the right-handed tunnels which are mostly encountered on the route from France to Italy."

GERMAN HEAVY TANK – Pz. Kw. 6

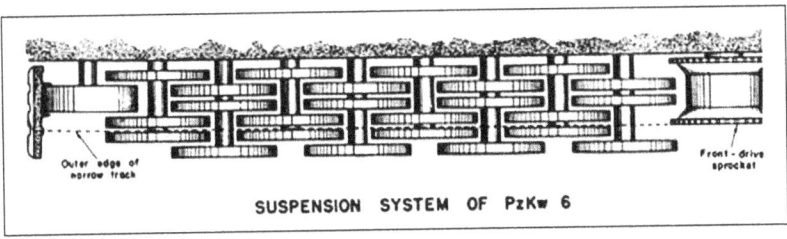

SUSPENSION SYSTEM OF PzKw 6

The accompanying sketch of the tank is based on photographs of a Pz. Kw. 6 knocked out on the Tunisian front.

The suspension system, which has only very briefly been described in Tactical and Technical Trends, is shown in the sketch The track is made of metal. To the far right in the sketch is the front-drive sprocket and to the far left, the rear Idler. There are no return rollers since the track rides on top of the Christie-type wheels, which are rubber rimmed. It will be noted that there are eight axles, each with three wheels to a side, or each with one single and one double wheel to a side. There are thus 24 wheels, or 8 single wheels and 8 double wheels, on each side of the tank. The system of overlapping is similar to the suspension system used on German half-tracks.

The tank is provided with two tracks, a wide one (2 ft, 4.5 in) and a narrow one (just under 2 ft). The wide track is the one used in battle, the narrow being for administrative marches and where manoeuvrability and economy of operation take precedence over ground pressure. The dotted line in the sketch of the suspension system indicates the outer edge of the narrow track. When the narrow track is used, the eight wheels outside the dotted line can be removed.

USE OF Pz. Kw. VI (TIGER)

(a) Information obtained from PW indicates that the Pz. Kw. VI was chiefly used in Tunisia to support other armoured units, and mention was made of its employment as mobile artillery. As a support tank it was always used in rear of lighter units. In one reported skirmish however, the lighter Pz. Kw. IIIs and IVs formed the spearhead of the advance; as soon as our tanks came within range the German 'spearhead' tanks deployed to the flanks, leaving the heavier Pz. Kw. VI tanks to engage.

(b) A PW who was with RHQ7 Pz. Regiment in Tunisia for sometime states that there were some 20 Pz. Lw. Vis in the regiment. When on the march ten of these moved with the main column, the others moving on the flanks. According to this PW, the tactics in the attack were to seek to engage enemy tanks from hull-down positions at short ranges, even down to 250 yards. On the other hand, this prisoner also reports an engagement in which two Pz. Kw. Vis brought indirect fire to bear, observation being carried out by an artillery FOO, each tank opening with one round of smoke. In confirmation of this there is another A.F.HQ. report which speaks of this exploitation by Pz. Kw. VI gunners of the great range of their 8.8 cm guns.

(c) 30 Military Mission also reports the use of Pz. Kw. VI in squadron strength on various parts of the Russian Front, especially the South-West.

(d) In conversation with Gerneral Martel, Marshal Stalin stated that in Russia, as in the desert, the Pz. Kw. VI went into battle in rear of a protective screen of lighter tanks.

(e) An A.F.HQ. training instruction states that the size and weight of the Pz. Kw. VI present many problems. PW indicated that extensive reconnaissance of terrain, bridges etc., was necessary before operations with this tank could be undertaken. Bridges had to be reinforced in many cases, and it was necessary for the 'going' to be good for the effective employment of the Pz. Kw. VI.

TIGERS BOLDLY USED

At first his Tigers were very boldly used and, once they were sure that their flanks were secured, they drove straight on. After several of these tanks had been knocked out, however, the crews appeared to be less enterprising and were inclined to use their tanks as mobile pillboxes. The fact remains, however, that in an armoured attack the Tiger tank must be regarded as a very formidable fighting component and, given adequate flank protection, will add very effective weight to the enemy firepower.

In the defensive the Pz. Kw. VI, usually well sited in a covered and defiladed position, was a particular danger. Despite the

This is a standard Tiger tank - or, as the Germans designate it, Pz. Kpfw. Tiger. (The Roman numeral "VI" has been dropped.)

A broken down Tiger I being towed by two Sd.Kfz. 9. The convoluted arrangement was the only means by which a broken down Tiger I could be officially recovered.

comparatively slow traversing rate of its turret, the Pz. Kw. VI proved an extremely good defensive weapon and could effectively cover a wide area with anti-tank fire. It was often used in good hull-down positions over very difficult ground, which made it hard for the Sherman to deal with it, and no amount of artillery fire could force it out.

Pz. Kw. VIIIs and IVs rarely took up good defensive positions on their own, but were used to watch the flanks of positions occupied by Pz. Kw. VIs. They were often used in small groups to counter-attack from concealed positions on the flank, from a cactus or olive grove or down a wadi. The terrain forced the enemy to employ rush tactics in close formation, and resulted in these counter-attacks being suitably dealt with.

Tank recovery requires a special note. It was often affected on the spot with speed and courage by attaching tow ropes to the casualties and towing them away by other tanks. Special trips at night were made by tanks to recover casualties (20 Jan BOU ARADA, and 1 Feb ROBAA). Where the enemy held the battlefield, tractors were brought up and the whole area cleared of recoverable casualties, both theirs and ours, in a very short time. The speed with which the recovery plan was made and carried out made action by our demolition squads very difficult, and where tank casualties were in no-man's land and unapproachable by day, the enemy would get out to them the moment darkness fell. Sometimes (eg ROBAA, BOU ARADA) as much as a company of infantry was used to hold off our patrols or stage a diversion while recovery was in progress. The enemy used tanks against our Churchills and was quick to take advantage of an unprotected flank.

GEAR BOX TROUBLE

If a Tiger tank has gearbox trouble, it is customary to dismantle the flexible couplings in the half-shaft drives and to tow it out of the immediate battle area by another Tiger, using two tow ropes secured in 'X' formation to correct the tendency of the towed tank to sway. Should, however, the track on a Tiger have ridden up over the sprocket teeth, the tractive effort required to move it is so great that two Tigers pull in tandem, each towing with crossed tow ropes.

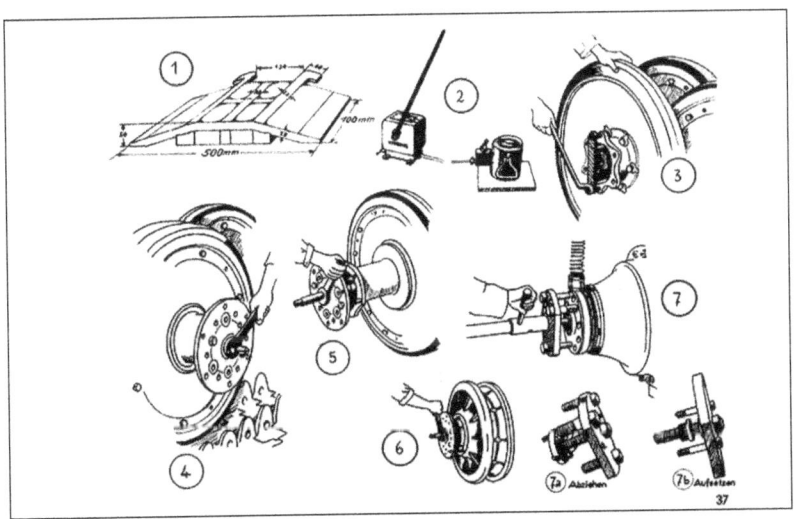

Illustration showing the tools and methods of running gear maintenance from Tigerfibel. Although the need to change road wheels was a frequent and frustrating occurrance, by far the largest share of the mechanical problems resulted from the gear box, the repair of which necessitated the removal of the turret by a mobile crane.

***

This Tiger of the 502nd overturned in the act of crossing a bridge in Russia, during November 1943. The tank commander was killed but the tank was recovered.

MOBILITY

Despite its drawbacks the Tiger was relatively manoeuvrable for its weight and size, and as it generated less ground pressure, it proved to be superior to the Sherman in muddy terrain,. The Tiger tank however was plainly too heavy to cross small bridges with certainty, so it was purpose designed with the built in mechanism to enable the tank to ford four-meter deep water while fully submerged. This required unusual mechanisms for ventilation and cooling when underwater. At least 30 minutes of set-up was required, with the turret and gun being locked in the forward position, and a large snorkel tube raised at the rear. Only the first 495 Tigers were fitted with this expensive and rarely used deep fording system; all later models were capable of fording only two meters.

The main source of mechanical breakdown of the Tiger I appears to have been the gearbox which is a recurring theme in relation to the numerous breakdowns suffered by these vehicles. Towing a Tiger was an enormous problem and frequently resulted in the breakdown of other Tigers assigned to tow broken down vehicle. The procedure was described in an R.A.C. liaison letter dated August 1944.

The real Achilles heel of the Tiger was the extent to which it was prone to mechanical breakdowns. Even when the vehicle was running smoothly vigilance and extreme care was required as the Tiger was exceptionally liable to becoming bogged down while moving across the difficult terrain which was particularly prevalent in Italy. It was here that the British discovered an inordinately large number of disabled Tigers. Initially these 12 machines were all thought to be victims of combat, but it was later discovered, through examination and prisoner interrogation, that the casualties were all as a result of either mechanical or terrain difficulties. This astonishing revelation was published in August 1944 in a report by the British Army's Technical Branch entitled *"Who Killed Tiger?"*

WHO KILLED TIGER?

As a fairly large number of Tiger tanks were reported to have been knocked out in the breakout from the Anzio bridgehead and the advance on Rome we thought it might be educational to try and find out what weapon or what tactics had been responsible, so that the dose might be repeated on other occasions.

Hearing that there was somewhat of a concentration of bodies in a certain area we made a reconnaissance on the 5th August in an area between Velletri and Cori some 30 miles S.E. of Rome.

In all during this reconnaissance 12 Tigers were found either on the road, by the roadside or within easy sight of the road. The following is what we found:

(1) On the Via Tuscolana. Pulled up at the side of the road near a bridge diversion. No sign of battle damage but both tracks were off and each had been cut with a gas torch. Blown up and

A Tiger I undergoing engine repair.

burnt out so the cause of the casualty could not be determined.

(2) On the village green of Giulianello. No sign of battle damage other than a penetration of the hull back plate by Bazooka. This is thought to have been done by following troops after the tank had been abandoned, because the engine cooling fan had been penetrated by the shot but was obviously not rotating at the time and, furthermore, several unused rounds of U.S. Bazooka ammunition were found lying near the machine. This tank had not been demolished by the crew and there was no indication of the cause of stoppage.

(3) By the side of the road one mile from Giulianello. Signs of two H.E. strikes on the turret and one on the cupola. A further H.E. had struck the upper side plate about track level and may have broken the track which was off on this side.

On the opposite side the three rear bogie spindles were bent upwards and the bogies were riding the track guides. A tow-rope was found in place and the tank had been demolished. If the right hand track had in fact been cut by H.E. it is possible that a recovery crew had been caught while extricating the tank which had become a casualty due to the suspension trouble on the other side.

(4) Halfway down a steep bank on the Guilianello-Cori road. No sign of any battle damage or suspension trouble. Tank had been demolished. In this case it is possible that the machine had either become ditched down the bank or had some internal mechanical trouble which could not be rectified.

An interesting point is that this tank had rubber bogie wheels on one side and steel on the other.

(5) Found in a small copse about 100 yards off the road. No sign of battle damage but tank appeared to have become ditched in a sunken lane where it had been trying to turn. Broken tow-ropes found in place. No important suspension defects so that the casualty must have been due to internal mechanical trouble possibly caused by trying to extricate itself from the lane. Blown up.

(6) Found off the road down a bank where it had been pushed to clear the road. Deep A.P. scoops on front of manlet and side of

The task of extricating a stricken Tiger from difficult terrain was beyond every vehicle except another Tiger. Activities of this nature placed a huge strain on the engine and could often result in both vehicles being lost and was officially against orders. However this type of activity, although frowned upon, was a daily occurrence for the men of the Panzerwaffe as there was simply no alternative.

Two Tigers of the 504th Schwere Abteilung irrecoverably stuck in a steep valley. This battalion suffered six total write-offs in four days while on a road march in Italy in September 1944.

turret. Penetration by unknown weapon through 3rd bogie from rear on left hand side. Tracks off, blown up and burnt out. Not enough evidence to deduce the cause of the casualty except that it was certainly not due to the A.P. strikes which were probably sustained in an earlier engagement.

(7) Off the road at the edge of an olive grove. Definite evidence of track trouble. Several track guide lugs broken. R.H. sprocket ring cracked in one place and L.H. ring in two places. Attempts to tow had been made. Demolished. Possibly on tow because of mechanical trouble and abandoned when tracks rode the sprockets and damaged them.

(8) On the level in an olive grove. There were signs of the area having been used by a workshop detachment. No apparent battle damage other than penetrations of bogie wheels by H.E. splinters. Casualty probably due to internal mechanical trouble. One demolition charge had been blown.

(9) Found up against a house in Cori where it would appear to have been left by a recovery team. Two H.E. scoops on front

plate. Tracks off and obvious signs of suspension trouble. R.H. front bogie bent and out of line. Tracks found near. These showed fractures of several links. Demolished.

(10) Off the road in Cori within 10 yards of No.9 above. One bogie wheel missing and others damaged. Sprockets cracked in three places. Tracks off and lying nearby showed evidence of trouble – cracked link and broken guide lug. Demolished.

(11) On the bridge at Cori. Within 50 yards of Nos 9/10. Tank had fallen through damaged arch of bridge. Both tracks off and laid out on the road behind. No battle damage to be seen. Demolished. The presence of Nos 9,10 and 11 tanks so close together suggests that Cori may have been a recovery point for tanks with mechanical trouble which were blown up when it was found impossible to repair them.

(12) Found on the road from Giulianello to Valmontone in a field by a stream some 300 yards off the road. No battle damage but two bogie wheels on one side were bent and out of line. Tracks were still on. There was evidence in the shrubs nearby that the crew of a recovery section had camped by the tank and had been attempting some mechanical repairs which could not be completed in time so that the tank had to be left and demolished.

Notes

Since the above examination was made some information has been received from a P.O.W. which suggests that these 12 tanks were the remnant of 3 Sqn, 506 Heavy Tank Battalion, which was given the job of resisting the Allied break-out from Anzio with 16 tanks.

Some were lost in the engagement while others suffered gearbox trouble and had to be towed out of action. The squadron was ordered to retreat on Cori and during this retreat so much trouble was experienced with the gearboxes and suspensions of towing tanks that attempts at extrication beyond Cori had to be abandoned.

Conclusion

Tiger is not yet sufficiently developed to be considered a reliable vehicle for long marches. He suffers from frequent suspension defects and probably also gearbox trouble. When pushed, as in a retreat, these troubles are too frequent and serious for the German maintenance and recovery organization to deal with.

***

TIGER RECOVERY

Due to its size and weight the high number of breakdowns and the recovery of battle damaged vehicles was to prove a real headache for the engineers. The tanks were immensely valuable and had to be recovered if at all possible. However, the infrastructure and, in particular the recovery vehicles, to support the easy recovery of such a heavy machine as the Tiger I was found to be severely wanting.

The main problem was that the standard German heavy Famo recovery half-track tractor could not actually tow the tank; up to three Famo tractors were usually the only way to tow just one Tiger. It was the case therefore that another Tiger was needed to tow a disabled machine, but on such occasions, the engine of the towing vehicle often overheated and sometimes resulted in an

Three famo 18t tractors were needed to drag this Tiger I into the workshop during the assault on Kharkov in 1943.

engine breakdown or fire. Tiger tanks were therefore forbidden by regulations to tow crippled comrades.

In practice this order was routinely disobeyed as the alternative was the total loss of a large number of tanks that could otherwise have been saved. It was also discovered too late that the low-mounted sprocket limited the obstacle-clearing height. The wide Tiger tracks also had a bad tendency to override the sprocket, resulting in immobilisation. If a track overrode and jammed, two Tigers were normally needed to tow the tank. The jammed track was also a big problem itself, since due to high tension, it was often impossible to disassemble the track by removing the track pins. It was sometimes simply blown apart with an explosive charge.

USE OF Pz. Kw. VI (TIGER)

(a) Information obtained from POW indicates that the Pz. Kw. VI was chiefly used in Tunisia to support other armoured units, and mention was made of its employment as mobile artillery. As a support tank it was always used in rear of lighter units. In one reported skirmish however, the lighter Pz. Kw. IIIs and IVs formed the spearhead of the advance; as soon as our tanks came within range the German 'spearhead' tanks deployed to the flanks, leaving the heavier Pz. Kw. VI tanks to engage.

(b) A POW who was with RHQ7 Pz. Regiment in Tunisia for sometime states that there were some 20 Pz. Lw. VIs in the regiment. When on the march ten of these moved with the main column, the others moving on the flanks. According to this

The illustration from the driver section from Tigerfibel.

A section of Tiger I tanks rolls into position prior to the battle of Kursk .

PW, the tactics in the attack were to seek to engage enemy tanks from hull-down positions at short ranges, even down to 250 yards. On the other hand, this prisoner also reports an engagement in which two Pz. Kw. VIs brought indirect fire to bear, observation being carried out by an artillery FOO, each tank opening with one round of smoke. In confirmation of this there is another A.F.HQ. report which speaks of this exploitation by Pz. Kw. VI gunners of the great range of their 8.8 cm guns.

(c) 30 Military Mission also reports the use of Pz. Kw. VI in squadron strength on various parts of the Russian Front, especially the South-West.

(d) In conversation with General Martel, Marshal Stalin stated that in Russia, as in the desert, the Pz. Kw. VI went into battle in rear of a protective screen of lighter tanks.

(e) An A.F.HQ. training instruction states that the size and weight of the Pz. Kw. VI present many problems. PW indicated that extensive reconnaissance of terrain, bridges etc., was necessary before operations with this tank could be undertaken. Bridges had to be reinforced in many cases, and it was necessary for the 'going' to be good for the effective employment of the Pz. Kw. VI.

(f) It would seem that the employment of this tank in a support role is not however invariable, because a German press report of the fighting round Kharkov in March seems to indicate that the Pz. Kw. VI were used offensively in an independent role.

(g) Another German press report states that during the German withdrawal from Schusselburg, 'a few' Pz. Kw. VI formed the most rearward element of the German rearguard, a role in which they were most successful.

(h) An interesting and detailed newspaper article, written towards the end of May, on events on the Leningrad Front, points towards the use of the Tiger as a mobile defensive front and as having been in action 'for days' (i.e. by inference, that they had been in the same area). These operations were carried out in close co-operation with the infantry manning the defensive positions.

In one particular operation a troop of tanks is described as taking up a defensive position forward of the infantry positions from which (presumably hull-down) advancing Soviet tanks and the following infantry were engaged. All this defensive fire

A rare shot of a Tiger actually engaged in combat during the battle of Kursk.

was put down at the halt including the fire from the MGs in the tanks. In order to move to an alternative position because of enemy arty fire it was necessary for the tank commander to obtain permission from the CO Battle Group, under whose command he was operating.

Conclusion

The use of Pz. Kw. VI tanks in both attack and defence seems, from all available information to hand, to be in a support role. The use of this type of tank in an independent thrusting role, even when supported by tanks of lighter types, would seem to be discouraged.

USE OF A F Vs IN NORTH AFRICA

(a) A POW has described how riflemen with MGs were employed for the protection of tanks when in harbour. On the following morning they were withdrawn from this task for rest and in preparation for other duties.

(b) A POW reports that German tanks were always able to intercept Allied radio traffic, on one occasion obtaining in this way an exact location. Pz. Kw. VI were immediately detailed to engage.

(c) Voluntary destruction of tanks. On 5th December 1942 the following orders were issued by OC 8 Pz. Regiment: "Tanks may be blown up in the following circumstances only:

The radio operator from the Tigerfibel.

Distant Tigers moving up to engage Russian forces during the Kursk offensive. The millions of anti-tank mines were the greatest danger facing the Tigers during the assault phase of the battle.

(i) If the tank cannot be moved

(ii) If the enemy is attacking, and then only,

(iii) If the tank has defended itself to its last round.

The Commander responsible for issuing the order to blow up the tank must make a report to R H Q detailing the circumstances".

(d) Another report describes as 'typical' a case in which a large concentration of tanks was observed opposite one area on our front, small parties of which were observed 'tapping' along our front, halting to fire from about 2,000 yards.

(e) On another occasion another report describes how an estimated total of 50 German tanks put in a counter-attack in the early evening in two groups, each under smoke cover.

***

A Tiger I painted in the original factory Dunkelgrau deployed on the Northern sector in January 1943.

Design review

TIGER COLOUR SCHEMES

In June of 1940 a general order was issued that stipulated all Panzers were to be painted Dunkelgrau (dark grey). This order was still in effect when the Tigers were initially deployed in August 1942. The very first Tiger I's were painted dark grey and as such are usually easy to identify in photographs.

In areas where winter camouflage was needed, the crews applied whitewash. When spring arrived, the crews had to scrub the whitewash off, which was a tedious, labour intensive chore.

In February 1943, a general order came down to change the base coat from dark grey to tan (Dunkelgelb nach Muster). Crews were issued cans of red brown (Rotbraun) and dark olive green (Olivgruen) to use in creating camouflage patterns over the basic tan colouration.

Some tigers were coated with the Zimmerit anti-magnetic

mine coating starting in July 1943. This paste was applied in recognizable grooved patterns and the paint was applied over the top of the coating. Vehicles coated with Zimmerit have a distinctive rough look to their surface.

Camouflage patterns varied from unit to unit, as did the placement and colouring of the vehicle numbers. In addition to good camouflage the tanks themselves required close protection from infantry squads at all times.

As the war wore on into 1944 the increasing volume of captured Tigers continued to yield invaluable intelligence information. With a number of complete machines now in the hands of the western allies it was possible to conduct increasingly scientific examinations. Practical testing of weapon systems and armour was soon undertaken to identify the strengths and weaknesses of the Tiger I. In November 1944 a series of gunnery trials was conducted by Major W. de L. Messenger and his report is summarized overleaf.

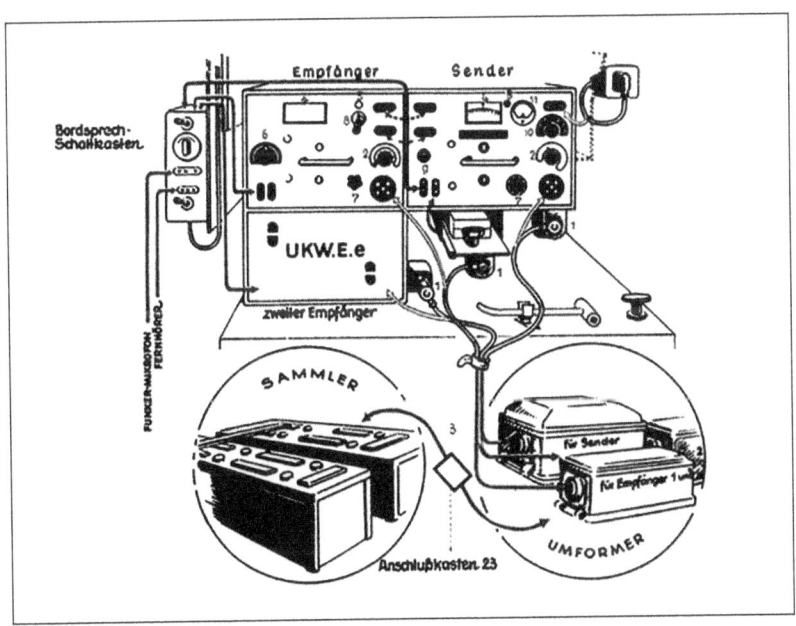

The Tiger radio set up from Tigerfibel which was split into a receiver and a transmitter.

DESIGN REVIEW

The design has been well thought out and it embodies a number of distinctly original features such as the heavy armament and armour, turret and hull construction, powered traverse layout and facilities for total submersion.

It appears that the user has not had the same influence on it as on British tanks since so many of the items, whilst basically good, are unsatisfactory and could well be improved from the user aspect by slight modification.

The outstanding features would appear to be:

GOOD POINTS

(1) 8.8cm gun with its smooth action and easily stripped breech mechanism.

(2) Heavy armour and method of construction (welding and front plates projecting above the roof plates).

(3) Stability as a gun platform.

(4) Ammunition stowage – quantity and accessibility.

(5) Electrical firing gear with safety interlocks and novel trigger switch.

(6) Flush turret floor without coaming or shields.

(7) Binocular telescope with fixed eyepiece.

(8) Mounting for periscopic binoculars in cupola and commander's hand traverse.

(9) Ability to superimpose hand on power traverse and absence of oil pipes and unions.

(10) Ample space for loader.

(11) Method of attaching stowage to turret walls (flexible strips).

(12) Spring assisted hatches.

(13) S-mine dischargers.

(14) 2-position commander's seat and backrest

The Tiger was a prized target and was as vulnerable as any other tank to strongly motivated tank hunting teams. Close support from well trained infantry was therefore crucial to the survival of the Tigers on the battlefield. The Tiger on the right is carrying its own close support team.

(15) Electrically fired smoke generator dischargers.

(16) Handholds on roof to assist gunner.

BAD POINTS

(1) Out-of-balance of gun and turret.

(2) Obscuration by smoke from flashless propellent.

(3) Ventilation of gun fumes

(4) Lack of intercommunication for loader.

(5) Cramped positions of gunner and commander.

(6) Powered traverse control – Lack of definite neutral position and awkward range of movement

(7) No armouring on bins.

(8) Small gun deflector bag.

(9) Awkward re-arming of co-axial M.G.

(10) Gunner's exit via commander's cupola.

(11) Head pad on auxiliary M.G.

The Pz. Kpfw. VI with its heavy armour, dual purpose armament and fighting ability is basically an excellent tank, and, in spite of the defects noted, constitutes a considerable advance on any tank that we have tried.

Its greatest weakness is probably the limit imposed on mobility owing to its weight, width and limited range of action. Taking it all round, it presents a very formidable fighting machine which should not be under-rated.

***

PRODUCTION RUN MODIFICATIONS

During the production run of the Tiger I a number of modifications were introduced in order to correct imperfections to improve automotive performance, firepower and protection. Any good measure which led to the simplification of the design was also implemented, along with forced adjustments as a result of shortages of war materials. Due to a rigid production flow policy at the Henschel factory, incorporation of the new modifications could take several months. In 1942 alone, at least six revisions were made, starting with the removal of the Vorpanzer (frontal armour shield) from the pre-production models in April 1942. In May, mudguards bolted onto the side of the pre-production run were added, while removable mudguards saw full incorporation in September. Smoke discharge canisters, three on each side of the turret, were added in August 1942. In later years, similar changes and updates were added, such as the addition of Zimmerit in late 1943.

Modifications continued as a result of combat experiences in Italy at a comparatively late stage in the life of the Tiger I. The RAC liaison letter for August 1944 revealed that POW integration sources were still providing valuable information regarding the on-going modification programme, which mentioned modifications in the Model E over its predecessors including the following:-

TURRET TOP ARMOUR

In early March'44 on the beachhead, a number of Tiger tanks were spotted from the air by an artillery recce aircraft and shortly afterwards a concentration of artillery fire was put down, during which the turret top of one Tiger was pieced by a direct hit from what appears to be an American "Long Tom."

This incident, which cost two dead of the crew, was duly reported and is considered to have been the reason for the thickening of the turret top armour back and front from 25mm to 40mm on the Model E Tigers which came down from Paderborn in late May 1944.

***

Combat History

As we have see the Tiger was first used in action on 28th September 1942 in marshy terrain near Leningrad. The action was a direct result of Hitler's desperation to see the Tiger in action. This resulted in the tank, which was still very much a prototype, being forced into action prematurely.

Unfortunately, on 22nd September 1942, as they entered the combat arena for the first time the Tigers were deployed single file over marshy terrain with the inevitable result that the machines began to bog down. It was to prove an ominous portent when, in their first day of combat, all four were knocked out. It is interesting to note however that the armour of the vehicles was not penetrated. Three of the Tigers which had been abandoned by their crews were later recovered.

In spite of this atrocious start the Tiger I was to become a fixture of a number of heavy units serving on the eastern front. Better tactics involving close co-operation with supporting infantry

An interesting study of two Tigers passing on a narrow forest track in northern Russia during the summer of 1943.

units were soon developed and other Panzer crews were quickly trained at Paderborn so that they too could be equipped with the Tiger I as the machines rolled off the production lines. The deployment of The Tiger I happened at a fairly rapid pace and by the end of 1942 the first Tiger formations had been deployed in Russia, Tunisia, and Italy. A further training centre was soon established in France. Tigers would eventually be in service with ten Heer heavy tank battalions and one training battalion as well as and the Grossdeutschland Panzer Grenadier Division.

In addition to the regular army units three Waffen-SS heavy tank battalions were also equipped with the Tiger I. A number of additional Heer formations received a smattering of Tigers though the numbers were generally very limited. The 14 Tiger equipped units were the backbone of the fighting force and were issued with the bulk of the available machines.

In the North African theatre, the Tiger first saw action near Robaa Tunisia. In the ensuing battle, a battery belonging to the 72nd Anti-tank Regiment of the British Army equipped with six-pounder managed to knock out three enemy Tigers and rout the remaining forces. The action soon found its way into the British and US intelligence reports reprinted elsewhere in this book. The next theatre in which the allies encountered the Tiger was to be Italy where Tigers were encountered both in Sicily and on the mainland. Following the D-Day landings the Tiger I was encountered during the Normandy battles where it was fielded by the Leibstandarte division.

ROAD MARCHES

The Tiger's extreme weight limited which bridges it could cross. It also made driving through buildings something of a lottery as basements were liable to collapse trapping the tank in the rubble. Another weakness was the slow traverse of the hydraulically-operated turret. The turret could also be traversed manually, but this option was laborious and rarely used, except for very small adjustments.

Early Tigers had a top speed of about 45 kilometres per hour (28mph) over optimal terrain. This was not recommended for

A Grenadier standing in front of a trio of captured Russian anti-tank guns scans the skies as a Tiger I in summer camouflage paint scheme rolls on towards the enemy.

normal operation, and was discouraged in training. Crews were ordered not to exceed 2600rpm due to reliability problems of the early Maybach engines with their maximum 3000rpm output. To combat this, the Tiger's top speed was reduced to about 38 kilometres per hour (24mph) through the installation of an engine governor, capping the rpm of the Maybach HL 230 to 2600rpm (HL 210s were used on early models). Despite being slower than medium tanks of the time, which averaged a top speed of about 45 kilometres per hour (28mph), the Tiger still had a very respectable speed for a tank of its size and weight, especially if one considers the fact that the Tiger I was nearly twice as heavy as a Sherman or T-34.

The Tiger had reliability problems throughout its service life; Tiger units almost invariably entered combat under strength due to various mechanical breakdowns. It was rare for any Tiger unit to complete a road march without losing vehicles due to breakdowns. The tank also had poor radius of action ie the distance which a combat vehicle can travel and return to the battlefield without refuelling. Although the Tigerfibel gave the

Another shot of a Tiger I encountering difficult terrain and insurmountable obstacles in the Army Group North sector.

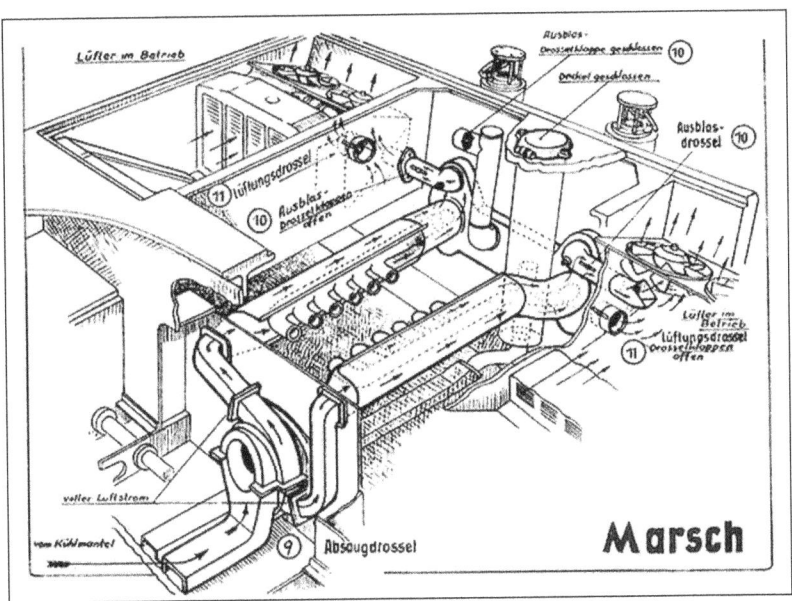

This diagram from Tigerfibel shows throttle and vent flap positions when the Tiger is moving on a road march.

figure of 42.5km in each direction the reality was much lower - 35km across country was considered to be the maximum on a full tank. However, the Tiger I was a remarkably efficient cross-country vehicle. Due to its very wide tracks however, the Tiger did produce a lower ground pressure bearing than many smaller tanks, the most notable exception being the Soviet T-34 which also ran on comparatively wide tracks.

NOTES ON TANK TACTICS
USE OF Pz Kw Vi (TIGER)

Information obtained from PW indicates that the Pz Kw VI was chiefly used in Tunisia to support other armoured units, and mention was made of its employment as mobile artillery. As a support tank it was always used in rear of lighter units. In one reported skirmish however, the lighter Pz Kw IIIs and

IVs formed the spearhead of the advance; as soon as our tanks came within range the German 'spearhead' tanks deployed to the flanks, leaving the heavier Pz Kw VI tanks to engage.

A PW who was with RHQ7 Pz Regiment in Tunisia for some time states that there were some 20 Pz Kw VIs in the regiment. When on the march ten of these moved with the main column, the others moving on the flanks. According to this PW, the tactics in the attack were to seek to engage enemy tanks from hull-down positions at short ranges, even down to 250 yards. On the other hand, this prisoner also reports an engagement in which two Pz Kw VIs brought indirect fire to bear, observation being carried out by an artillery F O O, each tank opening with one round of smoke. In confirmation of this there is another A.F.HQ report which speaks of this exploitation by Pz Kw VI gunners of the great range of their 8.8 cm guns.

30 Military Mission also reports the use of Pz Kw VI in squadron strength on various parts of the Russian Front, especially the South-West.

In conversation with General Martel, Marshal Stalin stated that in Russia, as in the desert, the Pz Kw VI went into battle in rear of a protective screen of lighter tanks.

An A.F.HQ. training instruction states that the size and weight of the Pz Kw VI present many problems. PW indicated that extensive reconnaissance of terrain, bridges etc., was

The loader from Tigerfibel.

necessary before operations with this tank could be undertaken. Bridges had to be reinforced in many cases, and it was necessary for the 'going' to be good for the effective employment of the Pz Kw VI.

It would seem that the employment of this tank in a support role is not however invariable, because a German press report of the fighting round Kharkov in March seems to indicate that the Pz Kw VI were used offensively in an independent role.

Another German press report states that during the German withdrawal from Schusselburg, a "few" Pz Kw VI formed the most rearward element of the German rearguard, a role in which they were most successful.

An interesting and detailed newspaper article, written towards the end of May, on events on the Leningrad Front, points towards the use of the Tiher as a mobile defensive pillbox. The tanks are described as operation on a defensive front and as having been in action 'for days' (i.e. by inference, that they had been in the same area). These operations were carried out in close co-operation with the infantry manning the defensive positions.

In one particular operation a troop of tanks is described as taking up a defensive position forward of the infantry positions from which (presumably hull-down) advancing Soviet tanks and the following infantry were engaged. All this defensive fire was put down at the halt including the fire from the MGs in the tanks. In order to move to an alternative position because of enemy arty fire it was necessary for the tank commander to obtain permission from the CO Battle Group, under whose command he was operating.

The use of Pz Kw VI tanks in both attack and defence seems, from all available information to hand, to be in a support role. The use of this type of tank in an independent thrusting role, even when supported by tanks of lighter types, would seem to be discouraged.

***

TACTICAL ORGANISATION

The Tiger I was usually employed in separate heavy tank battalions known as schwere-Panzer-Abteilung, and were so precious they were generally placed under army command. The heavy battalions would normally be deployed to critical sectors, for use either in breakthrough operations or, as the war wore on, more typically in local counter-attacks. A few favoured divisions, such as the Grossdeutschland and the 1st SS Leibstandarte Adolf Hitler, 2nd SS Das Reich, and 3rd SS Totenkopf Panzergrenadier Divisions at Kursk had a Tiger company in their tank regiments. The Grossdeutschland Division had its Tiger company increased to a battalion as the III Panzer Battalion in Panzer Regiment Grossdeutschland. 3rd SS Totenkopf retained its Tiger I company through the remainder of the war. 1st SS and 2nd SS tank regiments lost their Tiger Companies which were incorporated into a SS Tiger Battalion, the 101st SS Tiger Battalion, which was part of 1st SS Panzer Korps.

The commanders chosen to be granted command of a Tiger I represented the very best of the candidates who passed through the gates of the tank training facility at Paderborn.

The Tiger was originally designed to be an offensive breakthrough weapon, but by the time they went into action, the military situation had changed dramatically, and their main use was on the defensive, as mobile gun batteries known as "the mobile fire brigade". Unfortunately, this also meant rushing the Tigers constantly from location to location causing excessive mechanical issues. As a result, there are almost no instances where a Tiger battalion went into combat at anything close to full strength. Furthermore, against the Soviet and Western Allied production numbers, even a 10:1 kill ratio would not have been sufficient to turn the tactical tide. Some Tiger units did actually exceed the 10:1 kill ratio, including 13. Kompanie/Panzer-Regiment Grossdeutschland with a ratio of 16:1, schwere SS-Panzer-Abteilung 103 with a ratio of 12:1 and schwere Panzer-Abteilung 502 with a ratio of 13:1. These numbers must be set against the opportunity cost of the expensive Tiger. Every Tiger cost as much as four Sturmgeschütz III assault guns to build.

An English translation of a contemporary article from the Soviet Artillery Journal giving detailed instructions for the use of anti-tank weapons against the German Tiger tank, appeared in the U.S. intelligence periodical *Tactical and Technical Trends*, No. 40, December 16th, 1943. Vulnerability of various parts of the tank was cited in connection with directions for attack. At the time of publication, U.S. forces had only sporadically encountered the Tiger tank in Tunisia, Sicily, and Italy. The accompanying sketch shows vulnerable points and indicates weapons to be used against them. Material concerning the vulnerability of German tanks was published in Tactical and Technical Trends No. 8, p. 46 and No. 11, p.28. Detailed information about the Tiger tank was published in Tactical and Technical Trends No. 34, p.13. A translation of the Soviet Artillery Journal article follows overleaf:

THE RUSSIAN VIEW – Vulnerability of Tiger Tanks

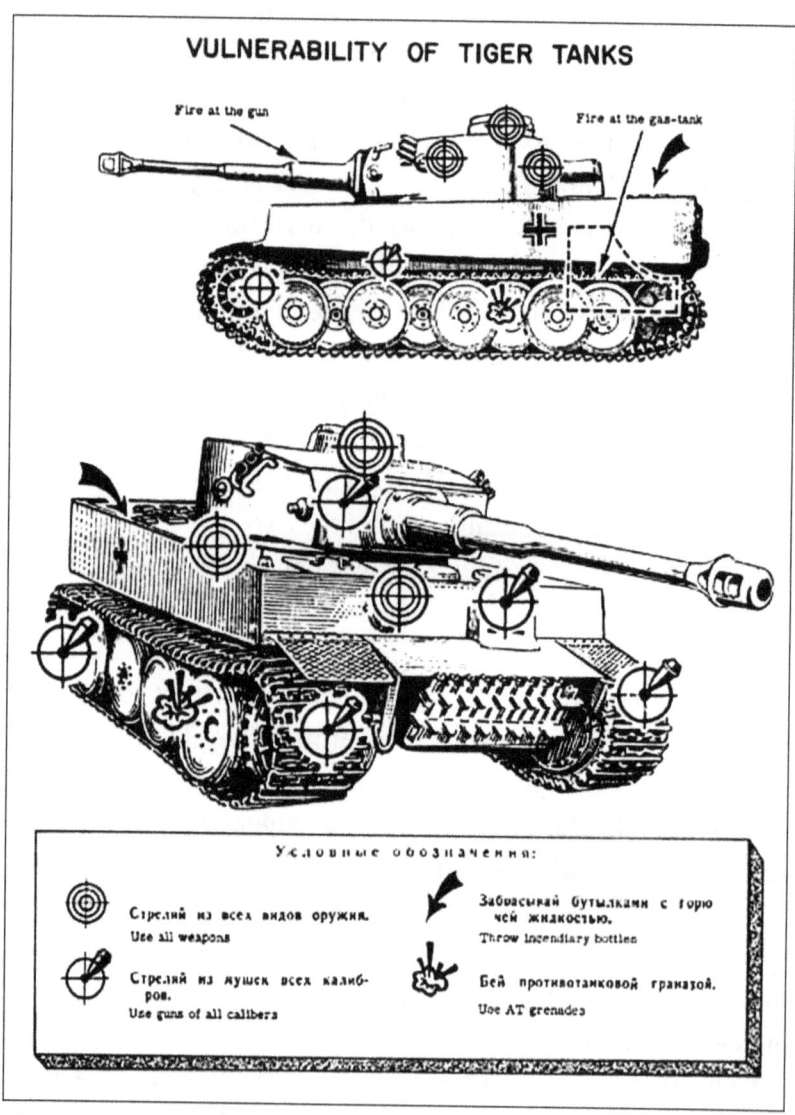

The Russian view on how to attack the Tiger was reproduced for the benefit of western Allied soldiers in the December 1943 version of Tactical and Technical Trends.

"The mobility of tanks depends upon the proper functioning of the suspension parts - sprocket (small driving wheel), idler (small wheel in the rear), wheels and tracks. All of these parts are vulnerable to shells of all calibres. A particularly vulnerable part is the sprocket.

"Fire armour-piercing shells and HE shells at the sprocket, the idler and the tracks. This will stop the tank. Fire at the wheels with HE shells. Also, when attacking a tank, use AT grenades and mines. If movable mines are used, attach three or four of them to a board and draw the board, by means of a cord or cable, into the path of an advancing tank.

"There are two armour plates on each side of the tank. The lower plate is partly covered by the wheels. This plate protects the engine and the gasoline tanks which are located in the rear of the hull, directly beyond and over the two rear wheels.

"Fire at the lower plates with armour-piercing shells from 76-, 57- and 45mm guns. When the gasoline tanks are hit, the vehicle will be set on fire. Another method of starting a fire within the tank is to pierce the upper plates on the sides of the tank, thus reaching the ammunition compartments and causing an explosion.

"The rear armour plate protects the engine as well as giving additional protection to the gasoline tanks. Shells from AT guns, penetrating this armour, will disable the tank.

"The turret has two vision ports and two openings through which the tank's crew fire their weapons. The commander's small turret has five observation slits. There are two sighting devices on the roof of the front of the tank, one for the driver, the other for the gunner. Also, in the front of the tank there is a port with a sliding cover.

"The turret is a particularly important and vulnerable target. Attack it with HE and armour-piercing shells of all calibres. When it is damaged, use AT grenades and incendiary bottles (Molotov cocktails).

A Tiger I camouflaged in a static defensive position.

"There is a 10mm slit all around the base of the turret. AT gun and heavy machine-gun fire, effectively directed at this slit, will prevent the turret from revolving and thus seriously impair the tank's field of fire. Furthermore, hits by HE shell at the base of the turret may wreck the roof of the hull and put the tank out of action.

"The tank's air vents and ventilators are under the perforations in the roof of the hull, directly behind the turret. Another air vent is in the front part of the roof, between the two observation ports used by the radio operator and the driver. Use AT grenades and incendiary bottles against these vents.

"Explode antitank mines under the tank to smash the floor and put the tank out of action."

***

Tiger Aces

The Tiger is particularly associated with SS-Hauptsturmführer Michael Wittmann of schwere SS-Panzerabteilung 101. He worked his way up, commanding various vehicles and finally a Tiger I. In the Battle of Villers-Bocage, his platoon destroyed over two dozen Allied vehicles, including several tanks.

Astonishingly given his enduring reputation Wittmann was not the highest scoring tank commander. Over ten Tiger tank commanders claimed over 100 vehicle kills each, including Kurt Knispel with 168, Walter Schroif with 161, Otto Carius with 150+, Johannes Bölter with 139+, and Michael Wittmann with 138.

Name	Tank Kills	Unit
Kurt Knispel	168	s.Pz.Abt. 503
Martin Schroif	161	s.SS-Pz.Abt. 102
Otto Carius	150+	s.Pz.Abt. 502
Hans Bolter	139+	s.Pz.Abt. 502
Michael Wittmann	138	s.SS-Pz.Abt. 101
Paul Egger	113	s.SS-Pz.Abt. 102
Arno Giesen	111	8./SS-Pz.Rgt. 2
Heinz Rondorf	106	s.Pz.Abt. 503
Heinz Gartner	103	s.Pz.Abt. 503
Wilhelm Knauth	101+	s.Pz.Abt. 505
Albert Kerscher	100+	s.Pz.Abt. 502
Balthazar Woll	100+	s.SS-Pz.Abt. 101
Karl Mobius	100+	s.SS-Pz.Abt. 101
Helmut Wendorff	95	s.SS-Pz.Abt. 101
Will Fey	80+	s.SS-Pz.Abt. 102
Eric Litztke	76	s.Pz.Abt. 509
Emil Seibold	69	s.SS-Pz.Abt. 502
Karl Brommann	66	s.SS-Pz.Abt. 503
Alfred Rubbel	60+	s.Pz.Abt. 503
Konrad Weinert	59	s.Pz.Abt. 503
Walter Junge	57+	s.Pz.Abt. 503
Bobby Warmbrunn	57	s.SS-Pz.Abt. 101
Jurgen Brandt	57	s.SS-Pz.Abt. 101

Heinz Kling	51+	s.SS-Pz.Abt. 101
Heinz Kramer	50+	s.Pz.Abt. 502
Alfredo Carpaneto	50+	s.Pz.Abt. 502
Heinz Mausberg	50+	s.Pz.Abt. 505
Oskar Geiner	50+	s.SS-Pz.Abt. 103
Johann Muller	50+	s.Pz.Abt. 502
Joachim Scholl	42	s.SS-Pz.Abt. 102
Franz Staudegger	35+	s.SS-Pz.Abt. 101

The Tiger I has been estimated to have an overall ratio of 5.74 kills to each loss, with 9,850 enemy tanks destroyed for a loss of 1,715 Tigers. It is important to note that the number of Tiger Is lost is higher than those produced (1,347), as the Wehrmacht included tanks that had undergone heavy repair and brought back into combat in the total of new machines.

The following chart demonstrates the estimated Tiger I kills to losses ratio:

Unit	Losses	Kills	Kill/Loss Ratio
schwere Panzer-Abteilung 501	120	450	3.75
schwere Panzer-Abteilung 502	107	1,400	13.08
schwere Panzer-Abteilung 503	252	1,700	6.75
schwere Panzer-Abteilung 504	109	250	2.29
schwere Panzer-Abteilung 505	126	900	7.14
schwere Panzer-Abteilung 506	179	400	2.23
schwere Panzer-Abteilung 507	104	600	5.77
schwere Panzer-Abteilung 508	78	100	1.28
schwere Panzer-Abteilung 509	120	500	4.17
schwere Panzer-Abteilung 510	65	200	3.08
13./Panzer-Regiment Grossdeutschland	6	100	16.67
III./Panzer-Regiment Grossdeutschland	98	500	5.10
13./SS-Panzerregiment 1	42	400	9.52
8./SS-Panzerregiment 2	31	250	8.06
9./SS-Panzerregiment 3	56	500	8.93
schwere SS-Panzer-Abteilung 101 (501)	107	500	4.67
schwere SS-Panzer-Abteilung 102 (502)	76	600	7.89
schwere SS-Panzer-Abteilung 103 (503)	39	500	12.82
Total	1,715	9,850	5.74

The cover illustration from Tigerfibel   *Kurt Knispel*   *Martin Schroif*

Otto Carius   *Hans Bolter*

Michael Wittmann   *Paul Egger*   *Heinz Rondorf*   *Heinz Gartner*

Wilhelm Knauth   *Albert Kerscher*   *Bobby Woll*   *Kurl Mobius*

Helmut Wendorff   *Will Fey*   *Eric Litztke*   *Emil Seibold*

Karl Brommann    Alfred Rubbel    Konrad Weinert    Walter Junge

Bobby Warmbrunn    Jurgen Brandt    Heinz Kling    Heinz Kramer

Alfredo Carpaneto    Heinz Mausberg    Franz Staudegger

A powerful study of Tigers in action near Orel.

This impactful study of a Tiger I on the move creates a strong impression of the power of the Tiger I. Faced with the prospect of engaging with a fast moving and strongly equipped monster such as this it is easy to understand how the Tigerphobia condition grew and spread.

TIGERPHOBIA

The Tigers forged an impressive combat record in Russia during 1943 and 1944. They destroyed tremendous amounts of enemy equipment especially anti-tank guns. Eventually it was held that often the mere sight of a Tiger was enough to cause Russian tank crews to withdraw from the battlefield. The Tiger enjoyed a similar psychological success in North Africa and Italy, creating a powerful negative effect on the morale of both British and US troops. The mere rumour that the troops were up against Tigers was often enough to spread panic.

The debilitating influence of the Tiger on allied morale was so widespread the condition was given its own name and was widely known as *Tigerphobia*. The grip which the Tiger held on the popular imaginations of allied soldiers was so severe that British Field Marshall Montgomery banned all reports of the Tiger which made any reference to its prowess in battle. There were times when even Monty couldn't prevail over

Panzer crewmen inspect the combat damage inflicted by enemy rounds which have just failed to pierce the strong side armour of the Tiger.

the cold facts. In the right hands the Tiger was a ferociously weapon system. The Tiger's greatest moment of fame was one such moment. Michael Wittmann gained lasting notoriety with his amazing exploits in a single action on 13th June 1944 in Normandy where the famous commander destroyed an entire column of 25 tanks, 14 half-tracks and 14 bren-gun carriers in a few short minutes with one Tiger I handled with deadly efficiency.

NOTES ON TIGER TANKS IN THE BATTLE FOR FLORENCE

In the battle for Florence, a New Zealand division had its first experience with standard Tiger tanks on a fairly large scale, and noted several useful points about the ways in which the Germans employed these vehicles.

As a rule, the Tigers were well sited and well camouflaged with natural foliage. To delay the New Zealand infantry and to pick off tanks, the Tigers were used in hull-down positions. Another enemy method was to send Tigers by covered routes to previously selected positions. From these positions the Germans would fire a few harassing rounds, withdraw, and move to alternate positions. Tigers also were used to provide close support for German infantry, to lend additional fire power to artillery concentrations, and to engage buildings occupied by the New Zealanders. These troops noted that almost invariably a Tiger would be sited with at least one other tank or a self-propelled gun in support. The supporting tank or gun would remain silent unless its fire was absolutely needed. Sometimes a Tiger would be accompanied by infantrymen - often only 6 to 12 of them - deployed on the flanks as far as 50 yards away from the tank.

The New Zealanders were of the opinion that the Tiger's heavy front and rear armour made it unlikely that the tank would be knocked out by hits on these parts. Simultaneous frontal and

This press photo does a great job of conveying the strength of the frontal armour of a Tiger I which, although not efficiently sloped, was strong and robust enough to deal with the direct hit from a large calibre shell, the evidence of which can be seen on the front mantlet to the right of the figure in the helmet.

A field conference in the summer of 1943, the half hearted camouflage and relaxed attitude suggest that soviet air cover was not perceived to be a threat by these tank men.

flank attacks were considered desirable. The New Zealanders found the Tigers' side armour definitely vulnerable to fire from 17-pounders. Other weak spots, it was reported, were the rear of the tank, just over the engines, and the large exhaust hole, also in the rear and just over the left of centre. Some commanders found high explosives the most effective ammunition against these rear parts.

As a rule, the Tigers were placed in position so skillfully that the New Zealanders found it difficult to employ a sniping anti-tank gun or a towed gun for stalking purposes. Unless very careful reconnaissance was carried out to site the gun to the best advantage, and so as to detect German supporting tanks or self-propelled guns, the effort was likely to be fruitless. For this reason, the New Zealanders concluded that maximum time for reconnaissance, and the maximum amount of information, were essential for a battery commander who was called upon to engage a Tiger. The German tank-and-gun combination seemed to be slow at manoeuvring and firing, and also very susceptible to blinding by U.S. 75mm smoke ammunition. On one occasion, two smoke rounds, followed by armour-piercing projectiles, were enough to force a Tiger to withdraw.

Sometimes the Germans used their Tigers with marked recklessness, the crews taking risks to an extent which indicated their extreme confidence in their vehicles. This rendered the latter vulnerable to New Zealand tank-hunting squads armed with close-range antitank weapons. When Tigers were closed down, and were attacking on their own at some distance from their supporting guns, the tanks' vulnerability to those close-range weapons was increased correspondingly.

Tigers were effectively knocked out, or were forced to withdraw, by concentrations of field artillery. It was clear that German tank crews feared the damaging effect of shell fire against such vital parts as tracks, suspension, bogie wheels, radio aerials, electrical equipment, and so on. The New Zealanders incorporated medium artillery in several of their artillery concentrations, and decided that medium pieces were suitable when a sufficiently large concentration could be brought to bear. However, owing to a dispersion of rounds, it was considered preferable to include a good concentration of field guns, to "thicken up" the fire. The division in question had no experience in using heavy artillery against Tigers.

It was admittedly difficult to locate stationary, well camouflaged Tigers which had been sited for defensive firing. Worth mentioning, however, is the performance of an artillery observation post, which was notified by Allied tanks that a Tiger was believed to be in a certain area. The observation post began to range. A round falling in the vicinity of the suspected tank blasted away the vehicle's camouflage, and the Tiger promptly retreated.

Several of the New Zealand antitank gunners' experiences in combating Tigers will be of special interest:

(1) A Tiger was observed about 3,000 yards away, engaging three Shermans. When it set one of the Shermans afire, the other two withdrew over a crest. A 17-pounder was brought up to within

A tank man inspects the combat damage inflicted by enemy rounds which have failed to pierce the strong side armour of the Tiger tank turret.

2400 yards of the Tiger, and engaged it from a flank. When the Tiger realized that it was being engaged by a high-velocity gun, it swung around 90 degrees so that its heavy frontal armour was toward the gun. In the ensuing duel, one round hit the turret, another round hit the suspension, and two near-short rounds probably ricocheted into the tank. The tank was not put out of action. The range was too great to expect a kill; hence the New Zealanders' tactics were to make the Tiger expose its flank to the Shermans at a range of almost 500 yards, by swinging around onto the antitank gun. The Tiger did just this, and, when it was engaged by the Shermans, it withdrew. The enemy infantry protection of half a dozen to a dozen men was engaged by machine guns.

(2) At the junction of a main road and a side road, a Tiger was just off the road, engaging forward troops in buildings. Another Tiger, about 50 yards up the side road, was supporting the first. A field-artillery concentration was called for. It appeared to come from one battery only. Although no hits were observed, both Tigers withdrew.

(3) A Tiger on a ridge was engaged by what appeared to be a battery of mediums. After the first few rounds had fallen, the crew bailed out. (It is not known why.) Shortly afterward, while the tank still was being shelled, a German soldier returned to the tank and drove it off. About 10 minutes later, the remainder of the crew made a dash along the same route their tank had taken.

(4) A tank hidden in the garage of a two-story house ventured out for about 20 yards, fired a few harassing rounds, and returned to its shelter. Many hits on the building were scored by 4.2-inch mortars firing cap-on, but little damage was visible. Each night the tank was withdrawn from the area, even though it was in an excellent concealed position and was protected by infantry. Later the house was examined. Although it had suffered appreciable damage — and there were several dead Germans about there was no evidence that damage had been done to the tank itself.

***

Inside The Tiger

The internal layout was typical of German tanks. Forward was an open crew compartment, with the driver and radio-operator seated at the front on either side of the gearbox. Behind them the turret floor was surrounded by panels forming a continuous level surface. This helped the loader to retrieve the ammunition, which was mostly stowed above the tracks. Two men were seated in the turret; the gunner to the left of the gun, and the commander behind him. There was also a folding seat on the right for the loader. The turret had a full circular floor and 157cm headroom.

The crews of the Tiger tank gained a feeling of invincibility and this mood of superiority on behalf of the German tank crews

This photograph from a contemporary British report shows the driving position of the Tiger I.

survived defeat and captivity as revealed by the interrogation of an veteran German tank gunner who had served in The Afrika Korps and in Italy and therefore could boast practical experience of both the Tiger and captured allied Sherman tanks.

THE TIGER vs THE SHERMAN

The gun layer- an experienced tank man- was inclined to be very boastful where German tanks were concerned. He had landed in Africa in May 1941 and stayed in the desert for nearly two years (no home leave and only the rarest visits to towns). His memories of the campaign are chiefly a record of the numbers of British AFVs knocked out by the invincible Mk IIIs and IVs, tinged with a reluctant admission that the same tanks were matched in October 43 at Alamein by General Grants and General Shermans. He was critical of the fact that the employment of these AFVs had not been appreciated by the

Germans and that the launching of the British push came as a surprise to the armoured Divs.

His confidence has been fully restored since he transferred to Tiger Tanks. On every occasion he stresses the great feeling of security which a crew has inside an AFV with such armour. Crews feel very certain of their ability to engage and destroy any target. He claims that he once ran into fire from the flank from seven 17 pdr A/Tk guns at close range and, having turned the hull of his tank so that a three quarter view was presented to the fire; proceeded to destroy five out of seven A/Tk guns with HE rounds. Several hits were registered on the frontal

From Tigerfibel

A Tiger I laden with grenadiers moves up towards the front during January 1944.

armour of the flaking from shell splinters.

The only situation in which he felt uncomfortable was to receive A/Tk gun fire from the flank and, having engaged the gun after having turned his AFV into the optimum position, to receive fire at right angles from an undetected A/Tk position in his rear. His reaction would then be to swing his turret as fast as possible and engage the more dangerous of the two targets.

The only time when a General Sherman stands a chance of knocking out a Tiger (in his opinion) is when it can close to less than 800 metres. He has observed that, even granted great superiority in numbers, Sherman tank crews do not venture willingly to close in, even on sides away from the principal preoccupation of the Tiger's fire. He claims that 3 Sqn has accounted for 63 Shermans since arrival in this theatre, 17 of which fall to his account.

The general opinion of the Sherman for its class was high. PW was instrumental in capturing two on the beachhead (one with a radial engine and one with twin Diesel engines) and the Bn had ample time to acquaint itself with these AFVs before removing the turrets and passing them back to 4 (workshops) Sqn for use as recovery vehicles, less turrets. His biggest criticism of the Sherman is of the visibility afforded to the commander when his hatch is closed down. He regarded the periscope as extremely poor.

***

"Yank" magazine

The following is an article on enemy vehicles tested at the Aberdeen Ordnance Research Centre from the January 21st, 1944 issue of Yank. The cover is an image of German Tiger I tank from the 1.Ko. of s.Pz.Abt. 504 which was captured by Allied forces in Tunisia.

The US Army did little to prepare for combat against the Tiger despite their assessment that the newly-encountered German tank was superior to their own. This conclusion was partly based on the correct estimate that the Tiger would be encountered in relatively small numbers. Later in the war, the Tiger could be penetrated at short range by tanks and tank destroyers equipped with the 76mm gun M1 when firing HVAP rounds, and at long range with the M2/M3 90mm AA/AT gun firing HVAP, and the M36 tank destroyer and M26 Pershing by the end of the war.

ENEMY VEHICLES FROM YANK

At Aberdeen's Ordnance Research Centre, inquisitive experts finds what makes an Axis vehicle tick, and their tests produce facts worth remembering.

By Sgt. MACK MORRISS and Sgt. RALPH STEIN, YANK Staff Correspondents

ABERDEEN, MD.

The first thing you learn at the Foreign Material outfit here is never, ever, to call a Nazi tank a "Mark Six" or a "Mark Four." The correct designation is Pz. Kw. VI or Pz. Kw. IV. "Mark" is a British way of saying model, whereas Pz. Kw. means what it says: Panzer Kampfwagen, or armoured battlewagon.

For more than a year captured enemy vehicles have been arriving here from every battle front on earth. The first was a half-track prime mover that came in sections and required three months

Changing the huge front sprocket on the Tiger I was a regular job as the sprocket itself was set too low to the ground without much clearance and as a result was frequently damaged by obstacles.

of trial-and-error tinkering to be completely reconstructed. Missing parts, which were requisitioned from North Africa, never arrived; mechanics in the Base Shop section made their own.

The worst headache for repair crews here is the difference in measurement caused by the European metric system. Nothing manufactured in the U.S. will fit anything in a Nazi machine unless it is made to fit. In reconstructing the captured stuff, it has sometimes been necessary to combine the salvaged parts of two or three vehicles in order to put one in running order. The mechanics have made their own pistons or recut foreign pistons to take American piston rings; they've cut new gears; they've had to retap holes so that American screws will fit them.

Specially assigned recovery crews, ordnance men trained to know and work with enemy material, roam the battlefields of the world to collect the captured rolling stock, which is being accumulated here. It arrives with the dust of its respective theatre still on it, plus the names and addresses of GIs who scratch "Bizerte" or "Attu" or "Buna Mission" in big letters on the paint.

Generally speaking, ordnance experts here have found German stuff exceptionally well made in its vital mechanisms, whereas the less essential parts are comparatively cheap. The motor of a Nazi personnel carrier, for example, is a well-built affair, while the body of the vehicle is little more than scrap tin. Japanese pieces of equipment for the most part are cheap imitations of American or British counterparts.

The engineers, who judge by the mass of detail employed in all German-built machines, are convinced that the Nazi idea has been to sacrifice speed for over-all performance and manoeuvrability. The German equipment, from the sleek motorcycle to the massive Pz. Kw. VI, is rugged.

The famous Tiger is the largest and heaviest German tank. Weighing 61 1/2 tons, it is propelled at a speed of from 15 to

Tigers training in perfect conditions in Normandy during May 1944.

18 miles an hour by a 600-to-650 horsepower Maybach V-12 cylinder engine. Maybach engines are used in many of the Nazi Panzer wagonen and in submarines. The Pz. Kw. VI has an armour thickness which ranges from 3 1/4 to 4 inches. An additional slab of steel mounted in conjunction with its 88mm forms frontal armour for the turret. Besides the long-barreled 88, it carries two MG34 (Model 1934) machine guns. Largest tank used in combat by any nation today, the Tiger is more than 20 feet long, about 11 3/4 feet wide and 9 3/4 feet high. It has a crew of five.

***

Tiger I Tanks in Sicily

In total 17 Tiger I tanks from schwere Panzer Abteilung 504 (s.Pz.Abt. 504) fought in Sicily in 1943 against the Allied invasion forces. All but one were lost in combat in the period from July 11th to August 10th 1943 when the German forces were finally forced to withdraw.

When the first elements of s.Pz.Abt. 504 with 20 Tiger I were

The reconnaissance element of a Tiger company had an equally difficult and dangerous job. This evocative study was taken in Russia during March 1944.

A Tiger rolls through a Sicilian town in July 1943. These machines had been destined to serve with the Afrika Korps but arrived too late to take part in the campaign. All but one of the 17 Tigers deployed in Sicily were lost in action.

sent to North Africa, the 2nd Kompanie remained behind in Sicily with nine Tiger I tanks. As a result of the surrender of German forces in North Africa, the nine Tigers of s.Pz.Abt. 504 were never actually shipped to Tunisia, but stayed behind on Sicily where they were soon called into action to repel the Allied assault which took place in July 1943. Prior to the Allied invasion eight additional Tiger I were shipped to the unit arriving early in the summer. By the time of the Allied invasion of Sicily, s.Pz.Abt. 504 with 17 Tiger I was attached to the Panzer Division Hermann Göring.

During the ill fated attack on the Allied beachhead near Gela, s.Pz.Abt. 504 was heavily engaged and lost ten Tigers in just two days of fierce fighting between 11th July and 12th July. Further Tigers were lost in action or abandoned during July and August as German forces slowly retreated across the island. In August, the unit's last surviving Tiger I bearing the tactical number 222 from managed to escape from the wreckage and was ferried across the Straits of Messina to Italy.

The following is an article on German tank trends, Panzer tactics, and how to fight the German heavy tanks from the October 1944 issue of the *Intelligence Bulletin*. The article includes suggestions from the Soviet Artillery Journal on combating the Tiger tank.

GERMAN TANK TRENDS

Just what can be expected from German tanks in the near future? Which models are most likely to be employed extensively? Are present models undergoing much alteration?

A brief summary of the German tank situation at the moment should serve to answer these and other pertinent questions.

There is good reason to believe that the German tanks which will be encountered most frequently in the near future will be the Pz. Kpfw. V (Panther), the Pz. Kpfw. VI (Tiger), and the Pz. Kpfw. IV. However, the Germans have a new 88mm (346-

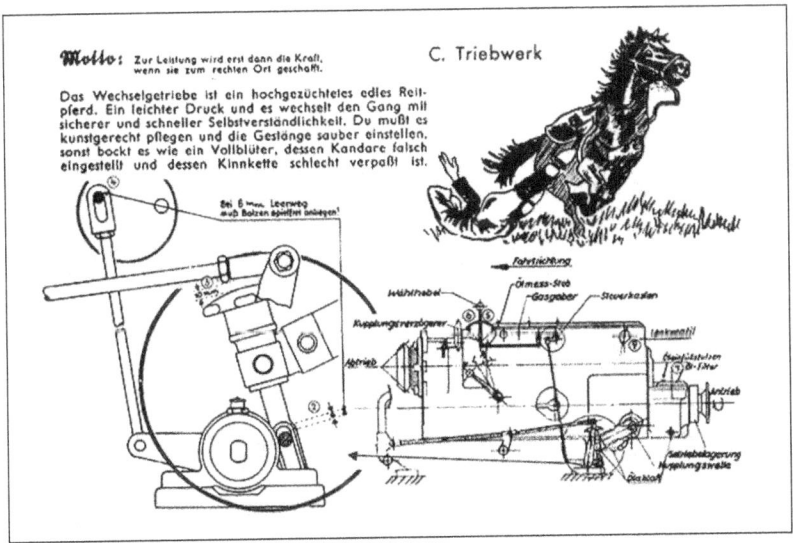

This page from the driver's section in Tigerfibel emphasizes the need for team work.

Officers plan the next move during a field conference in Normandy, June 1944.

inch) tank gun, the Kw. K. 43, which is capable of an armour-piercing performance greatly superior to that of the 88mm Kw. K. 36. According to reliable information, the Kw. K. 43 is superseding the Kw. K. 36 as the main armament of the Tiger. A new heavy tank, which has been encountered on a small scale in northwestern France, also is armed with the Kw. K. 43. This new tank looks like a scaled-up Panther, with the wide Tiger tracks. (Further information regarding this tank will appear in an early issue of the Intelligence Bulletin.)

During recent months both the Tiger and the Panther have been fitted with a slightly more powerful 690-horsepower engine in place of the 642-horsepower model. The principal benefit from this slight increase will be a better margin of power and improved engine life. The maximum speed will be increased by no more than 2 or 3 miles per hour.

Face-hardened armour, which was not used on the early Tiger tanks, has reappeared in certain plate of at least one Panther. On other Panthers which have been encountered, only machine-quality armour is used. There is no reason to believe that face-hardening would substantially improve the armour's resistance to penetration by the capped projectiles now in use against it.

It would not have been surprising if the Pz. Kpfw. IV had slowly disappeared from the picture as increased quantities of Panther tanks became available, but actually there was a sharp rise in the rate of production of Pz. Kpfw. IV's during 1943. Moreover, the, front armour of the Pz. Kpfw. IV has been reinforced from 50mm (1.97 inches) to 80mm (3.15 inches) by the bolting of additional armour to the nose and front vertical plates. And the 75mm (2.95-inch) tank gun, Kw. K. 40, has been lengthened by about 14 3/4 inches.

All these developments seem to indicate that the Pz. Kpfw. IV probably will be kept in service for many months. Recent organization evidence reflects this, certainly. In the autumn of 1943, evidence regarding provisional organization for the German tank regiment in the armoured division indicated that the aim was a ratio of approximately four Panther tanks for each Pz. Kpfw. IV. Now, however, the standard tank regiment has these two types in approximately equal numbers.

The possibility that Tiger production may have been discontinued has been considered. Although discontinuing the Tiger would relieve the pressure on German industry, it is believed that a sufficient number of these tanks to meet the needs of units equipped with them still is being produced.

Tiger tanks constitute an integral part of division tank regiments only in SS armoured divisions. However, armoured divisions of an army may receive an allotment of Tigers for special operations.

Early in 1944 a number of Pz. Kpfw. III's converted into flame-throwing tanks appeared in Italy. Nevertheless, it is believed that production of this tank ceased some time ago. Some of the firms which in the past produced Pz. Kpfw. III's now are making assault guns; others are believed to be turning out Panthers. It is extremely unlikely that production of Pz. Kpfw. III's as fighting tanks will ever be resumed, no matter how

A Tiger I rolls through the open countryside in Normandy in June 1944. The tank is obviously some distance from the combat zone as the crew have not taken any form of anti-aircraft precautions.

serious the German tank situation may become.

In an effort to combat attacks by tank hunters, the Germans have fitted the Tiger with S-mine dischargers, which are fired electrically from the interior of the tank. These dischargers are mounted on the turret, and are designed to project a shrapnel antipersonnel mine which bursts in the air a few yards away from the tank. Thus far these dischargers have been noted only on the Tiger, but the Germans quite possibly may decide to use them on still other tanks.

The Germans take additional precautions, as well. For protection against hollow-charge projectiles and the Soviet antitank rifle's armour-piercing bullet with a tungsten carbide core, they fit a skirting of mild steel plates, about 1/4- inch thick, on the sides of the hull. In the case of the Pz. Kpfw. IV, the skirting is suitably spaced from the sides and also from the rear of the turret. Finally, the skirting plates, as well as the hulls and turrets of the tanks themselves, are, coated with a sufficient thickness of non-magnetic plaster to prevent magnetic demolition charges from adhering to the metal underneath.

Despite the recent introduction of the new heavy tank which resembles the Panther and mounts a Kw. K. 43, it is believed that circumstances will force the Germans to concentrate on the manufacture and improvement of current types, particularly the Pz. Kpfw. IV and the familiar version of the Panther.

Evidence suggests that a modified Pz. Kpfw. II will shortly appear as a reconnaissance vehicle. Official German documents sometimes refer to it as an armoured car and sometimes as a tank.

***

Armour And Armament

The overwhelming advantage of the Tiger I lay in the quality of its main armament. From a 30 degree angle depending on the wind and weather conditions the Tiger's 88mm gun was capable of penetrating the well sloped front glacis plate of an American M4 Sherman at ranges up to 2,100m (1.3 miles). The better armoured British Churchill IV became vulnerable at a closer range of 1,700m (1.1 mile), the hardy Soviet T-34 could be destroyed at 1,400m (0.87 mile), and the Soviet IS-2 could only be destroyed at ranges between 100 and 300m.

The Soviet T-34 equipped with the 76.2mm gun could not penetrate the Tiger frontally at any range, but could achieve a side penetration at approximately 500 m firing BR-350P APCR ammunition. The T34-85's 85mm gun could penetrate the front of a Tiger between 200 and 500 m (0.12 and 0.31 mi), the IS-2's 122mm gun could penetrate the front between 500 and 1,500 m

A section of Tiger's deploying for combat operations in Russia during January 1943. The vehicle on the left still has the cover on the muzzle break which suggests this tank is not anticipating being forced into combat.

(0.31 and 0.93 mi).

From a 30 degree angle of attack, the M4 Sherman's 75mm gun could not penetrate the Tiger frontally at any range, and actually needed to be within 100 m to achieve a side penetration shot against the 80mm upper hull superstructure. However, the British 17-pounder as used on the Sherman Firefly, firing its normal APCBC ammunition, could penetrate the front armour of the Tiger I out to 1000m. The US 76mm gun, if firing the APCBC M62 ammunition, could penetrate the Tiger side armour up to a range of 500m, and could penetrate the upper hull superstructure at ranges up to 200m. Using HVAP ammunition, which was in constant short supply and primarily issued to tank destroyers, frontal penetrations were possible at ranges of up to 500m. The M3 90mm cannon used in the late-war M36 Jackson, M26 Pershing, and M2 AA/AT mount could penetrate its front plate at a range of 1000 m, and from beyond 2000m when using HVAP.

As range decreases in combat, all guns can penetrate more

armour. HEAT ammunition was the most effective round but this projectile was rare and in short supply. The great penetrating power of the Tiger's gun meant that it could destroy many of its opponents at ranges at which they could not respond. The issue which was compounding the Allied tank crew's problem was the superiority of German optics. This advantage increased the chances of a hit on the first shot and in tank to tank battles one shot was frequently all that mattered. In open terrain, this was a major tactical advantage as opposing tanks were often forced to change position in order to make a flanking attack in an attempt to knock out a Tiger.

GERMAN TANKS IN ACTION

A German prisoner observes that the following are standard training principles in the German tank arm:

(1) Surprise.

(2) Prompt decisions and prompt execution of these decisions.

(3) The fullest possible exploitation of the terrain for firing. However, fields of fire come before cover.

(4) Do not fire while moving except when absolutely essential.

(5) Face the attacker head-on; do not offer a broadside target.

(6) When attacked by hostile tanks, concentrate solely on these.

(7) If surprised without hope of favourable defence, scatter and reassemble in favourable terrain. Try to draw the attacker into a position which will give you the advantage.

(8) If smoke is to be used, keep wind direction in mind. A good procedure is to leave a few tanks in position as decoys, and, when the hostile force is approaching them, to direct a smoke screen toward the hostile force and blind it.

(9) If hostile tanks are sighted, German tanks should halt and prepare to engage them by surprise, holding fire as long as

possible. The reaction of the hostile force must be estimated before the attack is launched.

A German Army document entitled "How the Tiger Can Aid the Infantry" contains a number of interesting points. The following are outstanding:

(1) The tank expert must have a chance to submit his opinion before any combined tank-infantry attack.

(2) If the ground will support a man standing on one leg and carrying another man on his shoulders, it will support a tank.

(3) When mud is very deep, corduroy roads must be built ahead of time. Since this requires manpower, material, and time, the work should be undertaken only near the point where the main effort is to be made.

(4) Tanks must be deployed to conduct their fire fight.

(5) The Tiger, built to fight tanks and antitank guns, must function as offensive weapon, even in the defence. This is its best means of defence against hostile tanks. Give it a chance to use its unique capabilities for fire and movement.

(6) The Tiger must keep moving. At the halt it is an easy target.

(7) The Tiger must not be used singly. (Obviously, this does not apply to the Tiger used as roving artillery in the defence. On numerous occasions the Germans have been using single Tigers for this purpose.) The more mass you can assemble, the greater your success will be. Protect your Tigers with infantry.

***

The Two Extremes

The Tiger I enjoyed some spectacular triumphs on the battlefield, but it also endured its fair share of ignominious set backs. These two contrasting combat reports demonstrate the two extremes of the Tiger I experience.

A Tiger which has received a coating of anti-magnetic Zimmermit coating designed to prevent the application of magnetic mines by tank hunting teams.

On 21st April 1943, a Tiger I of the 504th German heavy tank battalion, with turret number 131, was captured after being knocked out on a hill called Djebel Djaffa in Tunisia. A round from a Churchill tank of the British 48th Royal Tank Regiment hit the Tiger's gun barrel and ricocheted into its turret ring. The round jammed the turret traverse mechanism and wounded the commander. Although the vehicle was still in a driveable condition the crew flew into a panic and bailed out.

The complete tank was captured by the British. The tank was repaired and displayed in Tunisia before being sent to England for a thorough inspection.

In complete contrast to the dismal performance of Tiger 131 the Tiger I commanded by Franz Staudegger enjoyed an amazing string of successes. On 7th July 1943, this single Tiger tank commanded by SS-Oberscharführer Franz Staudegger from the 2nd Platoon, 13th Panzer Company, 1st SS Division Leibstandarte SS Adolf Hitler engaged a group of about 50 T-34s around Psyolknee in the southern sector of the German thrust into the Soviet salient known as the Battle of Kursk. Staudegger used all his ammunition and claimed the destruction of 22 Soviet tanks, forcing the rest to retreat. For this amazing feat of arms he was understandably awarded the Knight's Cross.

HOW TO FIGHT PANZERS: A GERMAN VIEW

An anti-Nazi prisoner of war, discussing the various methods of combating German tanks, makes some useful comments. Although they are neither new nor startling, they are well worth studying since they are observations made by a tank man who fought the United Nations forces in Italy.

German tanks undoubtedly are formidable weapons against a soft-shelled opposition, but become a less difficult proposition when confronted with resolution combined with a knowledge not only of their potentialities but also of their weaknesses.

When dealing with German heavy tanks, your most effective weapon is your ability to keep still and wait for them to come within effective range. The next most important thing is to camouflage your position with the best available resources so that the German tanks won't spot you from any angle.

If these two factors are constantly kept in mind, the battle is

Two Tigers pictured just before they were to go into combat at Villers Bocage in June 1944.

half won. Movement of any kind is a mistake which certainly will betray you, yet I saw many instances of this self-betrayal by the British in Italy. Allow the enemy tank to approach as close as possible before engaging it — this is one of the fundamental secrets of antitank success. In Italy I often felt that the British opened fire on tanks much too soon. Their aim was good, but the ranges were too great, and the rounds failed to penetrate. My own case is a good illustration: if the opposition had held its fire for only a few moments longer, I should not be alive to tell this tale.

By letting the German tank approach as close as possible, you gain a big advantage. When it is on the move, it is bound to betray its presence from afar. Whereas you yourself can prepare to fire on it without giving your own position away. The tank will spot you only after you have fired your first round.

A tank in motion cannot fire effectively with its cannon; the gunner can place fire accurately only when the vehicle is stationary. Therefore, there is no need to be unduly nervous because an approaching tank swivels its turret this way and

The Tigerfibel emphasized the smooth ride of the Tiger I comparing it to a sports car.

that. Every tank commander will do this in an attempt to upset his opponents' tank recognition. If the tank fires nothing but its machine guns, you can be pretty sure that you have not yet been spotted.

Consider the advantages of firing on a tank at close range:

(1) In most cases the leading tank is a reconnaissance vehicle. Survivors of the crew, when such a short distance away from you, have little chance of escape. This is a big advantage, inasmuch as they cannot rejoin their outfit and describe the location of your position to the main body.

(2) Another tank following its leader on a road cannot run you down. In order to bypass the leading tank, it has to slow down. Then, long before the gunner can place fire on you, you can destroy the tank and block the road effectively. Earlier in the war, a German tank man I knew destroyed 11 hostile tanks in one day by using this method.

***

THE BRITISH RESPONSE

In contrast to the laissez-faire attitude of the Americans, who correctly assumed that there would never be enough Tigers in the field to present a potent threat, the more experienced British had observed the gradual increase in German AFV armour and firepower since 1940 and had anticipated the need for more powerful anti-tank guns. As a result of the lessons learned in France work on the Ordnance QF 17 pounder had begun in late 1940 and in 1942 100 early-production guns were rushed to North Africa to help counter the new Tiger threat. So great was the haste that they were sent before proper carriages had been designed and constructed, and the guns had to be mounted in the carriages designed for 25-pounder howitzers.

Hasty efforts were also made to get Cruiser tanks armed with 17 pounder guns into operation as soon as possible. The A30 Challenger was already at the prototype stage in 1942 and was pressed into service, but this tank was poorly protected, having a front hull thickness of only 64mm. It was unreliable, and was fielded in only limited numbers - only around 200 were ever built although crews liked it for its high speed. The Sherman Firefly, armed with the 17-pounder, was a notable success even though it was only intended to be a stopgap design. Fireflies were successfully used against Tigers. In one famous engagement, a single Firefly destroyed three Tigers in 12 minutes with five shots and as a result of the superior Allied product capability over 2,000 Fireflies were built during the war. Five different 17-pounder-armed British tanks and self-propelled guns saw combat during the war. These were the A30 Challenger, the A34 Comet, the Sherman Firefly, the 17-pounder SP Achilles and the 17-pounder SP Archer.

The gunner from Tigerfibel.

Tiger I Tanks in Normandy

Something like 130 Tiger Is were deployed in Normandy during June and July 19944. The machines were chiefly deployed by the three schwere Panzer Abteilung equipped with Tiger I tanks which fought in Normandy against the Allied invasion forces. In addition, a small number of Tiger I tanks also fought in Normandy serving with the Panzer Lehr Division.

s.Pz.Abt. 503 was a particularly formidable unit and was transferred to Normandy with a full complement of 33 Tiger I and 12 of the new Tiger II tanks. The unit went into action in early July 1944. The 33 Tiger Is were all shipped to the unit in June 1944. Photographs of the unit's Tigers are very limited. Technical features are, of course, identical to late Tigers shipped to the other units. However one possible distinguishing features is the fact that spare tracks do not appear to have been mounted on front plate as was customary elsewhere. Camouflage patterning was similar to other units, but on at least some vehicles, the Balkankreuz appear to have been unusually large in size. Tactical numbers were relatively thin, neatly stencilled with a white outline and a very dark, probably black, interior.

s.SS-Pz.Abt. 101 received 45 Tiger I in deliveries in total beginning with 10 in October 1943, nine additional late model machines were delivered in January 1944, and 25 in April 1944. The unit reached Normandy in early June and Michael Wittmann and the 1st and 2nd Kompanie fought in the celebrated battle of Villers-Bocage on 13th June 1944. The Tigers issued to this unit included both the rubber-wheel and steel-wheel variants. Unlike s.Pz.Abt. 503 spare track appears to have been mounted on the front plate of most, but it seems not all of the unit's Tigers. Each Kompanie carried the distinctive unit marking of crossed keys in a shield, on the front and rear. In addition, the 1st Kompanie also carried a Panzer lozenge with an "S" and a small "1" on

A knocked out Tiger I of s.SS-PzAbt.101 lies abandoned in the ruins of Villers Bocage.

the front and rear plates. Tactical numbers were fairly large and dark with white outline, except for the command tanks.

s.SS-Pz.Abt. 102 was transferred to Normandy with a full complement of 45 Tiger I and went into action for the first time in early July. The unit was originally issued with a mere six Tiger I in April 1944 but received a further batch of 39 Tiger I in May 1944. Photographs of this unit's Tigers are very rare. However, the unit appears not to have mounted spare track on the front plate. Camouflage was large patches of colour which on some vehicles leads to the appearance of lines of the original dunkelgelb. Tactical numbers were thin, neatly stencilled with white outline and dark interior. Tactical numbers on the turret sides were often sloped, being aligned with the slope of the turret roof. Some Tigers carried a single underlined "S" rune painted on the zimmerit on the front and/or rear plates.

Panzer Lehr Division was issued 10 Tiger I in September-October 1943 and five Tiger II in February-March 1944. Of the ten Tiger I, three Tiger were listed as still with the division in summer 1944. The division reported six of eight Tigers operational on June 1 and three Tigers operational on July 1st.

VULNERABILITY OF THE PZ. KPFW. VI

A tank is such a complicated weapon, with its many movable parts and its elaborate mechanism, that it is particularly valuable to know its points of greatest vulnerability. Recently the Soviet Artillery Journal published a number of practical suggestions, based on extensive combat experience, regarding the vulnerability of the Tiger.

All weapons now used for destroying German tanks - antitank guns and rifles, caliber.50 heavy machine guns, antitank grenades, and Molotov cocktails - are effective against the Pz. Kpfw. VI.

(1) Suspension System - The mobility of tanks depends upon the proper functioning of the suspension parts: the sprocket (small driving wheel), the idler (small wheel in the rear), the wheels, and the tracks. All these parts are vulnerable to shells of all calibres. The sprocket is especially vulnerable.

Fire armour-piercing shells and high-explosive shells at the

A late model Tiger I lies abandoned after being knocked out in action.

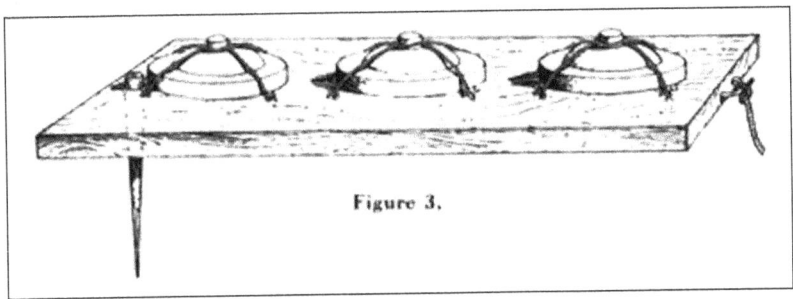

Figure 3.

sprocket, idler, and tracks.

Fire at the wheels with high-explosive shells. Use antitank grenades, antitank mines, and movable antitank mines against the suspension parts. Attach three or four mines to a board. Place the board wherever tanks are expected to pass. Camouflage the board and yourself. As a tank passes by, pull the board in the proper direction and place it under the track of the tank.

(A German source states that this method was successfully used on roads and road crossings in Russia, and that it still is taught in tank combat courses for infantry. The mine is called the Scharniermine (pivot mine). It consists of a stout length of board, 8 inches wide by 2 inches thick, and cut to a length dependent on the width of the road to be blocked. A hole is bored at one end, through which a spike or bayonet can be driven into the ground, thus providing a pivot for the board. A hook is fastened to the other end of the board, and a rope is tied to the hook, as shown in Figure 3. Tellermines are secured to the top of the board.

One man can operate this mine. After the board has been fastened down at one end with the spike (in emergencies, a bayonet) and a rope tied to the hook at the other end, the board is laid along the side of the road. On the opposite side of the road, a man is posted in a narrow slit trench. He holds the other end of the rope. When a tank approaches, the tank hunter waits until it is close enough to the pivoted board, and, at the very last moment, he pulls the free end of the board across the road.

The Tiger I that knocked out the first M26 Pershing in combat. The victorious Tiger then backed into a demolished building and became immobile. The crew then abandoned the tank which fell into Allied hands.

The rope and slit trench must be well camouflaged. A good deal of emphasis is placed on this point.)

(2) Side Armour Plates - There are two armour plates on each side of the tank. The lower plate is partly covered by the wheels. This plate protects the engine and the gasoline tanks, which are located in the rear of the hull — directly beyond and over the two rear wheels. Ammunition is kept in special compartments along the sides of the tank. These compartments are protected by the upper armour plate.

Fire armour-piercing shells from 76, 57, and 45mm guns at the upper and lower armour plate. When the gas tanks or ammunition compartments are hit, the vehicle will be set on fire.

(3) Rear Armour Plate - The rear armour plate protects the engine, the gasoline tank, and the radiators.

Use antitank guns. Aim at the rear armour plate. When the engine or the gasoline tanks are hit, the tank will halt and will begin to burn.

(4) Peepholes, Vision Ports, and Slits - The main turret has two openings for firing small-arms weapons, and two vision ports. The turret has five observation slits. There are two sighting devices on the roof of the front part of the tank - one for the driver, the other for the gunner. There is also a port with sliding covers in the front armour plate.

Use all available weapons for firing at the peepholes, observation ports, vision slits, and the ports for small-arms weapons.

5. Turrets - The commander's turret is an important and vulnerable target.

Fire high-explosive and armour-piercing shells of all calibres at the commander's turret. Throw antitank grenades and incendiary bottles after the turret has been damaged.

The tank commander, the turret commander, and the gunner ride in the turret. The tank gun and many mechanical devices are found in the turret.

Fire at the turret with 76; 57; and 45mm shells at ranges of 500 yards or less.

(6) Tank Armament - The turret is armed with a gun and a machine gun mounted coaxially. Another machine gun is found in the front part of the hull. It protrudes through the front armour plate, on a ball mount, and is manned by, the radio operator.

Concentrate the fire of all weapons on the armament of the tank. Fire with antitank rifles at the ball mount of the hull machine gun.

(7) Air Vents and Ventilators - The air vents and the ventilators are found under the slit-shaped perforations of the roof of the hull, directly behind the turret. Another air vent is located in the front part of the roof, between the two observation ports used by the radio operator and the driver.

Use incendiary bottles and antitank grenades to damage the ventilating system.

(8) Tank Floor - When an antitank mine explodes under the tank, the floor of the tank is smashed, and the tank is knocked out of action.

(9) Base of Turret - There is a 10mm slit going all around the turret, between the base of the turret and the roof of the hull.

Fire at the base of the turret with heavy machine guns and antitank guns, to destroy the turret mechanism, and disrupt the field of fire. Fire with high-explosive shells at the base of the turret in order to wreck the roof of the hull and put the tank out of action.

***

The Soviet Response

The initial Soviet response to the Tiger I was to order the restart of production of the 57mm ZiS-2 anti-tank gun. Production of this model had been halted in 1941 in favour of smaller and cheaper alternatives. The ZiS-2 which had better armour penetration than the 76mm F-34 tank gun which was then in use by most Red Army tanks, but it too proved to be all but inadequate when faced with the Tiger I.

A 2.52 firing APCR rounds could usually be relied upon to penetrate the Tiger's frontal armour. A small number of T-34s were fitted with a tank version of the ZiS-2, but the drawback was that as an anti-tank weapon the ZiS-2 could not fire a strong high-explosive round, thus making it an unsatisfactory tank gun. The Russians had no inhibitions about following the German lead and accordingly the 85mm 52-K anti-aircraft gun was modified for tank use. This gun was initially incorporated into the SU-85 self-propelled gun which was based on a T-34 chassis and saw action from August 1943. By the spring of 1944, the T-34/85 appeared, this up-gunned T-34 matched the SU-85's firepower, but had the additional advantage of mounting the gun with

A column of German infantry captured during the destruction of Army Group Centre file past an intact Tiger I now also in the hands of the Russians.

a much better HE firing capability in a revolving turret. The redundant SU-85 was replaced by the SU-100, mounting a 100mm D-10 tank gun which could penetrate 185mm of vertical armour plate at 1,000m, and was therefore able to defeat the Tiger's frontal armour at normal combat ranges.

In May 1943, the Red Army deployed the SU-152, replaced in 1944 by the ISU-152. These self-propelled guns both mounted the large, 152mm howitzer-gun. The SU-152 was intended to be a close-support gun for use against German fortifications rather than armour; but, both it and the later ISU-152 were found to be very effective against German heavy tanks, and were nicknamed Zveroboy which is commonly rendered as "beast killer" or "animal hunter". The 152mm armour-piercing shells weighed over 45 kilograms (99lb) and could penetrate a Tiger's frontal armour from 1,000 metres. Even the high-explosive rounds were powerful enough to cause significant damage to a tank. However, the size and weight of the ammunition meant both vehicles had a low rate of fire and each could carry only 20 rounds.

The tide was definitely turning against the Tiger I and the Tiger II was introduced as a replacement in mid 1944. In order to shore

Marshal Georgy Zhukov inspecting a captured Tiger

up the crumbling morale and maintain the sense of invincibility the German School of Tank Technology released re-assuring combat reports such as the detailed example below.

THE JOSEF STALIN

The new Soviet heavy tank, 'Josef Stalin', has caused the German tank experts no little worry. It is, therefore, of interest that the following unconvincing description of a 'Tiger' versus 'Stalin' engagement is printed in the official 'Notes for Panzer Troops' of September 1944, presumably as an encouragement to the German tank arm.

A 'Tiger' squadron reports one of a number of engagements in which it knocked out 'Stalin' tanks.

The squadron had been given the task of counter-attacking an enemy penetration into a wood and exploiting success.

At 1215 hours the squadron moved off together with a rifle battalion. The squadron was formed to move in file by reason of the thick forest, bad visibility (50 yards) and narrow path. The Soviet infantry withdrew as soon as the 'Tigers' appeared. The

A/tk guns which the enemy had brought up only three-quarters of an hour after initial penetration were quickly knocked out, partly by fire, partly by crushing.

The point troop having penetrated a further 2,000 yards in to the forest, the troop commander suddenly heard the sound of falling trees and observed, right ahead, the large muzzle brake of the 'Stalin'. E immediately ordered: 'AP fixed sights-fire' but was hit at the same time by two rounds from a 4.7 cm A/tk gun which obscured his vision completely. Meanwhile the second tank in the troop had come up level with the troop commanders's tank. The latter, firing blind, was continuing the fire fight at a range of 35 yards and the 'Stalin' withdrew behind a hillock. The second 'Tiger' had in the meantime taken the lead and fired three rounds at the enemy tank. It was hit by a round from the enemy's 122mm tank gun on the hull below the wireless operator's seat but no penetration was effected, probably because the 'Tiger' was oblique to the enemy. The 'Stalin', however, had been hit in the gun by the 'Tiger's' last round and put out of action. A second 'Stalin' attempted to cover the first tank's withdrawal but was also hit by one of the leading 'Tigers' just below the gun and brewed up.

The rate of fire of the 'Stalin' was comparatively slow. The squadron commander has drawn the following conclusions from all the engagements his squadron has had with 'Stalin' tanks:

(1) Most 'Stalin' tanks will withdraw on encountering 'Tigers' without attempting to engage in a fire-fight.

(2) 'Stalin' tanks generally only open fire at ranges over 2,200 yards and then only if standing oblique to the target.

(3) Enemy crews tend to abandon tanks as soon as hit.

(4) The Russians make great efforts to prevent 'Stalin' tanks falling into our hands and particularly strive to recover or blow up such of them as have been immobilized.

(5) 'Stalin' tanks can be brewed up although penetration is by no means easy against the frontal armour at long ranges

(another 'Tiger' battalion reports that 'Stalin' tanks can only be penetrated by 'Tigers' frontally under 550 yards).

(6) 'Stalin' tanks should, wherever possible, be engaged in flanks or rear and destroyed by concentrated fire.

(7) 'Stalin' tanks should not be engaged under any circumstances by 'Tigers' in less than troop strength. To use single 'Tigers' is to invite their destruction.

(8) It is useful practice to follow up the first hit with AP on the 'Stalin' tank with HE, to continue blinding the occupants.

The Inspector-General of Panzer Troops (who is responsible for this official publication) commented as follows on the above remarks:

(1) These experiences agree with those of other 'Tiger' units and are correct.

(2) Reference para. (4), it would be desirable for the enemy to observe the same keenness in all our 'Tiger' crews. No 'Tiger' should ever be allowed to fall into the enemy's hands intact.

(3) Reference paras (5) and (6), faced as we are now with the 122mm tank gun and 57mm A/tk gun in Russia and the 92mm AA/Atk gun in Western Europe and Italy. 'Tigers' can no longer afford to ignore the principles practiced by normal tank formations.

This means, inter alia, that 'Tigers' can no longer show themselves on crests 'to have a look round' but must behave like other tanks – behaviour of this kind caused the destruction by 'Stalin' tanks of three 'Tigers' recently, all crews being killed with the exception of two men.

This battalion was surely not unacquainted with the basic principle of tank tactics that tanks should only cross crests in a body and by rapid bounds, covered by fire – or else detour round the crest. The legend of the 'thick hide', the 'invulnerability' and the 'safety' of the 'Tiger', which has sprung up in other arms of the service, as well as within the tank arm, must now be destroyed and dissipated.

Hence, instruction in the usual principles of tank versus tank action becomes of specific importance to 'Tiger' units.

(4) Reference para (7), though this train of thought is correct, 3 'Tigers' do not form a proper troop. Particularly with conditions as they are at the moment, circumstances may well arise where full troops will not be readily available. And it is precisely the tank versus tank action which is decided more by superior tactics than superior numbers. However it is still true to say that single tanks invite destruction.

(5) It may be added that the 'Stalin' tank will not only be penetrated in flanks and rear by 'Tigers' and 'Panthers' but also by Pz. Kpfw. IV and assault guns.

***

Tigers In Italy

Due to Allied air superiority, the Tigers in Normandy and France were frequently employed mainly in a static defensive role. This conserved fuel as the Tiger normally consumed huge amounts of petrol. It also kept the mechanical breakdowns to a minimum. In other theatres such as Italy, Allied air cover was less comprehensive and the Tigers still enjoyed some freedom of action. This was not always a good thing however.

Although the Tiger was a formidable design and recognized as being such in a number of allied studies although the high fuel consumption and frequent mechanical breakdowns occasionally rendered its battlefield performance all but worthless. This was certainly the case with the 508 schwere Abteilung in May 1944 which the British report of which from August 1944 makes sobering reading and further deflates the myth of the invincible Tiger.

TIGER TANK IN ACTION
FIRST MAJOR REVERSE OF
3 SQN 508 HY TK BN

As an illustration of the difficulties encountered in the employment of Tiger tanks it is interesting to reconstruct one of the two mobile engagements on a Sqn basis which the Bn fought in Italy, when it won a victory and yet lost almost all its tanks.

The action took place between 23 and 25 May 44 in the general area of Cisterna. 3 Sqn, which had brought down 14 Tiger tanks from France, lost two burnt out at the end of Feb 4 — one through carelessness on the part of the crew and another by Allied A/tk action. It had received four of the latest pattern AFVs during May 44 and was two tanks over war establishment strength on 23 May 44, i.e. 16 instead of 14.

The Sqn formed up behind a railway embankment between the Mussolini Canal and the level crossing at G 063299 and engaged troop concentrations with HE. It then crossed the embankment and put three AFVs out of action in the attempt (one with gearbox trouble and two with tracks riding over the sprocket teeth). The remaining thirteen crews had all to stop on open ground because the guns had dug into the earth as the tanks came down the embankment and needed pulling through.

The Allied troops were driven back about three kms and a number of Sherman tanks surprised and knocked out.

The first loss sustained in action was a Tiger which had one radiator destroyed by an artillery round and had to limp back towards Cori in stages.

Twelve Tigers were thus left in action during the night 23/24 May 44. On the morning of 24 May 44 a retreat was ordered to everyone's surprise and A/tk fire accounted for one Tiger (hit on the right reduction gear and subsequently blown up by its crew).

Eleven Tigers withdrew to the embankment and the OC Sqn

The citizens of the liberated French town of Marle clamber around this Tiger I which was abandoned in the main street.

ordered five to continue to hold the enemy whilst the six were to tow away the tree tanks which had failed to cross.

Four of the six towing tanks experienced gearbox trouble and the OC then ordered the three towed tanks to be destroyed and tow out of the five fighting tanks to assist in towing away the breakdowns.

These eight AFVs were got back to an assembly point near Cori, leaving four Tigers only in fighting order. Of these four, one was hit by A/Tk gun fire and two more experienced gearbox trouble (all three were blown up), so that only one runner was left.

Two converted Sherman tanks came down from Rome during the night 24/25 May 44 and extricated the one runner which had also become u/s meanwhile, by towing it in tandem along the railway tracks.

By 25 May 44, the situation had so deteriorated that it was manifestly impossible to get towing vehicles through and the OC ordered the blowing up of the nine Tigers which had reached the assembly area.

Although a good many of the crews had gone back to Rome with the one runner, the OC and about 45 men were left near Cori. They had to march back to Rome and came under fire several times in the process, arriving in an exhausted condition.

PW states categorically that this action had a profound effect upon the Sqn's morale and also decided against the mass use of Tiger tanks. Of sixteen AFVs put into action, not one would have been lost, had adequate recovery facilities been provided.

Although the OC Sqn's personal courage was not in doubt, it was generally thought that he had not appreciated the situation and had created the disaster by attempting to salvage the three AFVs that jibbed at the embankment. Had he not done so, he might have saved about ten out of the original sixteen.

'Penny wise, pound foolish' was the criticism made of him. 3 Sqn also took a poor view of the fact that almost at once a new troop was formed from tanks drawn from 1 and 2 Sqn crews put in, the former crews going back to their Sqn pools.

***

Tank Losses

With such an important range of industries in operation the city of Kassel was targeted for destruction and was bombed around 40 times by the Allies during the course of the war. These unwelcome intrusions severely disrupted Tiger production. The most notable occasion took place in late 1943. During the night of October 22nd/23rd the RAF dropped an amazing 1800 tons of bombs which obviously causing severe damage at the Henschel facilities. In addition to the damage caused to the infrastructure of the factory itself and the local transport system the RAF bombers also killed or injuring a high proportion of its workforce.

Despite these set backs and the huge difficulties which had to be overcome Tiger production continued right up until almost the end of the war. The U.S. Third Army began the battle to capture Kassel on April 1st, 1945. The Henschel works continued working to the bitter end and, as US forces approached, the Henschel factory completed work on the final batch of 13 Tiger II tanks which were handed directly over from the factory to two companies of schwere Panzer-Abteilung 510 and 511. Three days later at 1200 hours on April 4th, 1945 the city was surrendered and Tiger tank production was ended forever.

Tank losses on the eastern front by year:

Year	German Losses	Russian Losses	Kill/Loss Ratio
1941	2,758	20,500	7.43
1942	2,648	15,000	5.66
1943	6,362	22,400	3.52
1944	6,434	16,900	2.63
1945	7,382	8,700	1.18
Total	25,584	83,500	3.26

The Elefant was deployed in Russia and also saw action during the Warsaw uprising in 1943, and finally ended its career in Italy.

The Ferdinand or Elefant, shown here in Italy in 1944, actually performed far better in combat than is generally perceived.

Notable Variants

In Italy, a field version of a demolition carrier version of the Tiger I was built by maintenance crews in an effort to find a way to clear minefields. It is often misidentified as a Berge Tiger recovery vehicle. As many as three may have been built. It carried a demolition charge on a small crane mounted on the turret in lieu of the main gun. It was to move up to a minefield and drop the charge, back away, and then set the charge off to clear the minefield. There is no verification any were used in combat although such a vehicle would have been of great value at Kursk.

During 1942, anticipating orders for his version of the Tiger tank, Ferdinand Porsche had actually gone as far as to build 100 chassis based on his Tiger prototypes. On losing the contract, the Porsche vehicles were used as the basis for a new heavy assault gun/tank hunter. In the spring 1943, ninety-one hulls were converted into the Panzerjäger Tiger (P), also known as Ferdinand. After Hitler's orders of 1st and 27th February 1944, the Elefant.

The Ferdinand represents a fascinating glimpse into what the Tiger might have been the Tiger had Porsche won the competition for the Tiger contract. This heavily armoured tank destroyer variant utilised all of the remaining redundant chassis which Ferdinand Porsche had ordered to be produced in anticipation of receiving the order for the Tiger I. These

The Sturmtiger with its 15in howitzer protruding. This calibre was as great as many a battleship's big guns.

vehicles were a scratch built solution introduced into combat in 1943. The Ferdinand has an unfair reputation as a complete failure and is widely held to have floundered then disappeared following an unsuccessful showing at Kursk where the poor performance has been ascribed as being due to the lack of a close defence machine gun. The reality is that the Ferdinand was a highly effective tank destroyer which performed very creditably in Russia and Italy. Mechanically the Ferdinand was to prove remarkably reliable and in many respects may actually have been a better machine than the Tiger I.

Among other factory variants of the Tiger I was the fearsome Jagdtiger which was one of the most formidable tank destroyers of the war however production was very low and only 160 machines were built. Also of note was the compact, armoured self-propelled rocket projector, today commonly known as Sturmtiger, only 16 of these machines built and when the first of these was captured by the Americans a great deal of attention was focused on this remarkably powerful weapon.

The end for the Tiger I came in May 1945, almost three years to the day from its birth.

ABOUT CODA BOOKS

Most Coda books are edited and endorsed by Emmy Award winning film maker and military historian Bob Carruthers, producer of Discovery Channel's Line of Fire and Weapons of War and BBC's Both Sides of the Line. Long experience and strong editorial control gives the military history enthusiast the ability to buy with confidence.

The series advisor is David McWhinnie, producer of the acclaimed Battlefield series for Discovery Channel. David and Bob have co-produced books and films with a wide variety of the UK's leading historians including Professor John Erickson and Dr David Chandler.

Where possible the books draw on rare primary sources to give the military enthusiast new insights into a fascinating subject.

www.codabooks.com

The English Civil Wars

The Zulu Wars

Into Battle with Napoleon 1812

Waterloo 1815

The Anglo-Saxon Chronicle

The Battle of the Bulge

The Normandy Campaign 1944

Hitler's Justification for WWII

Hitler's Mein Kampf - The Roots of Evil

I Knew Hitler

Mein Kampf - The 1939 Illustrated Edition

The Nuremberg Trials Volume 1

Tiger I in Combat

Tiger I Crew Manual

Panzers at War 1939-1942

Panzers at War 1943-1945

Wolf Pack - the U boats

Poland 1939

Luftwaffe Combat Reports

Eastern Front Night Combat

Eastern Front Encirclement

Panzer Combat Reports

The Panther V in Combat

The Red Army in Combat

Barbarossa - Hitler Turns East

The Russian Front

The Wehrmacht in Russia

Servants of Evil

www.ingramcontent.com/pod-product-compliance
Lightning Source LLC
Chambersburg PA
CBHW021139160426
43194CB00007B/628